Dynamic Democracy

CHICAGO STUDIES IN AMERICAN POLITICS

A series edited by Susan Herbst, Lawrence R. Jacobs, Adam J. Berinsky, and Frances Lee; Benjamin I. Page, editor emeritus

Also in the series:

Dynamic Democracy

Public Opinion, Elections, and Policymaking in the American States

DEVIN CAUGHEY AND
CHRISTOPHER WARSHAW

The University of Chicago Press
Chicago and London

The University of Chicago Press, Chicago 60637
The University of Chicago Press, Ltd., London
Published 2022
Printed in the United States of America

31 30 29 28 27 26 25 24 23 22   1 2 3 4 5

ISBN-13: 978-0-226-82220-4 (cloth)
ISBN-13: 978-0-226-82222-8 (paper)
ISBN-13: 978-0-226-82221-1 (e-book)
DOI: https://doi.org/10.7208/chicago/9780226822211.001.0001

Library of Congress Cataloging-in-Publication Data

Names: Caughey, Devin, author. | Warshaw, Christopher, author.
Title: Dynamic democracy : public opinion, elections, and policymaking in the
    American states / Devin Caughey and Christopher Warshaw.
Other titles: Chicago studies in American politics.
Description: Chicago : The University of Chicago Press, 2022. | Series: Chicago
    studies in American politics | Includes bibliographical references and index.
Identifiers: LCCN 2022012450 | ISBN 9780226822204 (cloth) | ISBN 9780226822228
    (paperback) | ISBN 9780226822211 (ebook)
Subjects: LCSH: Political participation—United States. | Political activists—
    United States. | United States—Politics and government.
Classification: LCC JK1764 .C395 2022 | DDC 323/.0420973—dc23/eng/20220422
LC record available at https://lccn.loc.gov/2022012450

♾ This paper meets the requirements of ANSI/NISO z39.48-1992 (Permanence of Paper).

Contents

1

Introduction

States have been at the forefront of policymaking throughout American history. In the nineteenth century, their capacious powers to further the people's welfare undergirded a huge range of activities, from building canals to banning "fornication."[1] By the early twentieth century, states had assumed a host of new responsibilities—highways, schools, parks—which they funded with new taxes on income, sales, and commodities such as gasoline.[2] The middle third of the century brought unprecedented government expansion at the national level, but states grew in tandem with the federal government.[3] Although federal laws and court decisions did impose new constraints on state governments, most notably by dismantling the South's system of racial segregation and exclusion,[4] states remained vibrant and innovative sites of policymaking. Indeed, action at the federal level often stimulated state-level policymaking, as the 1947 Taft-Hartley Act did for labor policy and the 1973 Supreme Court decision *Roe v. Wade* did for abortion.[5] For over half a century, right-wing activists have fought to retrench state governments, but despite conservative victories on issues such as taxes, welfare, and unions,[6] states remain as active and important as ever.[7]

Within these broad common trends, however, states have followed different developmental paths. Some states provide relatively generous needs-based welfare benefits and medical care; others do not. Some have crafted political economies predicated on low taxation, light regulation, and nonunion labor, but others have not. The criminal justice systems of some states are highly punitive; others are less so. Some have been at the vanguard of equal rights for women, racial minorities, and LGBT Americans, while others have brought up the rear. And at various times, some states have permitted alcohol, gambling, contraception, abortion, marijuana, and assault weapons, while others prohibited them. These policy differences across states have shaped the lives of their citizens in countless ways, from the taxes they pay to the medical care they receive, from where they can work to whom they can marry.

Consider the divergent trajectories of Idaho and Vermont. In the early 1930s, these two states had almost identical policies. Both taxed corporate and personal income, for example, but lacked a sales tax and a minimum wage, and neither allowed women on juries or banned racial discrimination in public accommodations. The policies of Idaho and Vermont remained similar until the 1970s, when Vermont began trending in a liberal direction relative to the nation and Idaho in a conservative one. Over the next couple of decades, Vermont adopted stringent environmental standards, repealed its antisodomy laws, and for the first time set its minimum wage above the national standard. Meanwhile, Idaho capped property taxes, passed a right-to-work law, and restricted access to abortion. By the twenty-first century, the two states had moved to opposite ends of the ideological spectrum. Vermont has continued to pioneer liberal policies like same-sex marriage, marijuana legalization, and single-payer health care, while Idaho has led the way on conservative ones such as work requirements for welfare recipients, "stand your ground" gun laws, and preemption of local minimum wages.

State governments, in short, are dynamic and diverse. While all have been transformed over the past century, each has followed its own path, with profound implications for the lives of its citizens. What explains these divergent trajectories? What is the motor that drives some states to adopt liberal policies, others conservative policies, and still others a mix of both? And, from the perspective of democratic performance, most importantly: Does state policymaking in some sense reflect the will of the people?

A venerable scholarly tradition in state politics answers in the affirmative. The exemplar of this perspective is Robert Erikson, Gerald Wright, and John McIver's classic *Statehouse Democracy*.[8] Based on data from around 1980, these authors argue that state policymaking, conceptualized along a liberal–conservative continuum, is highly responsive to public opinion.[9] They find that at a given point in time, the correlation between the liberalism of a state's policies and the proportion of its citizens who identify as liberal is nothing short of "awesome."[10] The primary mechanism for this responsiveness, they argue, is not that liberal states elect Democrats and conservative states elect Republicans—far from it. Rather, motivated by desire for electoral success, each state party adapts to the ideological leanings of its electorate. It is primarily by influencing state party positions that citizens exercise their strong influence over the ideological direction of state policymaking.

This optimistic interpretation, however, has been subject to multifaceted critiques. One, acknowledged by Erikson, Wright, and McIver themselves, is that "causation is not congruence": strong responsiveness to public opinion does not necessarily produce policies that match what the public desires.[11] In fact, Jeffrey Lax and Justin Phillips's study of thirty-nine state policies in the early twenty-first century finds that policies align with majority opinion no better than half the time—a sign, they argue, of a major "democratic deficit" in the states.[12] Nor does responsiveness to the public at large imply *equal* responsiveness to all citizens, for political influence is unequally distributed across racial and class lines.[13]

A second limitation of *Statehouse Democracy* is its temporal focus on state politics circa 1980.[14] Before the 1970s, many states had undemocratic institutions such as suffrage restrictions and severely malapportioned legislatures.[15] How did these institutions affect the quality of policy representation in the states? State politics has undergone major transformations since the 1980s as well. Americans today know and care much less about state politics than they do about national politics.[16] As party and ideology have aligned, geographic polarization has grown and partisanship has increasingly dominated state elections and policymaking.[17] These developments have undermined voters' capacity and willingness to hold state officials accountable for their actions, weakening the latter's incentives to cater to their constituents' wishes.[18] Perhaps most troublingly, critics have interpreted increasingly aggressive efforts to restrict voting rights and redraw constituencies for partisan advantage as signs of "democratic backsliding" in the states.[19]

The politics of Medicaid expansion under the 2010 Affordable Care Act (ACA) illustrates many of these concerning trends. A federal program that pays health care costs for low-income Americans, Medicaid is administered at the state level, and the experience of receiving Medicaid varies widely across states.[20] The ACA subsidized the expansion of Medicaid to cover millions more Americans, but thanks to the Supreme Court's partial invalidation of the ACA, states had the choice of whether to participate. Despite strong financial incentives from the federal government and majority support in every state, by the end of 2014 only twenty-six states had expanded Medicaid. Expansion decisions were strongly related to party control: nearly every Republican-dominated state initially refused to participate, regardless of public opinion.[21]

Wisconsin is a case in point. In 2010, 69 percent of Wisconsinites supported expanding Medicaid, a figure that rose to 75 percent by 2014 and 82 percent by 2020.[22] Yet the Republican-controlled state legislature steadfastly blocked expansion, even after Democrat Tony Evers replaced Republican Scott Walker as governor in 2019. Republicans have been aided by the strong partisan bias in Wisconsin's gerrymandered legislative map, which prevented Democrats from capturing control at any point after 2010 despite twice winning a popular majority. By thus thwarting the public will, Wisconsin has denied affordable health care to thousands of its residents.

But Wisconsin does not tell the whole story. Since 2014, twelve additional states have adopted expansion, bringing the total to thirty-eight by the end of 2021.[23] In some states, such as Alaska and Maine, this was the result of non-Republican governors implementing expansion through executive order.[24] In the others, however, expansion was accomplished through bipartisan cooperation (Montana, Virginia, and Louisiana), by Republican governors and legislatures (North Dakota and Indiana), or by ballot initiative (Idaho, Utah, Oklahoma, Missouri, and Nebraska). As a consequence of these actions, state Medicaid expansion policies' congruence with majority opinion increased from 52 percent in 2014 to 76 percent in 2021.

This larger story of Medicaid expansion suggests a more nuanced account of state-level democracy, which we elaborate in this book. Even in this polarized age, state policymaking *is* responsive to public opinion. Indeed, it is probably more responsive than it was when *Statehouse Democracy* was written and certainly more so than before the 1970s. But responsiveness is not immediate. Due to the prevalence of veto players and the scarcity of time and other political resources, barriers to policy change are often high.[25] As a result, change tends to be incremental, especially when a state's policies are viewed collectively.[26] Vermont's gay rights policies, for example, were completely transformed between the 1970s and the first decade of the twenty-first century, but the transformation occurred in stages: decriminalization of sodomy in 1977, stronger employment and public accommodations protections in 1991–1992 and again in 2007, legalization of civil unions in 2000, expanded definitions of hate crimes in 2001, and legalization of same-sex marriage in 2009. Due to the piecemeal and incremental nature of policy change, it often takes years or even decades for the force of public opinion to filter through the political process.

Elections are critical to responsiveness, but responsiveness does not require electoral turnover. As we saw with Medicaid expansion in Alaska and Maine, replacing officials of one party with ones from another is one mechanism of responsiveness. But as the experiences of other states attest, policy change—and thus responsiveness to public opinion—can also occur without change in party control, via the adaptation of state parties.[27] Elections facilitate such adaptation in two ways. First, they allow electorates to filter out candidates whose positions are out of step with their constituents. Second, by enabling voters to hold incumbents accountable, they incentivize officials to react preemptively to public opinion. While such selection and accountability mechanisms are far from perfect, they are important sources of negative feedback that help keep state policymaking in equilibrium.

Despite the forces pushing for responsiveness, policies are often out of step with public opinion. Pollsters' bias in coverage of divisive and controversial issues exaggerates the pervasiveness of policy incongruence, but it is nonetheless real and substantial. The ideological direction of incongruence depends on the issue. On Medicaid expansion, state policy is more conservative than what most citizens demand, but on issues such as required waiting periods for abortions, policy is biased in a liberal direction. More important than ideological bias, however, is pervasive bias toward the status quo.[28] If policy is currently liberal, then even with supermajority support for making it more conservative, the chance of doing so in any given year is very low. But thanks to incremental responsiveness, the match between policy and opinion tends to improve over time. When issues arrive on the agenda, policy matches majority opinion only 40 percent of the time; three decades later, policy congruence averages 70 percent. In the short term, states often exhibit a democratic deficit, but over the long term, state publics tend to work their will.

The quality of democracy in the states, however, has been far from even. Before the Second Reconstruction of the 1960s, southern states used poll taxes, literacy tests, racially restrictive primaries, and other legal and extralegal devices to exclude their Black citizens, along with many White ones, from the electorate. As a consequence, policy representation was poorer in the South for all citizens, but especially for Blacks, than it was outside the South at the same time or inside the South after 1970. Another undemocratic practice from the same era, this one widespread in all regions, was legislative malapportionment, which allowed legislative districts to vary hugely in population. The resulting overrepresentation of rural interests in state legislatures distorted state policymaking in a conservative direction, resulting in a poorer match with the average citizen's preferences. Although malapportionment was eliminated by the US Supreme Court's "one-person, one-vote" decisions of the 1960s, distortions of the correspondence between votes and seats live on today in the form of partisan gerrymandering. In states like Wisconsin, where the legislative map distributes one party's supporters more efficiently than the other's, policymaking is skewed toward the advantaged party, again worsening policy representation for the public as a whole.

✳

These weak points in American democracy raise a question: What can be done to improve democracy in the states? There is no shortage of potential answers: from liberal reforms like election-day registration and campaign contribution limits to conservative ones like voter identification laws and restrictions on public-sector unions. However, after examining the effects of eleven common reforms on voter turnout, partisan control of state offices, the conservatism of state policies, and various measures of the quality of representation, we find very few detectable effects. The only firm causal inferences we can draw are (1) that adopting forms of direct democracy, such as the initiative and the referendum, increases the conservatism of states' cultural policies (i.e., on issues such as abortion, gay rights, and gun control) and that right-to-work laws have the same effect (and may increase economic policy conservatism as well); and (2) that nonpartisan or bipartisan districting commissions reduce the partisan bias in legislative maps. But these effects notwithstanding, none of the reforms we examine reliably improve the quality of policy representation, though in many cases the uncertainty about reforms' effects is large. In short, while there are good reasons to believe that state-level democracy can be improved, there is not yet compelling evidence that any widely tried reforms do so.[29]

Although this book focuses on states, it holds important lessons for American democracy in general. It provides a counterpoint to the most skeptical accounts, such as Christopher Achen and Larry Bartels's *Democracy for Realists*, which levels a powerful argument against the "folk theory" that elections suffice for responsive government.[30] In one sense we agree: elections alone are not enough; they must be paired with an inclusive electorate, fair translation of votes into government offices, and other guarantees of free participation and contestation.[31] When these conditions are not met, as they were not in many US states before 1970, representation suffers. For skeptics like Achen and Bartels, however, even contemporary American democracy—plagued as it is by new political ailments, such as partisan polarization—is unresponsive and dysfunctional.[32] We respectfully disagree. American democracy is far from perfect, and responsiveness can be painfully slow and halting, but over the long term the public does exert a powerful influence—and even a substantial degree of control—over government policies. Such responsiveness is not inevitable, and its underpinnings are indeed threatened by partisan efforts to subvert democratic procedures, but neither should it be denied.

Finally, it is worth emphasizing what is most distinctive about this book: its dynamic perspective.[33] We mean this in several senses. First, state politics is dynamic, not static. Issues cycle on and off the agenda, political parties realign and polarize, and government institutions undergo formal reforms and informal evolution. Second, representation itself is a dynamic process: "a sequence, inherently structured in time."[34] For public opinion to change government policies, it must proceed through a series of steps—mobilization of supporters, recognition of public desires, replacement of incumbents, navigation of veto points, and implementation of legislation—each of which takes time. As a result, responsiveness is incremental, not immediate, though it can cumulate powerfully over the long term.

These theoretical and conceptual considerations dictate our empirical approach, which is dynamic as well. We have gathered an enormous amount of data on public opinion, election results, and state policies covering each state and year since the 1930s. To these data, we apply statistical techniques that stitch together disparate indicators into continuous time-series–cross-sectional (TSCS) measures. We then analyze these measures with statistical models designed to capture their dynamic relationships, accounting in particular for the stickiness of state policy over time. Together, these data, measures, and methods yield a wealth of descriptive and causal inferences about state-level democracy over a span of more than eight decades.

1.1 Plan of the Book

The remainder of the book is organized as follows. Chapter 2 outlines the measurement challenges posed by this project and describes the data and methods we use to address them. It is structured so that readers uninterested in technical details can skip most of the chapter without missing any key elements of our substantive argument.

Chapter 3 uses the measures described in chapter 2 to document the evolution of mass partisanship, mass ideology, and the relationship between them since the mid-twentieth century. It shows that the economic and cultural (as well as racial) conservatism of state publics have become much more tightly coupled and that conservatism in all three domains has come into alignment with support for the Republican Party. Moreover, as Democrats and Republicans have diverged ideologically within states, state parties have become more similar to their copartisans in other states, a phenomenon we refer to as the ideological nationalization of partisanship.

If chapter 3 covers the "inputs" to the political process, then chapter 4 describes the "outputs": public policies. This chapter summarizes patterns in state policymaking on economic and cultural issues, documenting a general liberalizing trend over time and an increasingly tight alignment between the two domains. We show that while mass ideology and policy ideology have always been correlated, mass partisanship and party control of government have only come into alignment with them in the last few decades.

Chapter 5 examines the relationship between state policies and the partisan control of state offices from a causal perspective. Using various approaches, it demonstrates that Democratic (relative to Republican) control of state offices has always caused state policies to shift leftward, especially on economics, but the causal effect of party control has roughly doubled since the 1980s. We find evidence that the increase in party effects is rooted in the ideological divergence between the mass constituencies of the two parties within states.

Chapter 6 considers determinants of elections to state offices. It shows that although partisan loyalties and national tides exert powerful effects on state-level elections, there is still substantial room for candidates and incumbents to shape their electoral fortunes. Relatively extreme candidates perform more poorly at the polls, and electorates seem to hold incumbents accountable by balancing against the majority party. These phenomena incentivize candidates and parties to adapt ideologically to their constituencies, which helps explain why mass ideology only weakly predicts shifts in party control. Together, the selection of moderate candidates and the incentives to avoid extreme policy-making are important sources of negative feedback in state politics.

Chapter 7 reaches a question at the heart of this work: How responsive is state policymaking to citizens' policy preferences? We begin by showing that the conservatism of elected officials is correlated with the conservatism of their electorates, both within parties and in the aggregate. We then demonstrate that the conservatism of state policies does respond dynamically to mass conservatism but that this responsiveness is incremental rather than instantaneous. Policy responsiveness is also substantially, if not predominantly, mediated by the adaptation of incumbent officials rather than partisan turnover. Policy responsiveness has increased over time, and it has been consistently weaker in southern states. Though the effects of mass ideology are small in the short term, over the long term they are much larger.

Chapter 8 considers the quality of representation from another angle, policy *proximity*: the match between state policies and citizens' preferences on individual policies. We first show that although states are highly responsive to issue-specific opinion, policy representation is often biased. Policy bias is more often conservative than liberal, but this is largely explained by bias toward the status quo. We also find that the average policy in our data set matches opinion majorities about 60 percent of the time, with proximity improving the longer a policy has been on the political agenda.

Chapter 9 examines three major exceptions to the relatively optimistic picture painted by the preceding chapters: the racially exclusionary politics of the Jim Crow South, legislative malapportionment in the era before equipopulous districts, and the partisan gerrymandering of recent decades. We document the damage caused by all three phenomena to the quality of democracy in the states, which in the case of gerrymandering is still ongoing. In particular, all three not only bias policymaking toward certain interests but also undermine policy representation of the public as a whole.

Chapter 10, the final empirical one, considers how various institutional reforms affect voter turnout, election outcomes, policymaking, and representation. Across a mix of liberal and conservative reforms in four categories— citizen governance, voting procedures, campaign finance, and union regulations—we find few reliably estimated effects. Direct democracy and right to work lead to more conservative policies, but for neither these nor any of the others can we conclude that they improve representation.

Chapter 11 concludes the book with a summary of the argument and a consideration of its theoretical, normative, and empirical implications. We discuss the limitations of our argument and what our conclusions suggest about the quality of American democracy, the prospects of institutional reform, and the future of state politics.

Measurement:
Public Opinion and State Policy

To chart the dynamic interplay of public opinion and policymaking, we need measures that cover all states over long stretches of time. Creating such measures requires both a great deal of data and solutions to several methodological challenges. This chapter describes the data sets we constructed and how we use them to operationalize the concepts in our theoretical model, most notably mass policy preferences and state government policies.

Because our approach is complex and technical, we have divided this chapter into two sections aimed at readers with different interests. The first section, designed to be accessible to all readers, provides a high-level overview of our approach. The second section, while nontechnical, goes into much more detail about our data sets and how we derived measures from them. We also include a technical appendix, aimed at graduate students and others interested in the statistical details, that describes the measurement models we use to infer values of the constructs of interest from the observed data. Only the first section is essential for understanding the evidentiary basis for this book. The second section and the technical appendix may be freely skipped without much damage to our substantive argument.

2.1 The Challenge of Measurement

The greatest barrier to a dynamic analysis of state politics is measuring the relevant concepts at the requisite level of analysis. For national coverage and cross-sectional comparison, we need variables measured in a consistent fashion across all states. To track political change and capture dynamic relationships, we need to measure them at multiple, preferably many, points in time. In other words, studying state politics dynamically requires time-series–

cross-sectional (TSCS) measures that are comparable across both states and years.

Devising these measures presents several major challenges. The first is variables' sparse and uneven availability, especially across time. For most variables we care about, there is no canonical list or data set that covers the entire time period. Policy ideas appear on the political agenda and then disappear; survey questions are asked in some years and not others. As a consequence, it is often impossible to construct a consistent time series for a given state policy or survey item, making it difficult to track issue-specific dynamics over long stretches of time.

The need to compile data from many disparate sources also presents challenges of comparability. To be compared across states and years, or between citizens and governments, measures must have a consistent meaning. A question asked in one survey, for example, must have a substantively identical meaning to that asked in another; otherwise, they cannot be coded as a single variable. Similarly, gauging whether a given state policy is congruent with mass preferences requires a survey question that is not merely on the same issue but also on the same policy. Ensuring sufficient comparability requires a nuanced understanding of the quality and context of the data and careful work to ensure that variables are coded consistently across sources.

A third challenge is measurement error, stemming from either random noise or systematic bias. Due to such error, we are often uncertain about the true value of a variable in a given state-year. For some variables, this uncertainty is negligible. Absent a coding or transcription error, there is typically little doubt as to whether a given policy was in place in a given state in a given year. But for other variables, measurement error is a much more serious and pervasive concern. This is especially true of state-level measures of public opinion, which are usually based on small poll samples that may not even be intended to be representative of state populations. The challenge is magnified when the construct of interest is not directly observable but rather is a "latent" trait, such as ideology, the value of which must be inferred from observable indicators.

Constructing the measures we require also entails important conceptual choices. One such choice is whether to conceptualize policy alternatives in ideological terms. Should favoring legal recognition of same-sex marriage be considered a "liberal" position and favoring the death penalty a "conservative" one, or should these variables be conceptualized nonideologically? If one adopts a pragmatic view of ideology as simply "what goes with what" in a particular political context,[1] assigning ideological labels to the kinds of policy positions we consider is usually fairly easy, but it can occasionally be problematic. This is especially true for long-standing policies whose ideo-logical valence has evolved over time (e.g., gun control[2]) or ones for which the alternative is unclear (e.g., is the alternative to a sales tax an income tax, or is it no tax at all?).

If we do conceptualize policy positions in ideological terms, another ques-tion arises: Should each policy issue be analyzed separately, or should a single holistic measure be used to summarize ideological variation across many is-sues? The former has several advantages. Issue-specific measures have a di-rect and intuitive interpretation—the proportion of Americans who favor the policy—whereas ideological summaries are more abstract. An issue-by-issue approach also avoids the sometimes problematic assumption of a single ideo-logical dimension, which rules out a person or state being liberal on some issues but conservative on others. Finally, even if ideological variation is one-dimensional, comparing the positions of citizens and elites or governments—that is, "jointly scaling" them—typically requires fewer assumptions when done issue by issue.[3]

That said, ideological summarization has advantages of its own. From a theoretical point of view, it is a better fit with this book's holistic perspective on state politics. Our primary focus is not policy-specific variation but rather the general tenor of state policymaking. Although there are alternative ways of summarizing policy variation across states—for example, in terms of an "innovation score" indicating how quickly a state adopts new policies[4]—we follow most of the state politics literature in conceptualizing variation in ideological terms.[5] Summarization has methodological advantages as well. If specific indicators (e.g., policies) share a common dimension of variation, aggregating across them will strengthen the common "signal" relative to indicator-specific "noise," yielding more precise indicators of the latent con-struct of interest.[6] Finally, as we explain below, focusing on the latent trait of domain-specific conservatism rather than policy-specific variation provides a solution to the problems posed by the sparsity of policy and opinion data. If we can estimate how specific indicators relate to latent conservatism, the fact that the different indicators are available at different points in time poses less of a problem.

Even if such biases are eliminated, however, a great deal of random error remains in our measures of public opinion. One source of error stems from variation in respondents' attention, the interview context, and other factors that, by influencing the salience of different considerations, make a given sur-vey instrument a less than perfectly reliable measure of each respondent's long-term preference.[7] Fortunately, our main interest is not the preferences of citizens considered individually but the *collective* preferences of state publics.

Owing to the so-called miracle of aggregation, random errors and fluctuations in individual survey responses tend to cancel out in estimates of the *average* response in the population.[8] As a consequence, public opinion tends to look much more stable and coherent at the collective level than at the level of individual citizens.[9]

Ultimately, the measurement approach we adopt in this book depends on the task at hand. For some purposes, we rely on a single indicator that directly captures the construct of interest. The description in chapter 3 of the partisan evolution of state publics, for example, relies on a single question series on party identification, some form of which has been asked in every year since 1942. Similarly, the analysis in chapter 8 of state policy proximity considers each policy's match with public opinion on an issue-by-issue basis. For other purposes, however, ideological summarization makes more sense. When describing trends in state policymaking (chapter 4), for instance, we focus mainly on the general liberalism or conservatism of states' economic and cultural policies. We do the same in chapter 7 when we examine states' policy responsiveness to their publics. Since each of these measurement strategies has its strengths and limitations, combining them provides a fuller picture of state politics than either on its own.

2.2 Data and Measures

We now turn to a more detailed description of our data and measures. Readers not interested in the specifics may wish to skip ahead to the next chapter.

2.2.1 POLICY AND SURVEY DATA

We begin by describing the collection of policy and survey data and the construction of standardized data sets from them. This process took many years and relied on the help of many research assistants and collaborators.

State Policies

Before collecting data on state policies, we had to decide what counts as a "policy." One criterion we used is that a policy must be something that a state government more or less directly controls. This rules out social outcomes such as high school graduation rates, which are influenced by government policy but not determined by it.[10] It also eliminates laws that, while on a state's statute books, are dead letters due to federal preemption or judicial invalidation, such as laws mandating segregation or outlawing abortion. We also exclude more fundamental institutions, such as the structure and powers of government offices, as well as the internal rules of state legislative chambers. Finally, on a more ad hoc basis, we exclude policies with direct effects on elections and representation, such as laws governing voting or districting. Beyond these restrictions, we defined the universe of state policies broadly to encompass a wide range of policy instruments (taxes, expenditures, mandates, prohibitions) and issue domains (economic, cultural, racial). As a consequence, the universe we examine includes a mix of dichotomous, ordinal, and continuous policies on issues ranging from abortion and education to gun control and civil rights.

From this universe, we sought to construct as large and as representative a sample of comparable policies as possible. Collecting a large number of policies was important to avoid basing general inferences on a small or unrepresentative subset of policies. To generate a list of potential policies, we canvassed a wide range of sources, including books and articles on state politics, legal surveys of state policies, state party platforms, governors' biographies, state-specific political histories, and government and interest-group websites. Based on this list, we collected data on the policies in place in each state and year from a wide variety of secondary sources, including government, academic, and interest-group publications as well as from state statutes themselves. Our data set covers the years 1935 to 2020, though for some policies we have data going back decades earlier. After excluding policies not applicable to all states, such as regulation of ocean beaches, and (with few exceptions) those for which data were available for fewer than five years, we are left with a total of 186 distinct policies. We classified 115 of these policies as economic, 62 as cultural, and 9 as racial. Given the constraints of data availability, we cannot claim to have constructed a random sample of state policies, but we are confident that the data set is broadly representative of available data on the salient policy activities of US states.[11]

Although our policy data set as a whole covers all eighty-six years between 1935 and 2020, this is not true of each individual policy. We were able to collect data in every year for only eleven policies. The policy data's uneven availability across time can be seen clearly in figure 2.1, which for space reasons includes a random sample of seventy economic policies, and figure 2.2, which includes all sixty-two cultural policies. On average, a given policy is measured in thirty-four out of eighty-six years. In the typical year, data are available for forty-two economic policies, with a minimum of twenty-nine per year, and for twenty-seven cultural policies, with a minimum of ten per year. Across all 15,996 policy-year combinations, 60 percent are missing data.

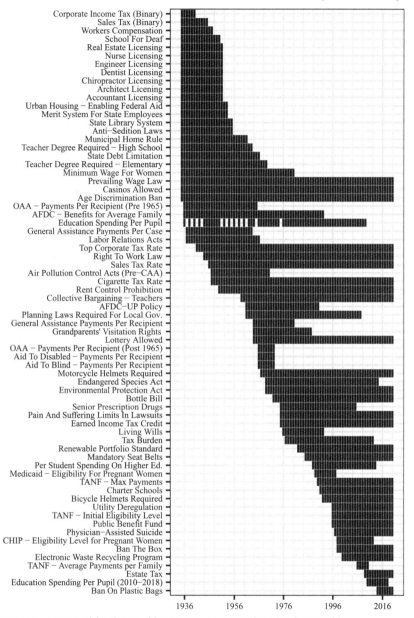

FIGURE 2.1. Temporal distribution of data on state economic policies (random sample).

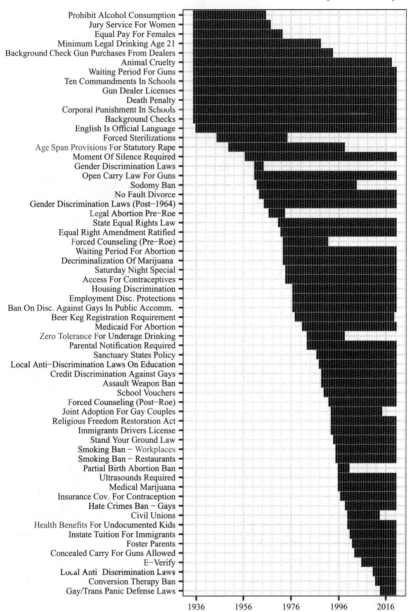

FIGURE 2.2. Temporal distribution of data on state cultural policies.

Opinion Surveys

Measuring policy preferences in the mass public presents some of the same challenges as measuring state policies, plus some additional complications. As with state policies, we must first define what we mean by *policy preferences*. This is more problematic than defining state policies, for many scholars dispute the very existence of mass preferences, or at least ones that satisfy the standards of logical consistency required by analytical democratic theory.[12] We employ a less strict definition of *preference*, however, using the term to mean an individual's tendency to evaluate a given object (e.g., a policy proposal) with some degree of favor or disfavor.[13]

Even under this looser definition of preference, responses to individual survey questions often exhibit a distressingly high degree of incoherence and instability.[14] Particularly disturbing is that seemingly minor differences in question wording can affect support for a given position.[15] To cite one well-known example: in the mid-1980s, over 60 percent of Americans said spending on "assistance to the poor" was too low, but only about 20 percent thought spending on "welfare" was too low.[16] It is not obvious which of these survey results better captures the public's support for, say, increasing Aid to Families with Dependent Children (AFDC) benefits. Even if such large wording effects are rare, their existence means we must be cautious about interpreting responses to any given survey item as the public's "true" support for a given policy.[17] In addition, when combining data from different polls, we must be careful to collapse into a single item only those questions framed sufficiently similarly across polls that wording effects are unlikely to be important. If we do not, then we might conflate differences due to alternative wordings with real differences in mass preferences.

Our data set itself is built on data from academic surveys, including the American National Election Studies (ANES), the General Social Survey (GSS), and the Cooperative Election Study (CES), and even more so from the hundreds of commercial opinion polls archived by the Roper Center for Public Opinion Research. Across these disparate sources, we identified a total of 296 distinct survey items related to economic issues, 70 related to cultural issues, and 44 related to race. The economic data set represents the opinions of 1.5 million distinct Americans; the cultural data set, 1 million; and the race data set, a quarter million. Nearly 1.6 million Americans contributed to an auxiliary data set of party identification. For each year between 1936 and 2019, the sample size in the economic data set is at least 3,000, with a median around 12,000; for the cultural data set, the annual minimum is 1,275 and the median 8,000.

Despite the richness of the data, survey questions are even more sparsely distributed across years than policies are. Figure 2.3 displays the temporal distribution of a sample of economics-related items, and figure 2.4 does the same for all cultural items. In the cultural domain, 92 percent of item-year combinations are missing; in the economic domain, 97 percent are. Only a few perennially controversial issues, such as universal health care and the death penalty, are polled regularly and with consistent question wording over long swaths of time. If we focused solely on these long-running question series, we would be ignoring the vast majority of survey data collected since the 1930s.

2.2.2 MEASURES OF STATE POLICY AND MASS PREFERENCES

We now turn to the transformation of the raw data into measures of our constructs of interest. We begin by describing how we created measures for specific policies and issues, followed by a discussion of ideological summaries of state policies and mass policy preferences.

Issue-Specific Measures

Constructing state-year measures for each state policy is the easiest task. The first step is coding each policy at an appropriate level of measurement. Most of the policies in our data set are best measured with a simple dichotomous indicator: either the state has the policy or it does not. Examples of dichotomous policies include a right-to-work-law, a legal drinking age of twenty-one years, or a ban on interracial marriage. Although a dichotomous coding may gloss over nuanced differences (e.g., whether a state without a statewide right-to-work law allows such laws at the local level), this is the price that must be paid for a measure that travels across states. Some policies, however, have several "levels" with a natural order. For instance, we code the policy *same-sex marriage* as having three ordinal levels: (1) the state has no legal recognition of same-sex unions, (2) the state recognizes same-sex civil unions but not same-sex marriage, and (3) the state recognizes full same-sex marriage. Each level indicates greater support for marriage equality.

Finally, about one-fifth of the policies in our data set—tax rates, per-capita expenditures, and so on—can take on so many values that they can be treated as varying continuously. Many continuous policies, however, are not immediately comparable across states or time. The real value of a $500 AFDC benefit, for example, varies greatly depending on the year and, to a lesser extent, on the state as well ($500 goes further in Mississippi than in Massachusetts). To

Economic Items (70 of 296)

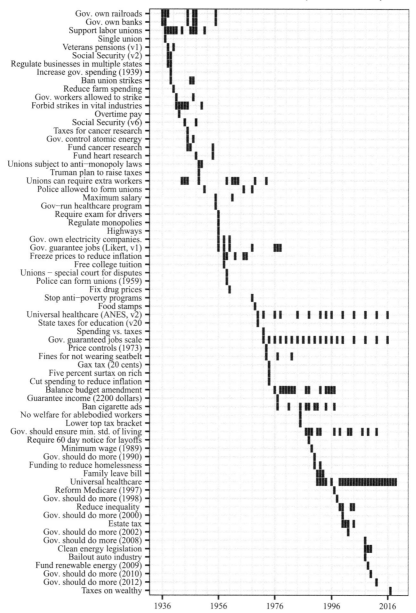

FIGURE 2.3. Temporal distribution of a random sample of survey items related to economic issues.

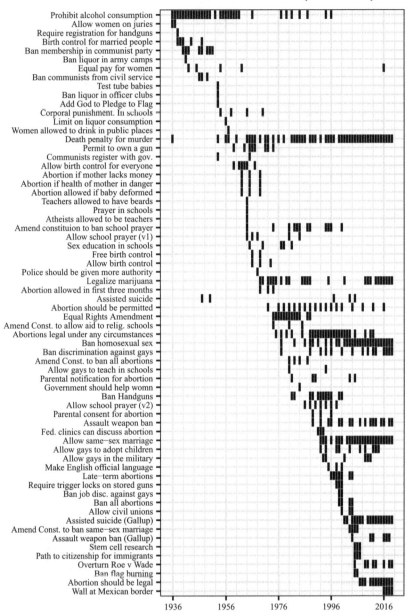

FIGURE 2.4. Temporal distribution of survey items related to cultural issues.

render such policies more comparable, we converted all monetary expenditure and welfare benefit policies into constant dollars and also adjusted for cost-of-living differences among states.[18] Our policy-specific measures thus comprise a mix of dichotomous, ordinal, and continuous policies, some of which have been normalized to enhance their comparability across time and space.

Measuring issue-specific public opinion at the state-year level is a more challenging task. The crux of the problem is that we want to know how much support a position has in the population, but we only observe a sample from that population. A sample estimate (e.g., the sample mean) can differ from a population quantity (e.g., the population mean) for two basic reasons: bias and variance. A biased estimator tends to yield estimates that on average are either too high or too low. If all members of the population have the same probability of being surveyed, the sample mean is an unbiased estimator of the population mean. Conversely, if the probability of being surveyed is correlated with the outcome of interest, the sample mean will be biased. Even unbiased estimators, however, generally do not return the same estimate in every sample but rather "bounce around" from sample to sample. The size of the bounces is captured by the variance. Among other things, variance is a decreasing function of the sample size (larger samples bounce around less) and of the estimator's explanatory power (the less residual variation around the estimator, the lower the variance). The best estimators have both low variance and no bias, but sometimes total error can be reduced by trading off a little bias for a large reduction in variance.

Estimating state-level opinion presents challenges with respect to both bias and variance. Sampling methods have varied greatly over the past eight decades.[19] In the 1930s and 1940s, pollsters generally sent interviewers to a diverse range of geographic locations and instructed them to select interviewees according to prespecified demographic quotas. Quota controls ensured that samples were representative with respect to the demographic variables in the quotas but not necessarily on uncontrolled variables.[20] At midcentury, commercial as well as academic surveys began to use probability sampling, which yields samples representative of unobserved as well as observed variables. Later, many pollsters replaced in-person samples with telephone surveys. This golden age of randomly sampled telephone surveys waned in the late twentieth century as response rates declined, and by the early twenty-first century many pollsters had adopted new techniques, such as opt-in internet-based surveys, which rely on purposive techniques similar to quota sampling to mitigate bias due to unrepresentative samples.

Variance is a particular concern in studies of subnational opinion. Until recently, almost all surveys were designed for inference at the national level.

Thus, for subnational inference, survey researchers had to disaggregate state or local samples from national surveys.[21] The typical national survey of one or two thousand respondents contains only a couple dozen respondents from each state. This problem is more severe in cluster-sampled in-person surveys, which are rarely designed to be representative within a state.[22] For some constructs, sufficiently large state-level samples can be obtained by combining data from many polls,[23] but since this typically requires pooling data from across multiple years, it is poorly suited for our interest in opinion *change*.

Rather, our solution to the twin problems of bias and variance relies on a combination of two techniques: adjustment weighting and Bayesian modeling. The specifics of our procedure are described in the technical appendix to this chapter, but in brief we follow a three-step process. The first step is to divide each survey sample into strata defined by the variables *State*, *Black*, *Urban*, and in some cases *Education*. Within each stratum, we weight survey respondents so that they are observably representative of the corresponding population stratum, typically with respect to the variables age, gender, and education. For example, if the sample underrepresents lower-education Americans relative to the population, they will receive larger weights than higher-education respondents. To the extent that the variables used to weight are good predictors of the outcome and of the probability of participating in the survey, the weighted stratum mean will be a nearly unbiased estimator of the population mean.

The second step is to fit a Bayesian model for the mean outcome in each stratum. The predictors in this model are the variables that define the strata— *State*, *Black*, and *Urban*—and, most importantly, the stratum mean in the preceding time period. In effect, this dynamic linear model (DLM) "borrows strength" from demographically similar strata, as well as from the stratum's own past, to predict the stratum mean. The actual estimate of the stratum mean is a compromise between this prediction and the stratum's sample average, where the weight of each component depends on how precise it is relative to the other. If the sample contains few observations in a given stratum, the sample average will have a high variance and will therefore receive little weight relative to the model's prediction.

The third step is to again weight, or "poststratify," the stratum-specific estimates in proportion to the size of the stratum in the state population. The estimate for the state mean—the ultimate quantity of interest—is the weighted average of stratum-specific estimates. The second and third steps just described are a dynamic variant on a procedure known as multilevel regression and poststratification (MRP).[24] Because it substitutes model-based stratum estimates for the stratum mean, which under ideal conditions is unbiased, MRP can increase bias, but even if it does, the bias is typically more than compensated for with a reduction in variance. For this reason, MRP has been shown to provide more accurate subnational estimates than simple disaggregation of national samples.[25]

Figure 2.5 illustrates the components of this estimation process for public opinion in the state of Wisconsin on three issues: Medicaid expansion under the Affordable Care Act, laws requiring a waiting period for abortions, and antimiscegenation laws. The tick marks along the x axis indicate years with survey data; estimates for intervening years are fully interpolated by the dynamic MRP model. "Support" is the liberal position on Medicaid and the conservative one on the other two issues. Demographic opinion cleavages differ across the three issues. Black Wisconsinites are more likely to support the liberal position on all three issues, but the racial gap in opinion is much larger on Medicaid and interracial marriage than on abortion. Urban residents, too, tend to be somewhat more liberal across the board. Educational cleavages are more complicated. Acceptance of interracial marriage increases with each education level, but on neither of the other two issues does education have a monotonically positive relationship with liberalism. Although these subgroup estimates are interesting in themselves, we use them primarily as inputs to our estimates of mean opinion in the state, which is a population-weighted average of the subgroup estimates.

Ideological Summaries

For many purposes it is sufficient to analyze public opinion and policymaking on an issue-by-issue basis. For example, if one wants to know whether individual policies are congruent with majority opinion, it often makes sense to examine each policy separately. These policy-specific results may then be summarized by reporting the average level of congruence across all policies.[26] In other cases, however, it is preferable to summarize across policies first before engaging in further analysis. In addition to its usual benefits of averaging out idiosyncratic variation and reducing measurement error, treating specific policies as indicators of a more general trait has the particular benefit for us of permitting the construction of consistent time series that are comparable across space and time.

Summarizing across policies with a single "ideology score" can be misleading if policy-specific variation is highly idiosyncratic—that is, if variation on each policy is unrelated to variation on others.[27] In our application, this problem is partially mitigated by our focus on aggregate rather than individual-level patterns, which reduces policy-specific "noise." Yet as figure 2.5 illustrates, even at the level of demographic groups, different policies

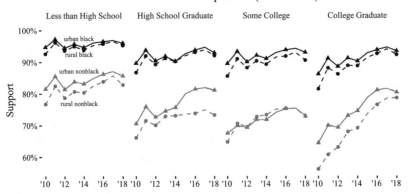

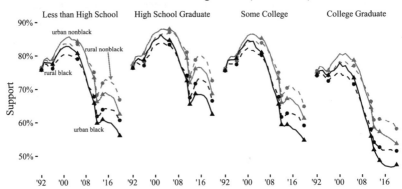

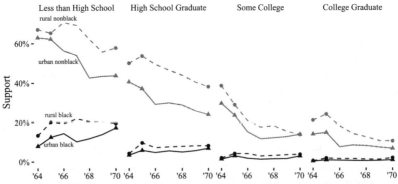

FIGURE 2.5. Dynamic MRP estimates of support for Medicaid expansion (*top*), abortion waiting periods (*middle*), and antimiscegenation laws (*bottom*) in subsets of the Wisconsin state public. Tick marks along the *x*-axis indicate years with survey data.

TABLE 2.1 Illustrative economic policies in five states, 1940 and 2020

Economic Policies (1940)

	NY	WI	MT	DE	MS
Urban Housing Aid	1	0	0	0	0
Minimum Wage for Women	1	1	0	0	0
Rate-Setting Utility Commission	1	1	1	0	0
Workers Compensation	1	1	1	1	0
State Labor Relations Act	pro-labor	balanced	none	none	none
Average ADC Benefit	$774	$685	$517	$509	$188
Economic Policy Conservatism	−1.75	−0.82	−0.05	0.86	1.74

Economic Policies (2020)

	NY	MN	VA	UT	MS
No TANF Work Requirement	1	0	0	0	0
No Right-to-Work Law	1	1	0	0	0
Earned Income Tax Credit	1	1	1	0	0
Age Discrimination Ban	1	1	1	1	0
Renewable Portfolio Standard	mandatory	mandatory	mandatory	voluntary	none
Maximum TANF Benefit	$575	$449	$373	$403	$168
Economic Policy Conservatism	−2.87	−1.21	0.12	1.15	2.58

can exhibit distinct patterns of support. It is thus valuable to distinguish policies into separate issue domains likely to be structured by a common dimension of variation. Following many previous scholars, we distinguish between
economic, cultural, and racial policy domains, though unfortunately there
are not enough racial policies in our data to generate dynamic estimates of
racial policy conservatism. Today, issue attitudes and state policies are quite
positively correlated across domains, but as we show in chapter 3, this was not
always true, especially in the mass public.

Summarizing states' conservatism in a given issue domain presents different challenges depending on whether we are examining state policies or the
mass public, and so we use related but distinct measurement models for the
two tasks (for details, see the technical appendix at the end of this chapter).
Each of these latent-variable models aims to characterize the relationship between an unobserved trait (mass or policy conservatism in a given domain)
and observed indicators of that trait (survey responses or state policies). The
models differ according to the differences in how the observed data are generated, but the basic idea is the same: to use the observed indicators to infer
the value of the latent trait.

Tables 2.1 and 2.2 illustrate the low-dimensional structure underlying
variation in state policies. Each table compares the economic or cultural policies of five states, ordered by their domain-specific policy conservatism, in

TABLE 2.2 Illustrative cultural policies in five states, 1940 and 2020

Cultural Policies (1940)

	NJ	PA	IA	NE	OK
Corporal Punishment Ban	1	0	0	0	0
Gun Dealer Licenses	1	1	0	0	0
Female Jurors Allowed	1	1	1	0	0
No Alcohol Prohibition	1	1	1	1	0
Cultural Policy Conservatism	−1.76	−0.85	−0.06	0.79	1.63

Cultural Policies (2020)

	NJ	ME	WI	KS	OK
No Open Carry Gun Law	1	0	0	0	0
Medicaid Covers Abortion	1	1	0	0	0
No Religious Freedom Restoration Act	1	1	1	0	0
Allows Local LGBT Protections	1	1	1	1	0
Ban on LGBT Hiring Discrimination	LGBT	LGBT	LGB	by govt.	none
Cultural Policy Conservatism	−2.86	−1.74	−0.01	0.99	2.01

1940 and 2020. The tables include a mix of dichotomous, ordinal, and (in the case of the economic domain) continuous policies. Some of the dichotomous policies separate ideologically extreme states from the others. In 1940, only the most economically liberal states, such as New York, provided direct aid for urban housing, and only the most conservative, such as Mississippi, did not have a workers compensation program. Analogously, in 2020, only very culturally liberal states such as New Jersey did not have an open-carry law, and only very conservative ones such as Oklahoma prohibited local LGBT antidiscrimination ordinances. Other policies, such as female jury service in 1940 and right-to-work laws in 2020, divided states more evenly. But all the dichotomous policies in the tables have a certain threshold that separates all states with the law and all states without. (In the language of item response theory, items whose threshold is high have a large "difficulty" parameter.) The fact that each of these items has a threshold that perfectly separates ones and zeros is a sign that they are well described by a single latent dimension.

Similarly, ordinal policies monotonically increase or decrease across each table. For example, in 2020, New Jersey and Maine both had laws prohibiting employment discrimination based on LGBT status; the next most liberal state in this regard, Wisconsin, had a law that protected homosexual but not transgender workers; Kansas's protections applied only to employees of the state itself; and Oklahoma had no protections at all. That same year, New York, Minnesota, and Virginia each had mandatory renewable energy standards, Utah had voluntary ones, and Mississippi had no such standards. The two continuous policies, which index the generosity of states' Aid to Dependent Children (ADC) and Temporary Assistance for Needy Families (TANF) programs, also decline with policy conservatism, though Utah's TANF benefits break the monotonic pattern. This exception is indicative of the fact that a state's policy conservatism does not perfectly predict what policies it will have. This is particularly true of policies that are not very ideological (e.g., licensing requirements for real estate agents), but even strongly ideological policies exhibit errors. Fortunately, our main goal is not predicting individual policies but rather aggregating many policies to estimate the general liberal-to-conservative direction of states' policymaking in a given domain.

Figure 2.6 conducts a similar exercise for the relationship between state-level mass conservatism and public opinion on specific issues. These survey items were chosen because the strength of their relationship with mass conservatism—their "discrimination," in the language of item response theory (IRT)—is close to the average across all items.[28] According to our model, about half the items in our data set are more ideological than these ones, and

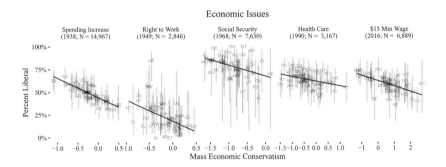

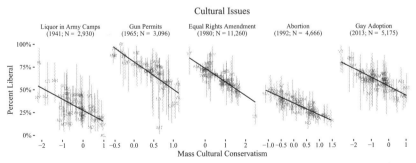

FIGURE 2.6. Mass conservatism and issue-specific opinion on a sample of survey items. Vertical axes indicate the estimated percentage of respondents in a state who supported the liberal position on the issue, with 95 percent confidence interval. Plot titles indicate the year the issue was surveyed and the sample size across all polls in that year that contain the item.

about half are less ideological. In contrast to figure 2.5, figure 2.6 plots the simple weighted averages within each state to provide a sense of the uncertainty of the unmodeled estimates.[29] Note that despite the fact that the sample sizes are larger than the typical national poll, the estimates for many states, especially smaller ones, are very imprecise. This measurement error attenuates the relationship between mass conservatism and issue-specific opinion. It also illustrates the downsides of relying on any single survey item as a proxy for general conservatism. Even if responses to that item are highly ideological, state-level samples will usually be too small for precise estimates. More information can be gained by aggregating many items together, even if some of those items are less than perfectly ideological.

2.3 Summary

The data and measures described in this chapter provide the foundation for the rest of the book. With them, we will describe how states have evolved ideologically over time, both in the mass public and in terms of policymaking. We will also be able to relate shifts in state policymaking to trends in the public's policy preferences and electoral choices and to evaluate how well states' policies match the preferences of their publics. Such analyses would be impossible without the data sets we have constructed and the methods we have developed to derive dynamic measures from them.

2.A Technical Appendix on Measurement Models

This appendix presents more formal derivations of the measurement models we discussed at a qualitative level earlier in the chapter. First, we describe our measurement model for mass policy preferences on individual issues. Second, we describe how we create indices of the ideological conservatism of mass opinion across entire policy domains. Finally, we discuss our approach for measuring the conservatism of public policies.

2.A.1 ISSUE-SPECIFIC OPINION

This section provides a more formal discussion of our dynamic MRP model for individual issues.[30] Consider a survey item q with K_q ordered response options. (In this book we dichotomize all items, so K_q is always 2, but we keep the notation general for consistency with the exposition of our measurement model for policy conservatism.) For each question, the quantity of interest is the population proportion of citizens in group (i.e., stratum) g who in year t

prefer response option k, which we denote π_{gqkt}. Let s_{gqkt} denote the number of respondents in group g who in year t selected response option k to question q. Assuming simple random sampling within groups, the number of responses in each category is distributed

(2.1) $s_{gqt} \sim \text{Multinomial}\,(\pi_{gqt})$,

Where $s_{gqt} \equiv (s_{gq1t} \ldots s_{gqK_qt})$ is the vector of group totals and $\pi_{gqt} \equiv (\pi_{gq1t} \ldots \pi_{gqtK_qt})$ is the corresponding vector of population proportions.

Although it is possible to estimate π_{gqt} directly, it will be convenient for us to specify it in terms of an unbounded variable, $\bar{\theta}_{gqt}$, and a standard-normal error term, $\varepsilon_{gqt} \sim \text{N}(0,1)$, where

(2.2) $\pi_{gqtk} = \text{Pr}(\alpha_{q,k-1} < \bar{\theta}_{gqt} + \varepsilon_{gqt} \leq \alpha_{q,k})$,

where $\alpha_{q,k}$ is the threshold for selecting response option k or above and the $K_q + 1$ thresholds are ordered $-\infty = \alpha_{q,0} < \alpha_{q,1} = 0 < \ldots < \alpha_{q,K-1} < \alpha_{q,K} = \infty$. The higher the threshold, the higher the value of $\bar{\theta}_{gqt}$ (group g's latent support for the issue) required to select above that response category.

Using the normal distribution function $\Phi(\cdot)$, equation (2.2) can be rewritten as an ordinal probit model,

(2.3) $\pi_{gqtk} = \Phi[\bar{\theta}_{gqt} - \alpha_{q,k-1}] - \Phi[\bar{\theta}_{gqt} - \alpha_{qk}]$.

In this formulation, the population proportion in category k is represented as the difference between the proportion above category $k - 1$, $\Phi[\bar{\theta}_{gqt} - \alpha_{q,k-1}]$, and the proportion above k, $\Phi[\bar{\theta}_{gqt} - \alpha_{qk}]$. In the case of $K_q = 2$ categories (where, for example, π_{gqt} is the proportion who favor rather than oppose a policy) equation (2.3) simplifies to the direct transformation $\pi_{gqt} = \Phi[\bar{\theta}_{gqt}]$.

One advantage of the ordered probit specification is that it enables us to use a DLM to specify a prior distribution for $\bar{\theta}_{gqt}$ and thus, indirectly, for π_{gqt}. DLMs are analogous to the hierarchical linear models used in classic MRP except that they include not only cross-sectional predictors x_{gt} (e.g., respondent race or education) but also $\bar{\theta}_{gq,t-1}$ (the value of $\bar{\theta}_{gqt}$ in the previous period). We use the following DLM for $\bar{\theta}_{gqt}$:

(2.4) $\bar{\theta}_{gqt} \sim \text{N}(\delta_t \bar{\theta}_{gq,t-1} + x'_{gt}\gamma_t, \sigma^2_{\bar{\theta}_q})$,

where the variance $\sigma^2_{\bar{\theta}_q}$ indicates how well the model predicts $\bar{\theta}_{gqt}$. The dynamic MRP estimate of $\bar{\theta}_{gqt}$ and thus π_{gqt} is a compromise between this model-based prediction and the maximum likelihood estimate implied by the data. As the size of the sample or the variance of the DLM increases, so does the likelihood's contribution to the estimate.

Mass Conservatism

The measurement model we use to infer mass conservatism in a given domain can be thought of as an extension of the ordered probit model described in section 2.A.1. In that model, we used s_{gqkt}, the observed number of respondents in group g who selected response option k to question q, to infer the value of the latent variable $\bar{\theta}_{gq}$, which represents the group's conservatism on question q specifically. Here, however, our interest is not groups' question-specific conservatism but their general conservatism in a given domain. We denote this variable $\bar{\theta}_{gt}$, which varies by group and period but not by question. If we substitute $\bar{\theta}_{gt}$ into equation (2.3), we obtain what is known in the language of item response theory as an ordinal Rasch model:

$$(2.5) \qquad \pi_{gqkt} = \Phi[\bar{\theta}_{gt} - \alpha_{qt,k-1}] - \Phi[\bar{\theta}_{gt} - \alpha_{qtk}],$$

where, as before, π_{gqkt} is the population proportion of group g who at time t favor response option k to question q. Because the thresholds α_{qt} vary by item, they allow questions to differ in their ideological "difficulty"—that is, in how conservative a respondent must be to be expected to choose a relatively conservative response option. As indicated by the index t, we allow the thresholds to vary across time periods to allow each item to have its own idiosyncratic time trend (e.g., the long-run increase in support for same-sex marriage, opinion on which has liberalized much more rapidly than on issues such as abortion).

Although it accounts for question difficulty, the Rasch model leaves out two important features of the relationship between groups' domain-specific conservatism and their question-specific responses. The first is that survey questions vary in how "discriminating" they are—that is, how well they distinguish liberals from conservatives. Highly salient issues with ideologically distinct policy alternatives—for instance, same-sex marriage—will feature large gaps in support between liberals and conservatives. Such cleavages will be much more muted on obscure or technical issues or ones that bundle ideologically ambiguous policies.[31] Due to differences in items' discrimination, we learn more about the latent trait from some questions than others. These differences can be represented with a question-specific parameter β_q, which captures the weight placed on $\bar{\theta}_{gqt}$ in determining response probabilities. The addition of this discrimination parameter results in a two-parameter ordinal IRT model:

$$(2.6) \qquad \pi_{gqkt} = \Phi[\beta_q \bar{\theta}_{gt} - \alpha_{qt,k-1}] - \Phi[\beta_q \bar{\theta}_{gt} - \alpha_{qtk}].$$

The second feature the Rasch model does not account for is within-group variation in conservatism.[32] A two-parameter ordinal IRT model would be sufficient if groups were internally homogenous—that is, if all individuals in the same group were equally conservative.[33] Since this is not plausible in our case, we accommodate within-group heterogeneity with the addition of a standard-deviation parameter, $\sigma_{\theta t}$, representing the residual variation in citizens' conservatism once group membership is accounted for.[34] The model that we actually use to estimate group-level conservatism, known as a group-level ordinal IRT model, incorporates both of these additional features:

$$(2.7) \qquad \pi_{gqkt} = \Phi\left[\frac{\beta_q \bar{\theta}_{gt} - \alpha_{qt,k-1}}{\sqrt{1 + \beta_q^2 \sigma_{\theta t}^2}}\right] - \Phi\left[\frac{\beta_q \bar{\theta}_{gt} - \alpha_{qtk}}{\sqrt{1 + \beta_q^2 \sigma_{\theta t}^2}}\right].$$

The main quantity of interest in this model is $\bar{\theta}_{gt}$, which represents the *average* conservatism of individuals in group g, with $\sigma_{\theta t}$ indexing variability around this within-group mean.[35] As in the dynamic MRP model, the population proportions π_{gqkt} are linked to the observed responses s_{gqkt} via the multinomial sampling model in equation (2.1), and the prior for $\bar{\theta}_{gt}$ is given by the DLM in equation (2.4).

To understand the substantive interpretation of this model, it may be helpful to focus on the probability of choosing the most conservative response option ($k = K$). Assuming that response options are coded so that higher values are more conservative, this probability, π_{gqKt}, is given by the first term in equation (2.7).[36] Since Φ is an increasing function, π_{gqKt} increases as the quantity inside the square brackets gets larger. Thus, as the difficulty $\alpha_{qt,K-1}$ increases, the probability of selecting the most conservative option decreases. By contrast, the probability is increasing in $\bar{\theta}_{gt}$, the mean conservatism of members of group g. The strength of the relationship between $\bar{\theta}_{gt}$ and π_{gqKt} depends on the question's discrimination, β_q. The larger the value of β_q, the more π_{gqKt} changes with group conservatism.[37] Finally, as the ideological heterogeneity within groups, indexed by $\sigma_{\theta t}$, increases, the bracketed quantity becomes smaller (closer to zero). This brings the expected proportion of responses in the two extreme categories (i.e., π_{gq1t} and π_{gqKt}) closer to equality, muting opinion differences between groups with different values of $\bar{\theta}_{gt}$. At the other extreme, as $\sigma_{\theta t}$ approaches 0 (homogenous groups), the denominator approaches 1 and the model simplifies to the individual-level IRT model in equation (2.6).

Policy Conservatism

This section provides a formal discussion of our measurement model for state policy conservatism. Because each state government is a single entity rather than a group, our model of state policy conservatism does not need to account for within-group heterogeneity ($\sigma_{\theta t}$). Thus, for an ordinal policy indicator $y_{stp} \in \{1, \ldots, K_p\}$ we can simply use the model:

(2.8) $y_{stp} \sim \text{Categorical}(\pi_{stp})$,

where s indexes states, p indexes policies, and

$$\pi_{stpk} \equiv \Pr(y_{stp} = k)$$
(2.9) $$= \Phi[\beta_p \theta_{st} - \alpha_{pt,k-1}] - \Phi[\beta_p \theta_{st} - \alpha_{ptk}].$$

In short, for ordinal policies the state policy model is essentially equivalent to the ordinal IRT model in equation (2.6). There is, however, an additional wrinkle that we do need to account for: the fact that some policies (tax rates, expenditure levels, etc.) take on a continuum of possible values. For these policies, rather than using an ordered probit model with a potentially infinite number of thresholds, we instead use a normal-theory factor analysis model:

(2.10) $y_{spt} = \beta_p \theta_{st} - \alpha_{pt} + \varepsilon_{spt}$,

where the error term $\varepsilon_{spt} \sim N(0, \sigma_q)$. In other words, for continuous policies we assume that the expected value of y_{spt} is given directly by $\beta_p \theta_{st} - \alpha_{pt}$ rather than being transformed by the probit link function. The value of this "mixed" factor analysis model is that it allows us to map policy indicators of any type—dichotomous, ordinal, or continuous—onto the same latent scale.[38]

2.A.3 COMMONALITIES AMONG THE IDEOLOGICAL MODELS

We have now introduced the three measurement models we use to summarize ideological patterns in policies and public opinion: the factor analysis model in equation (2.10), the ordinal IRT model in equation (2.9), and the group-level ordinal IRT model in equation (2.7). Each is designed for data of a different type: continuous policies, ordinal policies, and aggregated responses to ordinal survey questions, respectively. Nevertheless, their differences are much less significant than their commonalities.

All three models have the same purpose: to permit us to make inferences about the value of a latent trait (ideology) from observed indicators of that trait (policies or survey responses). Each uses two sets of parameters—the discriminations β and the difficulties α—to characterize the relationship between the trait and each indicator. The larger a policy or survey question's discrimination, the more sharply it distinguishes liberal and conservative states or groups. The greater its difficulty, the lower the expected score of the typical state or group. The crucial value of characterizing indicator-specific mappings in this way is that if we get the relationship right, then *it does not matter which specific indicators are available in any given year*. As long as there are enough overlapping indicators to bridge across years, then β and α tell us all we need to know to convert disparate indicators to the common scale of the latent variable. This in turn is what enables us to create TSCS measures of mass and policy conservatism that are comparable across time—a critical requirement for estimating the dynamic interplay between these quantities.

3

Preferences:
Partisanship and Ideology in State Publics[1]

In 1956, pitted for a second time against Democrat Adlai Stevenson, President Dwight Eisenhower cruised to reelection with over 57 percent of the popular vote. Like their contest in 1952, the 1956 campaign revealed few large differences in the candidates' domestic policy positions. President Eisenhower, a self-styled "modern Republican," generally opposed expanding the New Deal state he inherited, but unlike more reactionary conservatives, he showed little interest in cutting popular liberal programs such as Social Security. For his part, Stevenson, though he called for more spending on social welfare programs, eschewed the strident class-based appeals of the previous Democratic standard-bearer, Harry Truman. Rather, Stevenson insisted that the Democrats were the "truly conservative party of this country."[2] There was even less daylight between the candidates on civil rights, the prominence of which had increased after the Supreme Court's decision in *Brown v. Board of Education* (1954) invalidated racially segregated public schools. Both Eisenhower and Stevenson straddled the issue, expressing support for the principle but caution about its implementation.[3] Finally, neither devoted much attention to cultural issues such as prohibition of alcohol, which had fallen off the national agenda in the 1930s, or abortion, which would not become salient until the 1960s.

The 1950s, in short, were a low point in elite partisan polarization. On the economic issues that had cleaved Republicans and Democrats since the New Deal, the parties' presidential candidates had both converged toward the middle of the ideological spectrum.[4] On racial and cultural issues, over which the parties had not yet realigned, the candidates' positions were even less distinct.

If anything, the relationship between partisanship and policy positions was even more muddled in the mass public. We know this in part because the

Eisenhower elections coincided with the first two iterations of the University of Michigan's American National Election Studies (ANES), the longest-running academic survey of Americans' political attitudes. The early ANES surveys showed that although party identification (PID) played a dominant role in Americans' political perceptions and voting behavior, it had a much weaker relationship with their policy preferences, which tended to be unstable and ideologically inconsistent.[5] As was the case with presidential candidates, the most partisan issues were those related to economic policy. For example, 40 percent of Republicans disagreed with the statement, "The government ought to help people get doctors and hospital care at low cost," as compared to 22 percent of Democrats. On cultural and racial issues, however, Democratic and Republican identifiers were largely indistinguishable. A little over 40 percent of both parties agreed that "sex criminals . . . should be whipped in public or worse," and about half of each thought the federal government should "stay out of the question of whether white and colored children go to the same school."

Aggregating to the regional level magnifies some of these patterns and reveals others. As the left panel of figure 3.1a shows, the South (here defined to include Kentucky and Oklahoma) was by far the least Republican region of the country, followed by the West and then the Northeast and Midwest. Southerners were also the least likely to oppose government-assisted access to medical care (figure 3.1b, left panel), though not clearly less so than northeasterners. On the cultural issue of whipping sex criminals, which likely invoked respondents' preferences for moral regulation as well as punitiveness, the West was clearly the least conservative (figure 3.1c, left panel). The same is true for the racial issue of school desegregation, though the conservatism of the South is the biggest outlier (figure 3.1d, left panel). When aggregated geographically, then, mass attitudes did display some clear patterns. The South was the most Democratic region and the most liberal on economic issues but the most conservative on racial ones. The West, despite its middling partisanship, was the most culturally and racially liberal. Midwesterners leaned Republican and, on nonracial issues, toward conservative policy preferences.

Today, six decades later, partisanship and policy preferences are much more closely aligned, both among politicians and in the mass public.[6] In the 2016 ANES, for example, Republican respondents were sixty-seven points more likely than Democrats to oppose the Affordable Care Act, twenty points more likely to oppose allowing gays and lesbians to adopt children, and fifty points more likely to believe that "Blacks should help themselves" rather than receive assistance from the government. Policy preferences had aligned with partisanship at the regional level, too, as the right column of figure 3.1

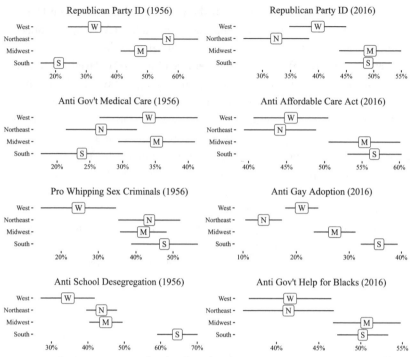

FIGURE 3.1. Partisan, economic, cultural, and racial preferences, 1956 versus 2016, ANES. Republican PID is defined as a percentage of major-party identifiers. Horizontal lines indicate 95 percent confidence intervals.

illustrates. In 2016, southerners and midwesterners not only were more likely to identify as Republicans than respondents from the other two regions but also held more conservative policy preferences in all three issue domains.

In short, by 2016, the politically muddled mass public of the 1950s had become much more sorted. Policy preferences in different domains, though still somewhat distinct, were now positively correlated. Americans with relatively conservative preferences on economics tended also to be conservative on race and culture. In addition, partisanship had largely aligned with policy positions: Republicans tended to have relatively conservative preferences in all three issue domains, and Republican-leaning regions did so as well. Thus, in contrast to the multidimensionality of the 1950s, variation in mass policy preferences in the 2010s was structured to a much greater extent by a single dimension.

How exactly did this "great alignment" of partisanship and policy preferences unfold over the past half century?[7] Did partisanship adapt to policy preferences or the other way around? And how did these dynamics play out within states as well as across them? The ANES is not well suited to answer these questions. It is designed to provide detailed election-year snapshots of the American public as a whole, not to follow individual respondents over long periods of time or support accurate inferences at the state level.[8] Instead, to chart this alignment in detail, we must take advantage of the rich data and measures described in chapter 2. The remainder of this chapter is devoted to this task.

The analyses that follow highlight three important features of this process of alignment. First, as the originally negative association between Republican partisanship and racial and cultural conservatism first reversed and then strengthened, its positive association with economic conservatism did not fade. Rather, partisanship became increasingly correlated with conservatism in all three domains.[9] Second, state publics have largely adapted their partisanship to match their operational ideology instead of the other way around.[10] This macro-level pattern, which contrasts with the typical finding in micro-level studies of individual citizens, suggests that in the aggregate and over the long term, Americans have responded to changes in the party system by updating their party identities to match their policy predispositions. Third, a major consequence of this alignment has been what we call the "ideological nationalization of partisanship." As states' partisan leanings have aligned with their ideological ones, cross-state differences within each party have diminished relative to within-state differences between parties, which have themselves increased. The increasing homogeneity of party brands across states has been an important contributor to the general nationalization of American political behavior in recent decades.[11]

3.1 Partisan and Ideological Trends in the States

3.1.1 PARTISANSHIP

At the individual level, party identification is among the most stable of political attitudes. When Americans are interviewed multiple times over a period of several years, their self-categorization as "Republican" or "Democrat" tends to be about as consistent as their identification as "Irish" or "Protestant."[12] One long-term study, spanning the years 1940–1977, found that between early adulthood and retirement age, only about a fifth of subjects changed their partisan leanings from one party to another.[13] Partisan stability also increases over the life course. Another panel survey, covering 1965–1997, found a 0.49 correlation between PID measured at ages eighteen and twenty-six, a 0.65 correlation between ages twenty-six and thirty-five, and 0.65 again for between thirty-five and fifty.[14] Few, if any, issue attitudes exhibit this degree of over-time consistency. It is this individual-level stability that undergirded the early Michigan School view of PID as an "unmoved mover"—profoundly shaping political attitudes and behavior while being largely immune to short-term political forces.

At the aggregate level, however, mass partisanship does evolve. There are two reasons for this. First, although PID is relatively stable at the individual level, it is not perfectly so. Some individuals do change their partisanship, and when they do it is usually in the direction of the party that better matches their policy preferences.[15] Second, the composition of the electorate itself changes over time. As relatively impressionable young adults reach political maturity, they bring into the electorate partisan affiliations more aligned with the current policy commitments and popularity of the two parties than those of the older adults they replace. Consequently, both the aggregate balance between the two parties—what MacKuen, Erikson, and Stimson[16] call "macropartisanship"—and the relative partisanship of different subpopulations can undergo major changes, especially over the long term.

With respect to national macropartisanship, the most important change since the mid-twentieth century has been the erosion of Democrats' once-massive advantage in partisan identification. As figure 3.2 shows, however, partisan trends have differed markedly across regions.[17] In the Midwest, Republican PID has oscillated around a long-term mean of about half of major-party identifiers. In the West, the Republican share increased from around 40 percent before 1980 to above 50 percent since then, while the Northeast has trended in the opposite direction. The most dramatic change, however, has occurred in the South, where Republican PID grew from around 20 percent of identifiers to over 50 percent. The South's realignment toward the Republicans has been driven entirely by the majority White population.[18] Black southerners, who before the 1930s were almost all Republicans, have been overwhelmingly Democratic since their reenfranchisement in the 1960s. It should be noted that these shifts in macropartisanship have coincided with a long-term increase in Independents, first largely at the expense of Republicans and then of Democrats.[19]

As figure 3.3 illustrates, even these regional comparisons conceal important differences in states' partisan trajectories relative to the nation. For example, the southern states of Louisiana and Virginia both trended Republican relative to the nation until the 1980s, after which Virginia began to drift back toward the Democrats while Louisiana's realignment continued unabated. In the West, Idaho and Oregon both leaned slightly Republican in 1940 but since then have trended in opposite directions. While Nebraska

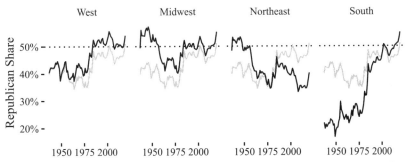

FIGURE 3.2. Republican share of major-party identifiers, 1937–2020. Black lines indicate Republican share averaged across states within region (not population weighted). Gray lines indicate Republican share in the average US state.

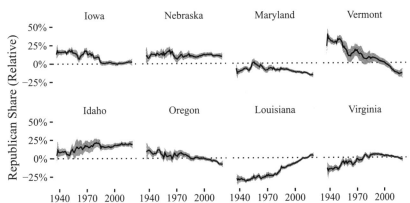

FIGURE 3.3. Partisan trends in selected states. Each plot shows Republican share of major-party identifiers relative to the average share across states in that year. Gray regions indicate 95 percent confidence intervals.

has remained solidly Republican, Iowa has become evenly divided between the parties. Traditionally Democratic Maryland flirted with Republicanism in the 1950s before returning to its partisan roots. Meanwhile, Vermont has transformed from the country's most Republican state to one that is fifteen points more Democratic than average.

As these examples show, partisan change does not occur overnight, but over the long run, state publics can dramatically alter their partisan complexion. This can be seen clearly if we examine the correlations between states' macropartisanship measured at different points in time. Suppose we take the cross-year average of each state's Republican PID share within three periods: 1936–1964, 1965–1992, and 1993–2020. Between the first and second periods, states' partisanship has a correlation of 0.74, indicating a fair degree of stability. By the third period, however, the correlation with the first falls to just 0.09.[20] In other words, a state's mass partisanship before 1965 provides almost no information about its partisanship after 1992. This instability contrasts markedly with the stability of PID at the individual level, suggesting that partisanship is much less of an "unmoved mover" for states than it is for individuals.

3.1.2 IDEOLOGY

In 1964, Philip Converse used data from early ANES surveys to argue that when it came to issue attitudes, most Americans were ignorant, unstable, and ideologically incoherent.[21] To many scholars, such attitudes have seemed to provide a shaky foundation for policy-based partisan affiliations if not for electoral democracy itself.[22] Indeed, though they may not realize it, Americans often hold policy positions inconsistent with their preferred party. If they do become aware of it, unless the issue is especially important to them, they are more likely to bring their issue preferences in line with their partisanship than the other way around.[23] From this perspective, PID seems to enjoy causal priority over policy preferences.

As we have noted, one counter to this perspective is to invoke the miracle of aggregation. Yes, at the individual level, issue opinions appear incoherent, but a reasonable structure emerges when responses are averaged across groups or the public as a whole. The structure and explanatory power of policy preferences also increases when individual issue questions are aggregated into an index or other summary measure. Our measures of domain-specific conservatism take advantage of both forms of aggregation: they summarize information from many issue questions and do so at the level of states, not individual Americans.

Aggregating in this way reveals patterns hard to discern at the individual level. One such pattern is the well-known tendency for the opinions of different subpublics to move in parallel with one another.[24] This tendency is clearly evident in figure 3.4, which superimposes regional trends in mass conservatism over national ones. Nationally, economic conservatism (top) has fluctuated sharply over time, especially since the 1960s, and the regional time series closely track the national one. The high points of economic conservatism—1942, 1982, 1995, 2014—coincide fairly closely with low points in James Stimson's measure of "policy mood," which captures the public's desire for increased government activity.[25] Generally speaking, economic conservatism seems to conform to the "thermostatic" model proposed by Christopher Wlezien.[26] It increases in response to periods of Democratic control and

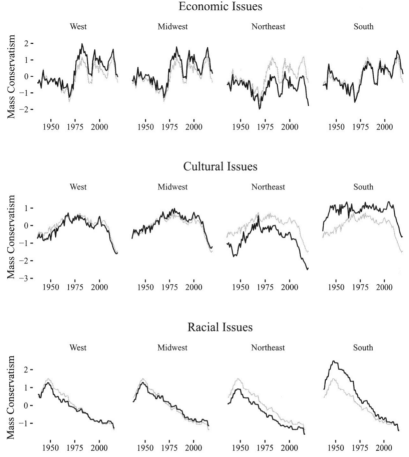

FIGURE 3.4. Trends in mass conservatism by issue domain. Black lines indicate the unweighted average across states in the region, and the gray lines indicate the unweighted national average. Measures are standardized to have zero mean and unit variance across state-years.

liberal policymaking and decreases in response to Republican control and conservative policymaking, exhibiting little long-term trend.

Over-time changes in mass economic conservatism have generally been larger than regional differences at any given point in time. This is especially true before 1970. Since then, regional contrasts have sharpened somewhat, with the Northeast emerging as clearly the most liberal region on economic issues. Interestingly, southern state publics closely tracked the nation as a whole until the Obama administration, when they shifted to the right of the average state.

The mass public's cultural ideology (figure 3.4, middle panel) has exhibited fewer fluctuations than its economic ideology. Nationally, mass conservatism

on cultural policies gradually increased until the late 1960s, when it began
a gentle decline that accelerated rapidly after 2000. Conservatism's apparent
upward trajectory early on should be viewed skeptically, as there are very
few high-discrimination items that bridge across years in this period (the
most consistently asked item is on support for alcohol prohibition, which
actually increased slightly over the 1940s before declining markedly in the
1950s–1960s). The cultural liberalization of recent decades, which was driven
in large part by steeply decreasing support for policies that discriminate
based on sexual orientation, is more credible and parallels similar trends in
European public opinion.[27] Regional differences stand out a bit more on this
domain, the Northeast being consistently liberal relative to the nation and the
South consistently conservative.

Finally, on racial issues, two patterns stand out. The first is the long-term
secular decline in racial conservatism in the American public. At midcentury, the average state was one standard deviation more conservative than
the long-run average (recall that these estimates are standardized across
state-years). Today, it is one standard deviation below average.[28] The second
pattern is the South's transformation from a racially conservative outlier to
parity with the rest of the nation. As was the case with partisanship, White
southerners drove this transformation. At midcentury, the policy attitudes
of White southerners were far more racially conservative than those of their
non-southern counterparts, but today they are only slightly so.[29] This small
difference is counterbalanced by the South's larger Black population, with
the net result of convergence between the South and the rest of the nation.
The South's liberalization has come largely at the expense of the West and
especially the Midwest, which is now the most conservative region. The one
region whose relative racial conservatism has not changed is the Northeast,
whose residents have always expressed the most support for civil rights and
other racially liberal positions.

3.1.3 EVOLUTION AND STABILITY

The long-term result of the changes described in the preceding section has
been a gradual evolution in the geographic distribution of mass partisanship
and ideology. This evolution is highlighted by the maps in figure 3.5, which
plot our four partisan and ideological measures on a common standardized
scale. Reading across the top row of graphs, we can clearly see the South's
transformation from a dark (Democratic) band of states in the 1936–1964 period to a middling gray in the years 1993–2020. The South's relative liberalization on racial issues (bottom panel) is obvious as well. Changes in economic

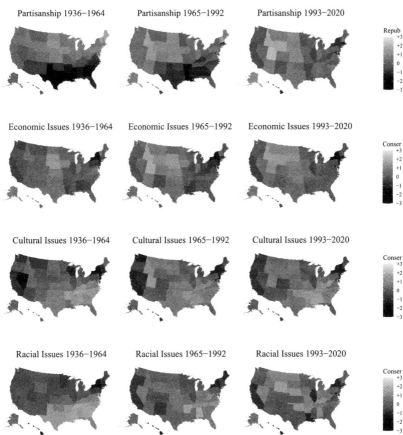

FIGURE 3.5. The geographic distribution of mass partisanship and ideology by era. Each measure is standardized within years and then averaged across years within eras.

and cultural conservatism tend to be subtler. Wisconsin, for example, has become more culturally conservative, and Vermont has become more liberal. On the whole, however, the dominant pattern with respect to states' economic and cultural conservatism has been stability relative to one another. Most southern states have remained fairly moderate on economic issues and conservative on cultural ones, while northeastern and Pacific Coast states have consistently leaned liberal on both domains.

The relative stability of partisanship and ideology can be compared more formally by correlating each measure with itself across time. The results of this exercise are reported in table 3.1. As we saw earlier, states' partisanship in the 1936–1964 period has only a 0.09 correlation with their partisanship in the 1993–2020 period. Economic and cultural conservatism, however, have

TABLE 3.1 Stability of partisan and policy preferences

	Partisan	Economic	Cultural	Racial
1936–1964 to 1965–1992	0.74	0.78	0.80	0.70
1965–1992 to 1993–2020	0.63	0.89	0.96	0.79
1936–1964 to 1993–2020	0.09	0.71	0.80	0.31

been far more stable, with analogous correlations of 0.71 and 0.80 respectively. Due to the South's convergence with the nation on racial issues, states' conservatism in this domain has exhibited greater flux ($R = 0.31$), but it has still been more stable than partisanship. In short, while neither states' relative conservatism nor their relative Republicanism has remained perfectly stable since the 1930s, mass partisanship has changed more than policy preferences.

3.2 The Alignment of Ideology and Partisanship

As mass partisanship and, to a lesser extent, mass ideology have evolved over the past eight decades, they have come into alignment with one another. In the 1930s, states' cultural and racial conservatism were poor predictors of their economic conservatism, let alone their attachment to the Democratic or Republican parties. Today, these variables are all positively correlated across states.

Figure 3.6 illustrates this process of alignment. As the plots in the top row show, economically conservative state publics have leaned Republican as far back as the 1936–1964 period. The positive relationship in the top-left panel fits with the dominance of economic issues in the New Deal party system, though the holdover of sectional conflict is visible in southern states' anomalously Democratic partisanship.[30] Far from erasing this positive association, however, the partisan realignments of the following decades only strengthened it. The cross-state correlation between economic conservatism and Republican PID increased from 0.22 in 1936–1964 to 0.89 in 1993–2020. The alignment of partisanship with cultural and racial ideology has been even more dramatic. In 1936–1964, mass Republicanism had a marked negative relationship with both cultural and racial conservatism (figure 3.6, middle and bottom rows). By the 1965–1992 period, these negative correlations had attenuated to near zero, and by 1993–2020 they were robustly positive.

As economic, cultural, and racial ideology have aligned with partisanship, they have also aligned with each other. In the 1936–1964 period, state economic conservatism had a 0.43 correlation with cultural conservatism and a 0.18 correlation with racial conservatism. In 1965–1992, the analogous correlations were 0.55 and 0.46, and by 1993–2020 they were 0.72 and 0.85. Thus, while states' conservatism has always been at least modestly associated across domains, these relationships are now much stronger, to the point where a single ideological (and partisan) dimension describes most cross-state variation.

These patterns are consistent with Geoffrey Layman and Thomas Carsey's argument that partisan realignments since the 1970s have not displaced the New Deal cleavage over economics but rather extended partisan polarization to the racial and cultural domains.[31] Based largely on individual-level data, these scholars have emphasized the degree to which conflict extension has been driven by party identifiers and activists bringing their issue positions into line with their partisanship, though they acknowledge that the reverse has also occurred.[32] From the perspective of states, however, the causal

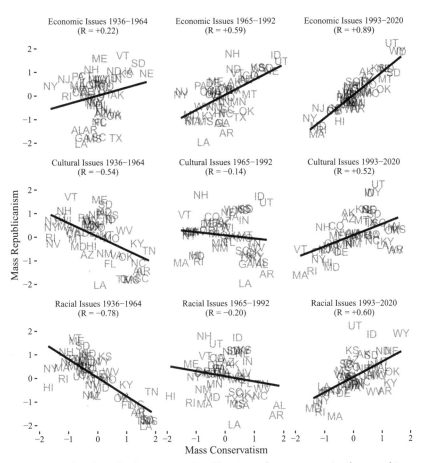

FIGURE 3.6. The relationship between mass Republicanism and mass conservatism by era and issue domain. "R =" indicates the Pearson correlation coefficient.

primacy of partisanship is much less clear. For instance, one study finds that state publics' support for the New Deal in 1940 is a better predictor of presidential elections half a century later than are the results of the 1940 presidential election itself.[33]

Our data yield similar results. States' mass partisanship in the 1993–2020 period has higher bivariate correlations with economic, cultural, and racial conservatism in 1936–1964 than with partisanship itself in 1936–1964. In fact, if post-1992 partisanship is regressed on all four pre-1965 measures, the only statistically significant predictor is economic conservatism, with a standardized coefficient of 0.74 (as compared to 0.18 for lagged partisanship). In short, consistent with Gerald Wright and Nathaniel Birkhead's evidence with respect to ideological identification, it appears that state publics, unlike individual citizens, have largely adapted their partisanship to fit their (economic) policy preferences rather than the other way around.[34]

3.3 The Ideological Nationalization of Partisanship

A major driver of the alignment of mass conservatism and mass Republicanism has been what we call the *ideological nationalization of partisanship*.[35] By this, we mean that the label "Democrat" has come increasingly to have the same ideological meaning everywhere in the country; the same is true of the label "Republican." Thus, whereas once the partisan identities "Southern Democrat" and "Rockefeller Republican" signaled ideological orientations that were clearly distinct from the national party brands, these labels are now much less meaningful. This is true not only of politicians (e.g., members of Congress), whose ideological positions are now more powerfully shaped by party than geographic constituency, but of citizens as well. Democratic identifiers are much more similar to Democrats in other states than they once were, and the same is true of Republican identifiers.

By the same token, ideological differences between Democrats and Republicans in the same state have grown, a phenomenon we call *mass partisan divergence*. On each issue domain, the within-state difference in mass ideology between identifiers for the two major parties has increased. Thus, in terms of their policy preferences, partisans in a given state have not only become more similar to copartisans from other states but also less similar to residents of the same state who identify with the opposite party.

Figure 3.7 illustrates these two phenomena by comparing the ideological evolution of Democratic and Republican identifiers in Illinois and Georgia. First, consider racial issues (right column). For most of the twentieth century, the two states differed massively in this domain; Georgians of both parties were

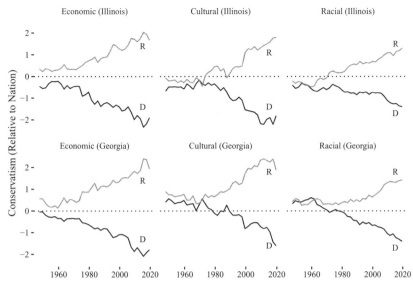

FIGURE 3.7. Partisan polarization in Illinois and Georgia. Vertical axis plots each party-public's conservatism relative to the average state-party public in the nation, with mass conservatism standardized across state-years.

much more conservative than Democrats and Republicans in Illinois. These cross-state differences dwarfed within-state ones, which in the case of Georgia were essentially nonexistent.[36] In other words, party explained almost none of the variance in racial conservatism across state-party publics. Contrast this with the end of the time series, when the opposite was true: Republicans in the two states exhibited very similar levels of racial conservatism, as did Democrats, but the two parties diverged markedly within each state.

Cultural issues (figure 3.7, middle column) exhibit a subtler variation on the same pattern. Throughout this time period, Democrats and Republicans in Illinois were modestly more liberal than their counterparts in Georgia. What changed is that the gaps between Democrats and Republicans in the same state were initially very small, but in the late 1970s they began to widen dramatically. By the twenty-first century, differences between the parties dominated within-state ones on cultural issues just as they did on racial issues. Finally, economic conservatism (left column) exhibits the same pattern of increasing divergence over time but from a more advanced starting point. In the 1930s, Democrats and Republicans in the same state were already somewhat polarized over economic issues, but the gap between them widened greatly over time. In short, all three domains exhibit a combination of partisan divergence and ideological nationalization as Democrats and

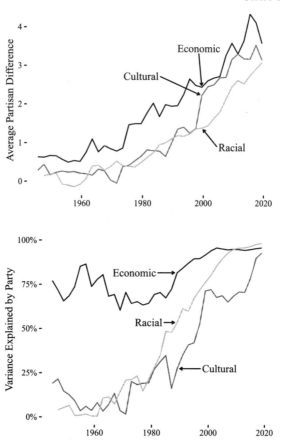

FIGURE 3.8. Trends in partisan divergence and ideological nationalization. Panel (a) plots the average within-state difference in standardized conservatism between Republicans and Democrats. Panel (b) plots the proportion of variance in state party publics' conservatism explained by party.

Republicans became more dissimilar from each other within states and more similar to their partisan brethren in other states.

These patterns are not unique to Illinois and Georgia. Figure 3.8a plots the average within-state difference in conservatism between Democrats and Republicans over this time period. In this plot, each measure has been standardized across state-party-years. The measures are comparable over time under the assumption that items' ideological "discrimination" has remained constant over this period.[37] Given this admittedly strong assumption, we can conclude that the ideological distance between the average Democrat and Republican in the same state has increased tremendously over time. This is obviously true of racial and cultural conservatism, where there were few partisan differences before the 1960s, but it is true as well of economic conservatism, where partisan divergence has increased eightfold since the mid-twentieth century. As we shall see in chapter 6, the increasing distance between partisan subconstituencies has magnified the incentives of politicians in each party to take ideologically extreme positions.

For a more direct and robust measure of ideological nationalization, we can use the proportion of ideological variation across state-party publics explained by partisanship.[38] Unlike partisan divergence, variance explained is "scale free" and thus does not rely on the assumption that items' discrimination is constant across years, and it also accounts for the possibility that differences across states may be changing at the same time as differences between parties. If the differences between parties are small relative to the differences across states, the variance explained by party will be near 0 percent. If they are large, the variance explained will approach 100 percent.

As figure 3.8b shows, party has always explained the bulk of ideological variation on economic issues. This is consistent with what we saw in figure 3.7: in the 1940s, Illinois Democrats were more liberal on economics than Georgia Democrats, but the difference between Illinois Democrats and Illinois Republicans was even larger. Nevertheless, beginning in the 1980s, the variance in economic conservatism explained by party increased markedly, from below 75 percent to well above 90 percent. On cultural and racial issues, ideological nationalization has been far more dramatic. Before 1980, less than a quarter of the variation across state-party publics was explained by party; by the 2010s, over 90 percent was. This, too, is consistent with figure 3.7, where state differences dominated early on, especially on racial issues, but were ultimately supplanted by partisan ones.

The upshot of these changes is that Democrats and Republicans today are far more ideologically similar across states than they once were. This does not mean that *states* are necessarily more similar. Rather, it means that ideological differences across states are, to a much greater degree, a function of differences in partisanship. Although Democrats in Georgia have become just as economically liberal as Democrats in Illinois, Georgia is still more conservative than Illinois because it is much less Democratic than it once was. As with partisan divergence, ideological nationalization changes both the incentives and the prospects of Democratic and Republican politicians. To the extent that state primary electorates favor candidates who represent their views, they are likely to select nominees that are more ideologically similar to their party's nominees in other states than they once were. In states where the party is a minority, however, these nominees face a double penalty: not only do most voters favor the opposite party but also their policy positions are more ideologically distant from the median voter than nominees in earlier eras. It is therefore no surprise that, as chapter 6 will show, the alignment of mass partisanship with mass conservatism has been accompanied by a parallel alignment of partisan election outcomes and control of state governments.

3.4 Summary

Why has mass ideology aligned with mass partisanship? There are no simple answers to this question, but several factors are worth highlighting. One is the New Deal–era realignment of African Americans and other racially liberal constituencies into Democratic parties outside the South, which, when combined with the subsequent reemergence of civil rights onto the political agenda in the 1940s–1960s, undermined the rationale for (racially conservative) White southerners' loyalty to the Democratic Party.[39] Among other things, the South's drift toward the Republican Party contributed to partisan polarization in Congress and sharpened the parties' ideological brands, making it easier for citizens to sort into the ideologically "correct" party. Polarization at both the national and state level was exacerbated by the decline of traditional party organizations and the growing importance of issue-oriented "amateur" activists motivated by policy rather than patronage.[40] Finally, due to changes in the media and other developments, Americans' political attention has increasingly focused on national politics over state and local politics.[41] Americans' focus on national politics has in turn increased the weight of parties' national brands in determining citizens' partisanship, fostering the ideological nationalization of partisanship.

The changes in mass opinion wrought by these shifts in national context have had knock-on effects on elections and politicians. As Republicanism and conservatism have aligned, fewer voters are cross-pressured by their partisan and policy preferences. This has decreased the fluidity of their electoral choices and increased their consistency across different offices. The nationalization of Americans' attention has also probably diminished the electoral rewards of moderation for state-level politicians (since voters are less likely to notice). At the same time, partisan divergence in the mass public has magnified the trade-off that politicians face between catering to the general electorate and satisfying their (now more extreme) partisan subconstituency. Mass-level partisan divergence therefore reinforces other factors contributing to elite-level partisan polarization, both at the national level and in the states.

4

Policies:
The Outputs of State Government

In some respects, Vermont and Idaho were political opposites in the 1930s. Vermont was a bastion of Republicanism, but Idaho typically floated with the partisan tide. In 1936, while Democratic president Franklin Roosevelt was being reelected in a landslide, his opponent Alf Landon won 56 percent of the vote in Vermont, one of only two states the Republican carried. In the same election, Vermont Republicans maintained control of all statewide elected offices along with four-fifths of state legislative seats. Meanwhile, Roosevelt swept Idaho with 63 percent of the vote. Idaho's state-level results, too, were the mirror image of Vermont's: Democratic control of all statewide offices and overwhelming majorities in the legislature.

At the same time, the public policies of these two states were remarkably similar. Both states taxed personal and corporate income but lacked a sales tax.[1] Unlike many states, neither Idaho nor Vermont had a minimum wage, a prevailing-wage requirement for government contractors, or a law enabling federal housing aid. Women could not serve on juries in either state, though both would reverse this policy within a decade. Neither Idaho nor Vermont mandated racially segregated school systems, but neither banned racial discrimination in public accommodations. Where their policies did differ, Idaho's tended to be slightly more liberal. In Vermont judges could enjoin labor unions from striking, but in Idaho antistrike injunctions were forbidden. Idaho also spent more per capita on education and welfare than the average state, whereas Vermont's expenditures were below the national average. On the other hand, interracial marriage was permitted in Vermont but not in Idaho. These differences notwithstanding, citizens living in the two states were governed by almost identical policies.

These patterns were not set in stone, however. Both the policies and the politics of these states evolved dramatically over the succeeding decades. Between the 1930s and 1960s, the size and scope of state government expanded greatly in both states, and in both it was Republican governors who presided over many of these new policy initiatives. In Idaho, the modernization and expansion of state government, especially in the realm of education, was spearheaded by Governor C. A. Robins, a Republican elected to a single four-year term in 1946. Governor Robert Smylie, another Republican who served from 1955 to 1966, built on Robins's initiatives, encouraging state action on parks, infrastructure, public schools, and social welfare.[2] Governor Smylie also engineered the creation of a permanent sales tax, which provided an enduring revenue stream for the state's expanded activities.[3] Although these Idaho governors mainly served with legislatures dominated by their fellow Republicans, both support and opposition to their proposals cut across party lines.

Vermont followed a similar policy trajectory. Although Republicans controlled the legislature continuously in this period, the state did elect its first Democratic governor since the Civil War, Phil Hoff, who served from 1963 to 1968. Under governors of both parties, the state gradually took on more responsibilities. For example, between the 1940s and 1970s, Vermont's inflation-adjusted state spending on public education steadily increased from around $1,500 per pupil to $5,000.[4] Over the same period, the state doubled the benefits it provided for need-based welfare programs such as Old-Age Assistance and Aid to Families with Dependent Children (AFDC).

In the 1960s and especially in the 1970s, the states began to move in opposite directions. Republican dominance in Vermont, in decline since the 1950s,[5] was further undermined by an influx of out-of-staters, many of them liberal Democrats from New York, Massachusetts, and other parts of New England.[6] It was weakened as well by the US Supreme Court's "one-person, one-vote" decisions of the early 1960s, which forced the state to draw legislative districts that increased the representation of more liberal urban voters.[7] Idaho, too, attracted emigrants from more progressive states, especially California, but these tended to be fleeing the taxes and regulations of their former homes rather than seeking to export them. The socially conservative Church of Jesus Christ of Latter-Day Saints (Mormons), long a salient constituency in Idaho, also grew robustly, roughly doubling its share of the state population over the second half of the twentieth century.[8]

The 1970s were a critical decade for the states' policy trajectories. In 1970, Vermont helped pioneer a "land use revolution" by passing Act 250, whose sweeping regulations "turned Vermont into the envy of environmentalists

across the nation."[9] The act was sponsored by Republican governor Deane
Davis, who also pushed through the state's first sales tax, as a means of fend-
ing off a primary challenge from a more liberal Republican.[10] Although Idaho
adopted a more modest land-use law not long after, its state government remained much more deferential to private property rights than Vermont's, as
evidenced by its relative hostility to environmental protections.[11] The 1970s
also saw Vermont's AFDC benefits and corporate tax rate exceed those of
Idaho for the first time. For Idaho, the key turning point was a 1978 "tax
revolt" and consequent limitations on local property taxes, which in turn
shifted the burden of public school funding onto the states, cannibaliz-
ing from other programs.[12] In the following decade, Idaho also repealed its
prevailing-wage requirement and passed a right-to-work law, reversing the
relatively pro-union stance it displayed in the 1930s. Around the same time,
Vermont increased its minimum wage to above the federal standard, while
Idaho's remained below it.

The two states diverged on cultural issues as well. In 1990, Idaho attracted
nationwide attention when its Republican legislature, spurred by a lobbying
campaign from a national "right to life" organization, passed what would
have been the strictest antiabortion law in the nation. Democratic governor Cecil Andrus, though avowedly pro-life, considered the bill so extreme
that he ultimately decided to veto it.[13] Nevertheless, Idaho's abortion laws,
through parental consent and other requirements, have remained about as
strict as constitutionally permissible. In contrast, Vermont has been among
the minority of states whose Medicaid system pays for abortions. Vermont attracted national attention for very different reasons in 2000, when it legalized
same-sex civil unions, and again in 2009, when the Democratic legislature
overrode the Republican governor's veto and made Vermont the first state
to allow same-sex marriage through legislative rather than judicial action.[14]
Thanks to the US Supreme Court, same-sex marriage is now legal throughout the country, but Vermont's laws on hate crimes, employment discrimination, and public accommodations continue to provide greater protections for
LGBT citizens than Idaho's do.

In short, the policy regimes of Idaho and Vermont, once nearly identical, now occupy different ends of the ideological spectrum. Moreover, their
policies now match their partisanship and voting patterns. In 2016, Republicans made up nearly two-thirds of major-party identifiers in Idaho but only
a little over one-third in Vermont. That same year, Donald Trump received
68 percent of the major-party vote in Idaho but just 35 percent in Vermont.
While Vermont has continued to elect Republican governors to balance the

increasingly large Democratic majorities in its legislature, Idaho Republicans
have enjoyed unified control of state government since 1995 and are in little
danger of losing it in the near future.

*

Vermont and Idaho are unusual among US states for the magnitude of
their policy transformations. As this chapter will show, most states' policy
ideology, like their mass ideology, has tended to be fairly stable over time—
substantially more so than their partisanship. Nevertheless, the two states do
illustrate several general themes in state policymaking.

The first theme is that state policies, even those in different issue domains,
do not vary independently of one another. Today, Vermont has not only a
more pro-union labor regime than Idaho but also larger welfare benefits,
stricter environmental regulations, and laxer abortion laws. The ideological
consistency of state policies is greater now than it was in the past, but for
as far back as our data extend, state policymaking has always had a strong
liberal–conservative structure. The direction of state policy *change* tends to
be ideologically consistent as well, at least when states are compared relative
to each other. For example, between 1970 and 1980, Vermont cut real AFDC
benefits by 19 percent and repealed its criminal sodomy law; over the same
period, Idaho cut AFDC by 44 percent and left its sodomy law in place. On
neither policy did the two states move in opposite directions in an absolute
sense. Relative to Vermont, however, Idaho became more conservative on
both policies—even though it made no change to its sodomy law. Because
state policymaking in a given domain often trends in a particular direction—
conservative on welfare in the 1970s and liberal on gay rights—we must account for these policy-specific trends to reveal states' overall ideological trajectory relative to the nation.

Second, even though a given state's policymaking often trends in a liberal or
conservative direction and states occasionally undergo bursts of policy change,
states' policy portfolios are never transformed overnight. Rather, policy change
is generally incremental. Sometimes this is true of individual policies. Vermont,
for example, increased its top corporate tax rate from 2 percent to 10 percent
between the 1940s and the 1990s, but it did so in seven steps that were roughly
evenly spread across time. Similarly, the real value of AFDC payments in Idaho
increased linearly between the late 1940s and late 1960s, from $800 to nearly
$1,500, then decreased linearly to less than $500 in the early 1990s. Even when
changes on individual policies are abrupt and large,[15] however, the overall liberalism or conservatism of a state's policies typically changes much more gradually. Thus, in Vermont, it was Governor Hoff who presided over large increases

in education and welfare expenditures, but the key shifts in environmental and land-use policy occurred in the Davis administration. In Idaho, the turning point for tax policy was 1978, but for labor policy it was 1985. The liberalization of Vermont's laws on homosexuality, too, occurred in stages: decriminalization of sodomy in 1977, strengthening of antidiscrimination protections in 1991–1992 and again in 2007, legalization of civil unions in 2000, passage of a hate crimes law in 2001, and state recognition of same-sex marriage in 2009. Viewed collectively, the policies of each state evolve gradually.

Third, Idaho and Vermont illustrate policy conservatism's changing relationship with partisanship. At midcentury, large differences in the states' partisan leanings had seemingly little impact on their policies. Moreover, important liberal policy shifts occurred under the auspices of Republican governors and legislators and were by no means uniformly supported by Democratic politicians, at least in Idaho. Partisan differences on cultural issues were even more muted than they were on economics, but both increased over time. By the 1980s, Republican officeholders were clearly to the right of same-state Democrats on issues such as abortion as well as on labor, taxes, and spending. Moreover, the partisanship of both states gradually aligned with their diverging policy conservatism. By the first decade of the twenty-first century, Vermont was among the least Republican states, especially in the mass public, and had among the most liberal policies; Idaho, on the other hand, was dominated by the Republican Party, and its policies were relatively conservative across the board.

The remainder of this chapter explores these themes systematically. We begin with an analysis of trends in state policy ideology over time, both collectively and in terms of individual states. We show that policy ideology has become increasingly one-dimensional, just as mass ideology has, though policy has consistently been more correlated across domains than has public opinion. We then examine the evolving relationship between policy and partisanship. We show that, consistent with classic findings in state politics, Republican states actually had more *liberal* policies than Democratic ones until the 1980s. In recent decades, however, both mass partisanship and party control of state government has aligned with policy ideology. In short, state policymaking has mirrored the mass public, becoming more correlated across issue domains while also aligning with partisanship.

4.1 Trends in State Policy Ideology

For the most part, our focus in this chapter and throughout the book is on states' policy evolution relative to each other. This is why, in our primary measurement model for policy ideology, we allow the "difficulty" of each policy to evolve between years (see the technical appendix to chapter 2). This flexibility improves the fit of the model but at the cost of dampening year-to-year changes in policy ideology scores.[16] It is therefore useful to set the scene with a brief examination of an alternative version of the policy measurement model that constrains the difficulty of each policy to be constant across years and thus attributes all over-time policy differences to shifts in policy ideology. The constant-difficulty version of the model highlights national trends in policy ideology better than the evolving-difficulty version.

Using the constant-difficulty estimates, figure 4.1 plots the policy evolution of the median state along with the cross-state distribution in each year. As this figure makes clear, the long-term trend in both domains has been toward less conservative (more liberal) policies over time. Because we normalize monetary indicators to account for the cost of living, this secular decline is not due to inflation. Rather, it is largely because, in the economic domain, the size and scope of government activity has generally increased, and in the cultural domain, moral regulation has generally become less restrictive. On economics, the rate of change was greater before the 1980s than after, and on cultural issues liberalization accelerated in the 1960s. Also visible in this figure are local bumps and dips in policy conservatism, such as the rare increase in the median state's economic conservatism after the wave of Republican state-level victories in the 2010 elections.[17]

A second trend highlighted by figure 4.1 is that policy variation across states has grown over time, especially in the economic domain.[18] In the 1930s, the ninetieth–tenth percentile interval of economic policy conservatism was about one standard deviation (the measures are standardized to have zero-mean and unit-variance across state-years); by the 2010s, the interval had doubled in size. One consequence of this increasing variation is that since 2000, unlike most earlier points in time, the most conservative states have exhibited little decline in conservatism, but the most liberal states have continued to liberalize rapidly. It should be noted that this does not necessarily imply that policy differences have become substantively larger. Indeed, as table 2.1 illustrated, cross-state differences on policies such as welfare benefits have actually shrunk in real terms. Rather, the increasing variance in policy conservatism is at least partly due to increasing policy "constraint": states now have more consistently liberal or consistently conservative policies, with fewer exceptions to their general ideological orientation.[19]

Having used the constant-difficulty variant of policy conservatism to highlight national trends, we now turn to our main measure, which allows each policy's difficulty to evolve independently across years. The evolving-difficulty

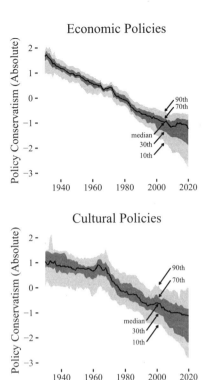

FIGURE 4.1. National trends in policy conservatism. The estimates in these plots are derived from a variant of the policy measurement model that does not allow difficulty parameters to evolve across years. Black lines indicate the median state, and light and dark gray ribbons, respectively, indicate intervals between the tenth and ninetieth and the thirtieth and seventieth percentiles of the cross-state distribution.

measure is designed to capture the *relative* liberalism–conservatism of states' policies at each point in time. The time series it yields can be best interpreted as how states have evolved relative to each other over the past eight decades.

Figure 4.2 plots these policy time series for a sample of five states: two we have already discussed in detail (Idaho and Vermont) plus Wisconsin, New York, and Mississippi. The last two were selected because in nearly every year they respectively anchor the liberal and conservative ends of both policy scales. As the figure shows, policy conservatism usually exhibits small fluctuations from year to year, though there are occasional large shifts. For example, between 1963 and 1970, Vermont's economic policy conservatism decreased by 1.5 standard deviations—a reflection of such liberal policy changes as an air-pollution control act, the extension of collective bargaining rights to state employees, and a 70 percent increase in the state's real per-pupil education spending. Between 2010 and 2017, Wisconsin's economic policy conservatism increased by a similar magnitude—a shift that coincided with the Republican

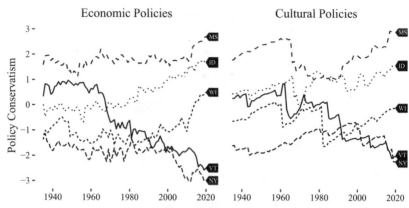

FIGURE 4.2. Trends in policy conservatism in five states, 1935–2020. Each measure has been standardized to have mean zero and variance one across state-years.

Party's capture of state government and the consequent passage of a right-to-work law, spending and tax cuts, and other conservative policy changes.

Because there are fewer cultural policies and none vary continuously, sharp changes in cultural policy conservatism have been somewhat more common. In the period 1965–1968, when Mississippi became the last state to legalize alcohol and allow women on state juries, its cultural policy conservatism decreased by 1.5 standard deviations (though its policies still remained among the most conservative in the nation). Idaho's cultural conservatism increased by a similar amount between 1972 and 1977 as it imposed abortion restrictions in the wake of *Roe v. Wade*, rescinded its ratification of the Equal Rights Amendment (ERA), and declined to imitate liberal policy changes adopted in other states, such as Vermont's repeal of criminal sodomy laws. Between 2014 and 2019, New York moved sharply in the opposite direction: strengthening its gay rights laws, loosening its regulation of contraceptives, and relaxing laws targeting undocumented immigrants.

As much as these sharp shifts stand out, however, the cumulative effects of many small changes can be even more impressive. The massive policy gap between Vermont and Idaho that exists today did not open up overnight. Rather, the two states diverged gradually over the course of half a century. In 1968, for example, the two states had nearly identical economic policy scores. By 1978, Idaho was almost a standard deviation more conservative than Vermont. The gap had increased to 1.5 by 1988, 2.3 by 1998, 2.9 by 2008, and 4.0 by 2018. The normally incremental nature of policymaking does not preclude large changes, as long as political pressures push in the same direction over many decades.

As we have noted, Vermont and Idaho are unusual for the duration and extent of their policy transformations. In other states, it is more common for policy ideology to fluctuate around a relatively stable equilibrium that changes slowly if at all. Mississippi and New York exemplify this tendency. For as far back as our data extend, New York has been one of the most liberal states in both policy domains, and Mississippi has been one of the most conservative. This policy stability reflects the stability of the states' socioeconomic profiles: New York as a rich urban state and Mississippi as a poor rural one. Yet it is remarkable that Mississippi's transition from a racially exclusionary one-party regime to a two-party democratic one, enfranchising half its population along the way, left seemingly so little trace on its policies apart from a mid-1960s drop in cultural conservatism from which it eventually recovered. We shall return to the puzzling policy stability of Mississippi and other southern states in later chapters, but for now we highlight it as an indication of the persistence of state policy regimes.

A more complete picture of states' policy stability can be seen in figure 4.3. As these maps show, a few states have undergone policy transformations comparable to Idaho and Vermont. Louisiana, for example, was once a liberal outlier within the South in terms of economic policy. This likely reflects the unusual influence of the powerful Long (Huey and his political heirs) faction within the Louisiana Democratic Party, which was much more committed to New Deal–style policies than others in the region.[20] That said, by the end of the century, the Long faction's legacy had been largely erased and Louisiana had joined its southern brethren on the conservative end of the policy spectrum.

States like Louisiana are the exception. In general, the geographic distribution of policy ideology has been remarkably stable since the 1930s. Southern states have been consistently conservative in both policy domains, and most northeastern and Pacific Coast states have been consistently liberal.

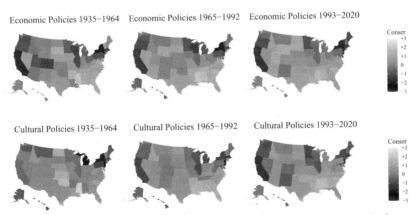

FIGURE 4.3. The geographic distribution of policy conservatism, 1935–2020. To accentuate visual contrasts, each measure has been standardized within eras.

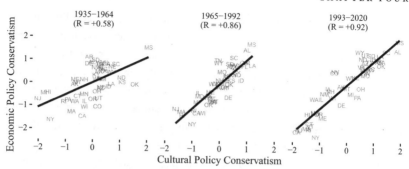

FIGURE 4.4. The relationship between policy conservatism on economic and cultural issues by era.

This impression is confirmed by the robust correlations between policy conservatism scores from different eras. Across all states, economic policy conservatism in the years 1935–1964 has a 0.79 correlation with the same measure in 1965–1992 and a 0.64 correlation with the 1993–2020 measure. For cultural policy conservatism, the analogous correlations are 0.75 and 0.65. Policy conservatism has thus been nearly as stable across time as mass conservatism (see chapter 3) and much more stable than state partisanship.

Like mass conservatism, policy conservatism has aligned across domains, though from a higher starting point. As figure 4.4 shows, in the 1935–1964 period, the cross-state correlation between economic and cultural policy conservatism was 0.65 (the analogous correlation for mass conservatism was 0.43). This correlation increased to 0.88 in 1965–1992 and 0.93 in 1993–2020 (compared to 0.55 and 0.72 for the corresponding opinion measures). Thus, even more than mass conservatism, policy conservatism has always been robustly correlated across domains. Their relationship has only strengthened over time, and today the main dimension underlying economic policy variation is essentially identical to that structuring cultural policies.

4.2 Policy, Preferences, and Party

One of the classic puzzles of state politics is the absence of a positive relationship between measures of state conservatism and measures of state partisanship.[21] Indeed, it was the lack of such a relationship that encouraged some scholars to downplay the importance of political factors, such as mass policy preferences or partisan control of government, in determining state policies.[22] As figure 4.5 indicates, however, this puzzle is now a historical artifact.

Each panel of figure 4.5 plots the cross-sectional correlation between policy conservatism in a given domain and one of three other measures: mass conservatism in the same domain, the Republican share of major-party identifiers in the public, and an index summarizing the extent of Republican control of state government.[23] The correlations are summarized by decade and are calculated on two samples: all states and all states outside the thirteen-state South. As the left panels in each row show, mass and policy conservatism have been correlated within domain for as far back as our data extend. In the economic domain, this correlation has been consistently stronger outside the South than in the nation as a whole, which, as we will see in chapter 7, is due to the fact that as a group southern states are conservative policy outliers relative to the rest of the country. Even with the South included, however, states with relatively conservative mass publics have always had more conservative policies, a relationship that has strengthened considerably over time.

Both policy scales' correlations with the two partisan measures have increased as well, but from a far lower baseline (see figure 4.5, middle and right panels). Indeed, through the 1970s states with Republican-leaning publics and Republican-controlled state offices tended to have more *liberal* policies in both domains. This was partly attributable to the conservative South's

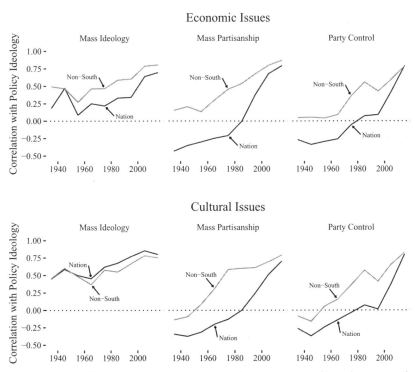

FIGURE 4.5. Policy ideology's correlations with mass ideology, mass partisanship, and party control, 1930s–2010s. Measures are averaged within decade. Black lines indicate correlations across all states, and gray lines indicate states outside the thirteen-state South.

anomalous attachment to the Democratic Party, but even outside the region the party-policy relationship was negligible. The 1980s—the focus of Erikson, Wright, and McIver's *Statehouse Democracy*—were a transitional decade, during which this relationship was in the process of inverting. The party-policy correlations grew rapidly between the 1990s and 2010s. They have now reached rough parity with the relationship between mass and policy ideology: today, all the correlations in figure 4.5 are 0.7 or higher.

In other words, the incongruous relationship between state partisanship and ideology that motivated much of the classic state politics literature has resolved itself. This happened first in non-southern states, where the party-policy association had become clearly positive by the 1960s and continued to strengthen thereafter. The same transformation occurred among all states about three decades later, in the 1990s. By the early twenty-first century, all the major variables of state politics—mass conservatism in each domain, mass Republicanism, Republican control of government, and policy conservatism in each domain—had come into rough alignment. Whereas once most states were buffeted by cross-cutting pressures, now most political winds push them in the same direction.

What we have not yet explored, however, are the causal relationships between these variables. Does the negative correlation between Republican control and policy conservatism before the 1980s indicate that electing Republicans caused the passage of more liberal policies? Have the policy effects of party control grown in tandem with their increasing cross-sectional association? What are the substantive policy consequences of electing Republicans rather than Democrats? We answer these questions in the following chapter.

5

Parties:
The Policy Effects of Party Control[1]

On January 4, 2018, James Alcorn, secretary of the Virginia State Board of Elections, reached into a ceramic bowl and pulled out one of the two film canisters inside. He opened it and read aloud the name on the slip of paper it contained: David Yancey. By this act, Yancey, the Republican incumbent in the Ninety-Fourth District, was reelected to the Virginia House of Delegates, his tie with Democratic candidate Shelly Simonds broken by a random draw. Not only that—Yancey's election also gave Republicans a slim 51–49 majority in the House of Delegates. Partisan control of one chamber of the Virginia state legislature was thus determined by the equivalent of a coin flip.[2]

Virginia Democrats were understandably disappointed. Fueled by popular anger against President Donald Trump, they had made large gains in the 2017 elections (Virginia holds state elections in odd years), nearly erasing Republicans' 66–34 majority in the state's lower chamber while also holding on to the governorship. Though the state senate, which was not up for reelection, was narrowly Republican, Democrats had still hoped that control of the lower house would give them leverage to pursue policy initiatives long resisted by the GOP legislature, such as opting in to the 2010 Affordable Care Act's expansion of Medicaid coverage.[3]

As it happened, Virginia ended up expanding Medicaid anyway, extending health care coverage to four hundred thousand low-income adults. After some concessions to conservatives, including work requirements for beneficiaries, the House of Delegates passed Medicaid expansion by a wide margin, with support from twenty Republicans. Then, thanks to four Republican defections to the pro-expansion side, the Senate of Virginia followed suit.[4] According to the *New York Times*, the Republican defectors "dropped their opposition after their party almost lost the House of Delegates in elections last fall and voters named health care as a top issue."[5]

What would have happened had James Alcorn pulled a different name out of the hat? Would Virginia have passed the same expansion law or a more liberal one without work requirements, or perhaps even none at all? And would Republican senators have changed their minds had not the election been interpreted as a signal of public support for expansion? These are all questions of causality—of what would have occurred had a given cause (a Republican victory, a shift in public sentiment) not been present. Answering causal questions is difficult in many social settings, but it is particularly so when, as is often the case in politics, strategic actors have incentives to anticipate the reactions of others and to conceal their true beliefs and motivations. Nevertheless, in this section we transition from the correlational focus of the first half of this book and attempt to make inferences about the determinants of state policymaking. We begin by generalizing the case of the Yancy–Simonds race in Virginia, examining systematically how much it matters whether Republicans control state offices rather than Democrats and how these party effects have changed over time. This analysis will set the stage for chapters 6 and 7, which will examine how public opinion affects election outcomes and, ultimately, state policymaking.

5.1 Theoretical Framework

Our basic theoretical framework for conceptualizing the policy effects of party control of state governments is a model of two-party competition over a policy space. In a perfectly Downsian world, in which electorally motivated parties adopt the positions of the median voter, party control of state offices has no effect on state policies. Only if the parties diverge from the median voter do partisan policy effects—counterfactual differences in policy liberalism under Democratic versus Republican control—actually emerge.

Given that candidates cannot perfectly predict election outcomes and often care about influencing policy in addition to winning office, we should in general expect some degree of ideological divergence between the two parties.[6] In fact, as John Gerring has shown, national party conflict has had a strong ideological component throughout US history.[7] The parties diverge at the subnational level as well: Democratic activists, candidates, and officeholders[8] all take more liberal policy positions than their Republican counterparts in the same state or district.

In light of this evidence for partisan divergence, the more interesting question is not whether partisan effects exist but how large they are. If centripetal pressures dominate, then the parties in each state will converge closely on the state's median voter and differ only modestly in their policy platforms. Policy effects will be further attenuated by the limitations imposed by the minority party and other constraints on the majority party's capacity to implement their preferred policies.[9] Governors, for example, cannot simply implement their ideal points but rather must compromise with a legislature in which the opposing party probably has at least some influence. Such limitations on Democrats' and Republicans' desire and capacity to implement divergent policies lead us to the expectation that policy effects should generally be small relative to, say, the policy variation across states.

Nevertheless, there are also good reasons to expect partisan effects on state policy to have increased over the period we examine. At the national level, Democratic and Republican officials have become increasingly ideologically polarized, especially since the 1970s.[10] Policy conflict between the national parties has become increasingly aligned with what is now defined as "liberalism" and "conservatism."[11] As we saw in chapter 3, the mass public has followed suit, increasing the ideological distance between the parties' electoral coalitions.[12] This growing ideological divergence between parties' primary electorates increases the electoral incentives for party nominees to diverge from the median voter.[13] Moreover, if candidates are drawn from the set of party identifiers, their own sincere policy views should become more extreme as well.[14] Mass polarization between the parties has thus reinforced and exacerbated elite polarization,[15] resulting in larger policy effects of the partisan composition of government.[16]

These theoretical results and empirical trends give rise to several expectations. On one hand, the centripetal pull of electoral competition and the limitations on officials' capacity to fully implement their policy preferences lead to the expectation that policy effects will be modest, at least relative to policy differences between states. On the other hand, given the growth of partisan polarization, partisan effects on policy are likely to be larger now than in the past. To the extent that this growth has been driven by the diverging policy preferences of Democratic and Republican officials, and elite polarization is rooted in ideological divergence between the parties' electoral coalitions, we should also expect policy effects to be larger where Democrats and Republicans are more ideologically polarized.

5.2 Policy Effects of Party Control

If we naively applied a causal interpretation to the correlations in figure 4.5, we might conclude that, until the 1980s, electing Republicans instead of

Democrats *decreased* state policy conservatism rather than increased it. Given what we know about the policy commitments of the parties—that Republican officials have consistently been more conservative than Democrats in the same constituency (see chapter 6)—this is implausible. The true relationship was likely confounded by the fact that, for reasons dating back to the Civil War, Democratic partisanship was strong in many conservative states and Republicanism was strong in many liberal states. It is more plausible, however, that the policy effects of party control are negligible, as they would be if both parties cared solely about pleasing the median voter. Indeed, this is the conclusion of much of the empirical literature on state politics.[17]

How can we distinguish correlation from causation? In this chapter, we use two basic empirical strategies. The first strategy is a generalization of the randomly decided Virginia House of Delegates election, called an electoral regression discontinuity (RD) design.[18] If tied elections were sufficiently numerous, we could analyze them as if they were data from a randomized experiment, with some constituencies randomly assigned to be represented by one kind of official (e.g., a Democrat) and other constituencies by another kind (e.g., a Republican).[19] The great advantage of randomization is that it ensures that the causal variable (in our case, party control of a given office) is assigned independently of all other determinants of the outcome of interest (policy conservatism). This means that any differences in the outcome are, up to statistical uncertainty, attributable to the cause of interest. To approximate this ideal experiment, an RD design uses data from elections that are narrowly decided to estimate what the expected outcome would be in the case of a tie that broke for one party versus a tie that broke for the other. The difference in these estimates is our estimate of the average causal effect of party control (in close elections), independent of factors such as public sentiment, state partisanship, national tides, and so on.

Our second empirical strategy is a dynamic panel (DP) model. This model includes separate intercepts for each state and year, plus a control for first-order lag of policy conservatism. In essence, a dynamic panel model estimates the correlation between Republican control of state offices and change in state policy conservatism, with all variables measured relative to other states in that year and to the state in question's own long-term average. If Republican control is associated with conservative policy change, over and above what is expected for that year and state, then this provides evidence that Republican control causally affects policy conservatism. Although the effect estimates from a dynamic panel are more vulnerable to bias than those from an RD design,[20] they can be much more precise. This added precision allows us to examine more nuanced questions, such as how much party effects have changed over time. We therefore report results from both designs, first using the RD estimates to establish the existence of party effects and then using the panel estimates to take a closer look at them.

5.3 Regression Discontinuity Estimates

For the outcome of elections to affect the ideological valence of policymaking, candidates typically must differ with respect to their policy goals.[21] In the context of US states, this generally means that Democratic and Republican candidates for a given office or legislative seat must take ideologically divergent policy positions. We can evaluate this condition empirically by using an electoral RD design to estimate the effect of Republican victory on the conservatism of state officeholders. Unfortunately, systematic data on candidate conservatism are available only since the 1990s, but in that era the results are unambiguous: electing a Republican rather than a Democrat results in an officeholder with much more conservative policy positions.

Figure 5.1 shows this using three measures of officeholders' conservatism, all of which are standardized to be zero-mean and unit-variance. The upper left panel uses governors' DW-DIME scores, which are derived from the donation patterns of their campaign contributors.[22] As indicated by the dots on either side of the vertical line at 0 percent, the average standardized DW-DIME score of Democratic governors who win by less than a percentage point is around −1 ; for narrowly elected Republican governors, it is +0.8. This difference in close elections roughly agrees with the formal RD estimate of 1.6, which is based on the difference in regression lines at the threshold itself (i.e., in a tied election).[23] These estimates indicate that over the past three decades, Democratic and Republican gubernatorial candidates have taken very different positions, even in the most narrowly balanced states.

The upper right panel of figure 5.1 conducts a parallel analysis of state house members using a more direct measure of their policy positions: their ideal points as estimated from legislative voting records.[24] Since there are so many more legislators than governors, the house estimates are also much more precise than the ones for governor. They are nevertheless quite consistent with the gubernatorial results. In the years between 1994 and 2018, electing a Republican makes the roll-call representation a state house district receives about a standard deviation more conservative.

Finally, the bottom panel of figure 5.1 shifts the unit of analysis from the legislator to the chamber as a whole, using what is called a multidimensional RD design.[25] In essence, this design estimates how much the median ideal point in the chamber is affected by electing a Republican to the seat that decides

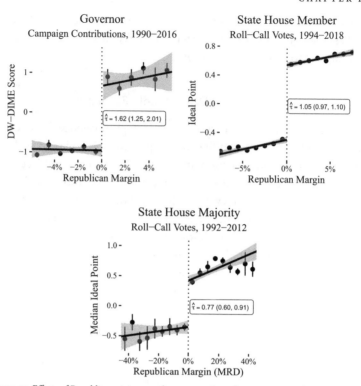

FIGURE 5.1. Effects of Republican victory on the conservatism of governors, state house members, and state house medians. The upper left panel plots the effect on the governor's DW-DIME score, a measure of conservatism derived from the donation patterns of contributors to the governor's campaign. At upper right is the effect on the roll-call conservatism of an individual member of the state house of representatives. At bottom is the effect on the roll-call conservatism of the *median* member of the state house. Estimated effects and confidence intervals are indicated with $\hat{\tau}$.

majority control of the chamber,[26] just as occurred in Virginia in 2017. Since the location of the median legislator has a powerful effect on policymaking,[27] this effect is more directly analogous to that for governor. As was the case with governors, we find that electing Republicans has a large effect on the location of the state house median, increasing its conservatism by around 0.8 standard deviations.

Since our direct measures of state officials' policy positions go back only to the 1990s, we have to rely on indirect evidence for the decades before then. Combining various cross-sectional measures, Erikson, Wright, and McIver show that party elites already diverged ideologically within states by the 1970s–1980s, but it is unclear how the magnitude of this divergence compares to later periods.[28] Data on the roll-call voting of senators, who of course share electoral constituencies with governors, provides additional indirect evidence.[29]

On economic issues, opposite-party senators from the same state have taken markedly divergent positions since midcentury, though divergence declined until 1980 and then rose to new heights thereafter. On racial and cultural issues, Democratic senators began the period only modestly more liberal than same-state Republicans, but the gap between them widened greatly over the rest of the century. As we saw in chapter 3, Democrats and Republicans in the mass public followed a similar pattern of within-state divergence over the same period. Taken together, this indirect evidence strongly suggests that the ideological distance between Democratic and Republican candidates for state offices has increased substantially, especially over the last half a century.

Officials do not, however, translate their policy positions directly into policy outcomes. For one thing, these positions are not necessarily sincere: politicians have incentives to downplay their differences with the opposing party in some circumstances[30] and to exaggerate them in others.[31] Further, even if politicians' positions are honest statements of their policy goals, they must compromise with officials with different values and priorities. Changing the law typically requires the acquiescence of the governor and both houses of the legislature, meaning that any one of those veto points can block policy change. Even if all the pivotal actors broadly agree, policy change can still be averted by legislative obstructionism, the mobilization of opponents, and shifts in political circumstances. For all these reasons, we should expect party effects to be smaller on policies than on positions.

This is in fact what we find. Figure 5.2 replicates the RD analyses for the governor and house median, using state policy conservatism as the outcome instead of politicians' conservatism. In other words, it estimates the expected change in state policies due to the bare election of a Republican governor or state house majority between the year of the election and the following year. To maximize the precision of the estimates, we define the dependent variable as the average of the change in economic policy conservatism and cultural policy conservatism.[32]

First consider the top panels in both columns which present the results for governor (left) and state house (right) during roughly the same period as that covered by figure 5.1 (1990s–2010s). In those years, the effect of Republican control of both institutions was unambiguously positive, but at around 0.1 the estimate is an order of magnitude smaller than the effects on officials' policy positions (the measure is again standardized so that policy conservatism in each domain is zero-mean, unit-variance across all state-years). More remarkably, the middle panels indicate that Republican control had no detectable effect on policy conservatism in the 1965–1993 period, though the confidence intervals do not rule out effects as large as those in later periods. Because district-level

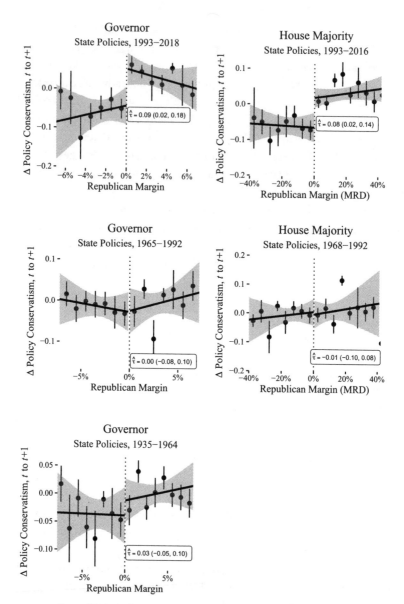

FIGURE 5.2. Party effects on policy conservatism by era, for governor (*left*) and state house (*right*). In all panels the dependent variable is the average change in a state's economic and cultural policy conservatism between the election year and one year later.

data on state legislative elections is not available before 1968, in the 1935–1964 period we can estimate the effect only for governors (lower-left panel). Though not clearly distinguishable from zero, the estimate is about halfway between the estimates for the other two periods, suggesting that the years 1965–1992 were a low point for party effects. Given the imprecision of these estimates, it is hard to draw firm conclusions about how policy effects vary across time, domain, or offices; for these, we will need to rely on the dynamic panel model. One thing the RD results do make clear, however, is that even the largest plausible policy effect of a year of Republican control is far smaller than both the effect on officials' policy *positions* and the policy variation across states.

5.4 Dynamic Panel Estimates

In order to ask more nuanced questions of the data, we need to switch to our second empirical strategy, a dynamic panel design. Our baseline model is specified as follows:

$$(5.1) \qquad y_{st} = \alpha_s + \gamma_t + \rho y_{s,t-1} + \beta^G R_{st}^G + \beta^H R_{st}^H + \beta^S R_{st}^S + \varepsilon_{st},$$

where y_{st} is policy conservatism; α_s and γ_t are state and year intercepts; $\rho y_{s,t-1}$ is lagged policy conservatism; and R_{st}^G, R_{st}^H, and R_{st}^S are indicators for Republican control of the governorship, state house, and state senate. In some models, we aggregate the three party control indicators into a Republican control index, $RC_{st} = R_{st}^G + R_{st}^H + R_{st}^S$, which runs from zero to three. Some models also allow party effects to vary by era, in which case we interact the lagged dependent variable and state intercepts with era as well. In all specifications, we cluster standard errors by state.

Dynamic panel models rely on stronger assumptions than RD designs, the most important of which is that there are no omitted variables that vary within states and affect both Republican control and change in policy conservatism. A plausible candidate for such a variable is mass ideology, but as chapter 6 will show, mass ideology is a weak predictor of short-term shifts in party fortunes. Consistent with this weak correlation, including lagged mass conservatism in the dynamic panel specification barely alters our estimates of the effects of party control.

The credibility of the DP results is further strengthened by their consistency with the corresponding RD estimates, where they are available. As the Governor and House panels of figure 5.3 show, the DP estimates (black) are generally smaller than the corresponding RD ones (gray), but in none of the pairs are the two estimates statistically distinguishable. One difference figure 5.3 does highlight is the much smaller confidence intervals around the

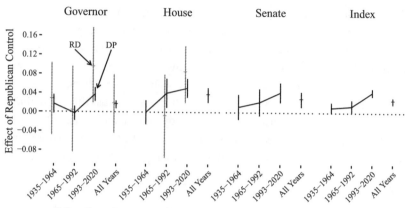

FIGURE 5.3. Policy effects of party control by office and era.

DP estimates. This greater precision enables us to draw more refined and confident conclusions about variation in party effects across different conditions.

One such dimension of variation is time. Although the RD and DP point estimates show similar patterns of change, with the DP estimates we can describe these changes more precisely. Across all three institutions (governor, state house, and state senate), the DP estimates suggest that the policy effects of party control roughly doubled between the first era (1935–1964) and the third one (1993–2020). Like the RD estimates, the DP estimates indicate that the policy effects of partisan control of the governorship actually fell to near zero in the second era (1965–1992) before rebounding afterward. This suggests that the period examined by Erikson, Wright, and McIver's *Statehouse Democracy* was a low point in the policy effects of party control. The DP estimates for the state house and senate, however, do not exhibit this pattern, so they should probably be viewed with some skepticism.

In addition to the era-specific estimates for each institution, figure 5.3 also reports the estimated effects pooled across all years as well as the ones based on a single zero-to-three index of Republican control. The results for the Republican control index (rightmost panel) summarize the institution-specific ones but with greater precision. They indicate that the effect of Republican control of the governorship, house, or senate increased policy conservatism by 0.018 (±0.012) in 1935–1964, by 0.016 (±0.017) in 1964–1992, and by 0.042 (±0.008) in 1993–2020. It is clear that since the 1980s, the ideological direction of state policymaking has come to depend much more heavily on which party controls state government.

Table 5.1 examines two additional dimensions of effect variation: issue domain and region. As the first column indicates, Republican control increased

TABLE 5.1 Policy effects of party control, by domain and era

	Dependent Variable: Policy Conservatism (t)			
	Economic, 1936–2020 (1)	Economic, 1936–2020 (2)	Cultural, 1936–2020 (3)	Cultural, 1936–2020 (4)
Repub. Control$_t$ 1935–1964	**0.026**	**0.026**	−0.001	−0.001
	(0.008)	(0.008)	(0.007)	(0.007)
Repub. Control$_t$ 1965–1992	**0.024**	**0.024**	0.007	0.007
	(0.008)	(0.008)	(0.009)	(0.009)
Repub. Control$_t$ 1993–2020	**0.049**	**0.051**	**0.045**	**0.046**
	(0.004)	(0.005)	(0.005)	(0.007)
Repub. Control$_t$ × South		−0.004		−0.002
		(0.010)		(0.010)
Lagged DV × Era	yes	yes	yes	yes
State × Era Fixed Effects	yes	yes	yes	yes
Year Fixed Effects	yes	yes	yes	yes
Observations	4,209	4,209	4,209	4,209
Adjusted R^2	0.978	0.978	0.972	0.972

Note: The coefficients on lagged policy conservatism range from 0.70 (economic policy conservatism 1935–1964) to 0.93 (cultural policy conservatism 1993–2020). Standard errors are shown in parentheses. Bold coefficients are statistically significant at the 10% level.

economic policy conservatism in all three eras, though the effect doubled after 1992. By then party effects on cultural policy (column 3) were just as large as on economics, but whether party control mattered on cultural policies in the first two eras is much less certain. This difference between domains is consistent with the evidence on mass and elite partisan divergence, which before the 1990s was only a fraction as large on cultural issues as it was on economic ones.

There is no evidence that the policy effects of party control differ between southern and non-southern states. The interaction coefficients in columns (2) and (4) of table 5.1 are small and statistically insignificant. Note also that the estimated main effects of Republican control in the first two eras do not budge at all when Republican control is interacted by South. This is because prior to the 1990s, the Democratic Party controlled southern state governments almost without exception, and thus the effect estimates for those years are driven entirely by partisan alternation in non-southern states. By the time the South became competitive enough for Republicans to take control, the ideological distance between the two parties differed little across regions.

What has driven this growth in the policy effects of party control? As we saw in chapter 3, the policy preferences of Democratic and Republican identifiers in the same state have increasingly diverged from one another. By making primary electorates and activist networks more extreme, partisan divergence

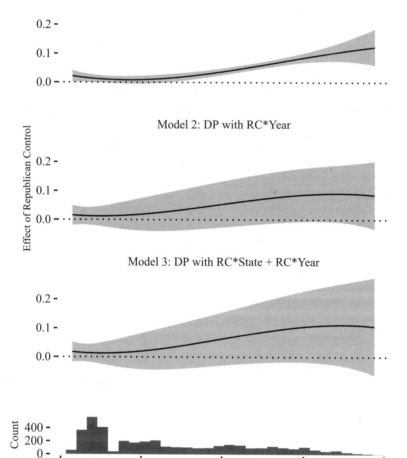

FIGURE 5.4. Party effects by mass divergence. In each plot, the horizontal axis indicates the difference in mean conservatism between Democratic and Republican identifiers in a state-year, averaged across economic and cultural conservatism. The vertical axis is the estimated effect on policy conservatism (also averaged across domains) of Republican control at a given level of mass divergence. Histogram indicates the marginal distribution of mass divergence scores. Model 1 (*top*) is the baseline DP specification plus Republican control interacted with a cubic polynomial in mass divergence and with state FEs. Model 2 (*middle*) includes an interaction with year FEs instead of state, and Model 3 (*bottom*) includes both state and year interactions.

in the mass public has in turn reinforced and probably exacerbated partisan divergence among political elites.[33] All else equal, we should expect increased partisan divergence among politicians to lead to larger partisan differences in policymaking, which is what we have seen over the past several decades.

To test this explanation more directly, we estimated dynamic panel models that interact Republican control index with mass partisan divergence, averaging across the economic and cultural domains (see chapter 3 for a description of the mass divergence measures). If our explanation is correct, the effect of Republican control should be larger in states and years where the mass constituencies of the two parties are further apart ideologically. Figure 5.4 confirms this expectation. The top panel, which accounts for state-specific differences in party effects, shows that mass divergence and the effect of Republican control are correlated within states over time. The middle panel, which accounts for year-specific effect differences, shows that in each year party effects are larger in states where divergence is larger. The bottom panel reports the results of an even more demanding test: whether party effects and mass divergence are correlated conditional on both year- and state-specific interactions. Though much more uncertain, the estimated relationship is qualitatively similar to that in the top panel: when and where Democrats and Republicans in the mass public have been more ideologically distant, party effects have been larger. Together, these results suggest that the divergence in policy outcomes between Democrat- and Republican-controlled states in recent decades is due at least in part to the increasing ideological distance between the parties' core supporters.

5.5 How Much Does Party Control Matter?

Whether measured by campaign platforms, financial donations, or roll-call records, the ideological distance between the policy positions of Democratic and Republican candidates and officials has grown greatly in recent decades. This partisan polarization has been driven by a combination of an increase in constituencies' tendency to favor the party that matches their ideological orientation and ideological divergence between Democratic and Republican politicians within each constituency.[34] States have polarized in similar fashion. The policies of "red" states are now much more consistently conservative than are those of "blue" states, which have become more consistently liberal.[35] This, too, has been driven by a combination of alignment and divergence: not only are conservative states now much more likely to elect Republicans and liberal states Democrats, but the policy consequences of party control are substantially larger.

These policy differences have real substantive consequences. For a low-income American, it can matter a great deal whether or not their state's Medicaid program provides coverage for abortions or requires them to work as a condition of eligibility.[36] Nevertheless, the causal effects of party control per se should not be overstated. For example, in the 1993–2020 period, Republican control in a given year is estimated to increase economic policy conservatism by 0.05 standard deviations. In 2020, this effect corresponded to about a 0.2 percent increase in the probability of a state ban on age discrimination, a 0.9 percent decrease in the probability of a mandatory renewable energy standard, a 1.3 percent increase in the probability of a right-to-work law, and a $1.94 decrease in the real value of the maximum TANF benefit. Analogously, party control's 0.04 effect on cultural policy conservatism translates to a 0.6 percent increase in the probability of an open-carry law or Religious Freedom Restoration Act, a 0.9 percent decrease in the probability of Medicaid coverage for abortions, and a 1.0 percent decrease in the probability of a ban on LGBT employment discrimination. These differences are not meaningless, but neither are they the "wide swings in policy" that would seem to be implied by differences in roll-call records or other measures of officials' policy positions.[37]

As we saw in figure 5.1, the ideological *positions* of the occupant of a given office depend very strongly on whether a Democrat or Republican is elected. Across a variety of measures and offices, national as well as state, Republican control increases officeholders' conservatism by at least one standard deviation.[38] By comparison, even in today's more polarized age, the standardized effect of party control on state policy conservatism is at least an order of magnitude smaller than its effect on policy positions. There are several reasons for this discrepancy, including politicians' incentives to play up partisan differences, the fact that policy change requires the assent of many actors, and the difficulty of bridging roll-call scales across states. Regardless, the important point is that measures of policy positions dramatically exaggerate the policy consequences of party control. Rather than wide swings in policy, alternation in party control usually results in incremental shifts in policy conservatism. These shifts pale relative to the policy differences among states: it would take many decades of Republican governors and legislatures to make the policies of New York as conservative as those of Mississippi.

5.6 Summary

In November 1948, the Ohio Democratic Party gained control of state government for the first time in ten years. With the popular Frank Lausche at the top of their ticket, the Democrats defeated the incumbent Republican governor and won majorities in both houses of the legislature. During their two years of unified control, however, Ohio Democrats did not pass any major liberal legislation. In fact, Governor Lausche, a fiscal conservative who had defeated a more liberal candidate in the Democratic primary, proposed a budget that cut state expenditures, and the liberal initiatives he did support, such as a ban on racial discrimination in employment, failed to make it through the Democratic legislature.[39]

Over six decades later, in 2012, North Carolina Republicans experienced a similar triumph when the election of Governor Pat McCrory completed their takeover of the state, initiated two years earlier with their capture of the legislature. Though reputed to be a moderate, Governor McCrory did not govern as one. Unlike Ohio Democrats in 1948, North Carolina Republicans took advantage of their newfound control by passing a flood of conservative legislation: cutting unemployment insurance, repealing the estate tax, "flattening" the income tax, relaxing gun laws, and tightening restrictions on abortion.[40]

This contrast between Ohio in 1948 and North Carolina in 2012 illustrates the differences between their two eras of state politics. The first occurred at a time when the parties were still internally heterogeneous and relatively hospitable to moderate politicians such as Ohio's Governor Lausche. Not coincidentally, it was a time when dramatic changes in partisan control did not necessarily lead to large changes in state policy. The second took place in a much more polarized era, when parties' positions were more extreme and consistent across issues. So, too, were parties more willing and able to leverage control of state government into large policy shifts. Although party control has always mattered for state policymaking, it matters much more now than it once did.

Do voters notice whether elected officials pursue moderate versus extreme policies? The contrast between governors Lausche and McCrory is again suggestive. The moderate Lausche was reelected in 1950 and twice again thereafter, surviving a Republican presidential landslide in 1952. He then served two terms in the Senate before being denied renomination in the 1968 Democratic primary. By contrast, the more extreme McCrory lost his 2016 reelection bid—the first North Carolina governor to do so since 1850—even as the state voted for Republican presidential candidate Donald Trump. These examples suggest that pushing policies too far to the left or right has electoral costs, giving officials incentives to avoid them. Whether this pattern holds more generally is the subject of the next chapter.

6

Elections:
Selection, Incentives, and Feedback

The 1994 elections were tough for Democrats up and down the ballot.[1] Bill Clinton, the Democratic president, was fairly unpopular and the economy was middling, setting the party up for a substantial midterm loss. Democrats' once-massive identification lead in the mass public had dissipated over the course of the 1980s, leaving them little cushion on that front. Moreover, Americans had turned decidedly to the right. According to Stimson's measure of policy mood, the public's desire for more government activity was at its lowest point in more than a decade.[2] Furious opposition to a number of President Clinton's policy proposals on health care, guns, and other issues—fanned, of course, by conservative opponents—had arisen in the mass public, stymieing several of them. On November 8, Democrats braced themselves for a bad night.

The results were even worse than Democrats feared. The Republicans' shocking capture of Congress for the first time in four decades received the most attention, but the GOP made major gains in the states as well. Republicans flipped fourteen state legislative chambers, giving them control of more than half for the first time since 1970, though Democrats continued to occupy a majority of state legislative seats. The GOP also netted eleven governorships, increasing their total to thirty. A number of moderate Republican governors, including California's Pete Wilson, Illinois's Jim Edgar, Minnesota's Arne Carlson, and Massachusetts's William Weld, rolled to reelection in left-of-center states, while in New York George Pataki unseated Democrat Mario Cuomo, a liberal firebrand. Equally impressive were Republicans' inroads in more conservative states where Democrats had long dominated gubernatorial elections. These victories occurred mainly in the South, such as George W. Bush's defeat of Texas governor Ann Richards, but some were in non-southern states like Idaho, where a Republican won for the first time in nearly three decades.

More than a few Democratic governors did manage to hold on, however, and not just in liberal strongholds. In Florida, for example, Governor Lawton Chiles beat back a strong challenge from Republican Jeb Bush. Bush campaigned on a tough-on-crime platform, which Chiles blunted by citing his administration's expansion of state prisons.[3] In Colorado, Governor Roy Romer, a pragmatic centrist endorsed by independent presidential candidate Ross Perot, was returned to office as well.[4] Governor Ben Nelson of Nebraska cruised to reelection on the strength of a record of prison construction and cuts to state taxes and expenditures.[5] Despite his opponent's attempts to tie him to President Clinton, Georgia governor Zell Miller—a conservative Democrat who would leave the party a decade later—eked out a victory.[6] Close Clinton ally Jim Guy Tucker was comfortably reelected in Arkansas, as were Bob Miller in Nevada and Howard Dean in Vermont. Democratic challengers, however, faired much more poorly than incumbent governors. Aside from open-seat races in Oregon and Alaska, the only state to elect a nonincumbent Democrat to the governorship was Hawaiʻi, which had not elected a Republican since 1959.

The 1994 elections illustrate several important themes. One is the strong influence of national tides on state elections. It is no accident that at the same time that Republicans made massive gains in Congress they also greatly increased their power in the states. Nor is it coincidental that the Democrats' devastating midterm came two years after the party had achieved unified control of the national government for the first time in twelve years. Democratic control of government is regularly followed by a conservative backlash in the public, and vice versa for Republican control.[7]

In addition to these dynamic patterns of national tides and backlash, the 1994 elections also illustrate the important, though contingent, influence of the partisan and ideological leanings of state publics. The imprint of partisanship was strongest among state legislatures. For both state houses and senates, the share of seats won by Republicans had over a 0.8 correlation with Republican PID share in the public. In contrast, gubernatorial elections were almost unrelated to state partisanship. In fact, only fourteen of thirty-six gubernatorial elections held in 1994 were won by the party that carried the state in the previous presidential election. As for ideology, state legislative results in 1994 were moderately correlated with mass economic conservatism ($R = 0.44$ for senate, $R = 0.60$ for house) but barely at all with cultural conservatism. Like partisanship, mass ideology was only weakly predictive of gubernatorial election outcomes. Thus, although the aggregate Republican swing in 1994 paralleled the relatively conservative national mood in that year, electoral variation across states bore at most a modest relationship to cross-sectional differences in mass policy preferences.

One explanation for this loose connection between mass partisanship and electoral outcomes, especially for governors, is that candidates adapted their positions to suit their electorate, and voters noticed and rewarded them. It is doubtful that Democratic governors in states such as Nebraska and Florida, as well as Republicans in Massachusetts and Illinois, would have been re-elected had they not taken more moderate positions than their copartisans elsewhere. By the same token, unpopular stances clearly hurt some candidates, including New York's Mario Cuomo, whose opposition to capital punishment was a salient campaign issue, and Eddie Basha in Arizona, where the Republican incumbent "used Mr. Basha's support for homosexual marriages to undercut the challenger's popularity among conservative Democrats."[8]

The remainder of this chapter provides a more systematic examination of state elections' role in policy representation. We begin by reviewing the logic of electoral democracy, focusing on the two main mechanisms by which elections can induce representation: selection and incentives. We describe the conditions under which these mechanisms are effective and consider how they interact with one another. Next, we address the argument that important features of state elections, especially the dominant role of partisanship and national conditions, weaken representational linkages in the states. We show empirically that although state elections are powerfully shaped by exogenous forces, state-specific factors also matter a great deal.

We then examine the state-level evidence for the first mechanism of representation, selection, focusing specifically on *partisan* selection. Consistent with more skeptical accounts, we find that partisan turnover in state offices has a weak and ambiguous relationship with mass conservatism, especially compared to the powerful impact of mass partisanship. We also show, however, that state electorates punish candidates who take relatively extreme positions, which both tends to select relative moderates into office and incentivizes politicians to project moderate images to the public. Finally, we present evidence that at least some voters engage in partisan balancing, switching their votes to the opposition as a check against ideologically extreme policy-making. Manifested in phenomena such as gubernatorial midterm slumps, balancing provides negative feedback that helps maintain state policymaking in a relatively stable equilibrium. We find, in sum, that despite the importance of exogenous forces and the weakness of partisan selection, elections do provide state publics with effective means of influencing the actions of their governments.

6.1 Selection and Incentives

Agency theory highlights two basic means by which citizens (the principals) can use elections to induce officeholders (their agents) to act in accord with their preferences. The first is the *selection* of officeholders who personally share those preferences. The second is the use of *incentives* to align office-holders' preferences with those of citizens. In theory, either of these strategies on its own can induce good representation, but in practice elections typically serve a mix of the two functions.[9] When used in concert, selection and incentives interact in subtle ways. Even if voters care only about selecting good representatives, their use of incumbents' performance to distinguish good from bad "types" incentivizes bad representatives to act like good ones. Effective incentives can therefore make it more difficult to distinguish ideological types but also make it less necessary to do so.[10]

In a two-party system such as that of the United States, selection typically entails choosing one of two partisan types: the Democratic candidate or the Republican one. Under this mechanism, citizens can change the representation they receive through the *replacement* of officials from one party with ones from the other. Partisan selection and replacement are blunter tools of democratic control than, say, choosing from the pool of all citizens,[11] for the parties themselves define the choices by choosing whom to nominate. Even if each party's pool of nominees tends to be relatively extreme, however, voters may still be able to influence the ideological composition of officeholders within each party by electing only relatively moderate nominees.[12] Thus, in addition to the blunter tool of partisan selection, voters may also be able to engage in ideological selection within each party. The efficacy of electoral incentives requires not only that incumbents desire reelection but also that citizens be able to condition electoral sanctions and rewards on performance in office. That is, it requires that voters have the information and the will to hold candidates *accountable* for their policy positions and actions. If politicians know they will be sanctioned for being out of step with their constituents, they have incentives to adapt their positions to fit their constituents' preferences. When the electoral incentives are strong enough, adaptation can result in policy responsiveness without the replacement of any incumbent officials.

This, of course, is an idealized view that may not be realized in practice. Indeed, there are reasons to suspect that states in particular fall short of the conditions required for effective representation. Chief among these conditions is that voters have sufficient information about candidates and political conditions to select representative types and punish poor incumbent performance.[13] Since at least the mid-twentieth century, citizens have paid less attention to state politics than national politics, an imbalance that has only increased in recent decades.[14] Partly as a result, state election outcomes have long been powerfully shaped by national partisan and economic factors beyond the control of state-level parties and politicians.[15] To the extent that such exogenous forces determine the outcome of state elections, they weaken politicians' incentives to cater to the electorate relative to alternative goals, such as satisfying their party's core constituencies. In short, whether and how state elections do in fact induce policy responsiveness are empirical questions.

6.2 National Tides and Partisanship

One of the most important distinctions between state and national politics is that states cannot be treated as independent political systems. Rather, because states are embedded in a larger political system, state politics is strongly shaped by national politics as well as by other states. A stark illustration of this fact is provided by figure 6.1, which compares changes in Republican seat share for state houses versus for the US House.[16] As this figure suggests, partisan shifts at the two levels are very highly correlated ($R = 0.90$); when Republicans gain or lose seats at the national level, they nearly always do the same in the states. Furthermore, other research has shown that state elections respond to the same national forces that drive congressional elections, most notably presidential approval and the health of the US economy.[17]

Another, much more stable influence on state elections is mass partisanship. The more Republican a state public is, the more likely Republicans are to occupy state offices. Figure 6.2 shows this visually by plotting the relationship between mass Republicanism on the x axis and an index of Republican control of state government on the y axis.[18] These measures are centered across states within each year, thus removing the effect of national partisan tides. Though the correlation of 0.72 is not quite as high as that for the partisan swings plotted in figure 6.1, mass partisanship and Republican control are still strongly related. When a state public is 10 percent less Republican than the average state in that year, the Republican Party controls one fewer institution of state government, and vice versa for publics that are 10 percent more Republican than average. Moreover, despite the changes in states' partisanship that have taken place over the past seven decades, the strength of the relationship between mass and government Republicanism has remained quite stable over time.

The strong influence of national tides and state partisanship on subnational elections poses problems for democracy in the states. As Daniel Hopkins and Steven Rogers have argued, if state elections are determined by

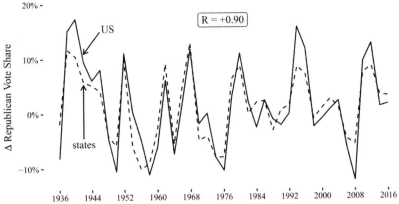

FIGURE 6.1. Interelection change in average Republican two-party seat share, state houses (dashed) and US House (solid).

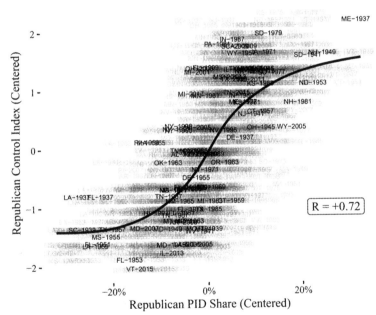

FIGURE 6.2. Partisan identification and party control, 1937–2019. Each observation is a state-year, a random 5 percent sample of which have been highlighted. Horizontal axis indicates Republican share of major-party identifiers and vertical axis the 0–3 government control index, both centered within year.

national rather than state-specific factors, state officials have little electoral incentive to cater to the preferences of their constituents, which will not affect their reelection probabilities either way.[19] That the state-level balance of partisan preferences also exerts a powerful effect on state elections is not in itself very reassuring, for as figure 3.6 showed, partisanship and policy preferences were only loosely related to each other for much of the twentieth century. Though partisanship does seem to respond on the margin to political conditions,[20] it typically evolves gradually over time. Moreover, Americans' "partisan hearts and spleens" (to quote Achen and Bartels) bias their political perceptions and generally hinder voters from reaching the standards of rationality assumed by some democratic theories.[21]

Fortunately for state-level democracy, state elections are not completely determined by national tides and state partisanship. In fact, these two factors together explain only about half the variance in partisan control of state governments.[22] In principle, this leaves plenty of scope for state parties and officials to influence their own fate and thus for citizens to incentivize good representation. Whether this occurs in practice is the subject of the remainder of this chapter.

6.3 Partisan Selection

Do state publics select officials whose policy positions are aligned with their own preferences? For a first cut at an answer, we examine the relationship between mass ideology and party control across states. If partisan selection were the dominant mechanism of representation, we would expect conservative state publics to favor the election of Republicans and liberal publics to do the opposite. In earlier eras, conservatism in the economic domain (where the parties have long taken divergent positions) should be a more powerful predictor of party control than cultural conservatism, and in both domains the relationship should be stronger in today's more partisan era than in earlier ones.

Figure 6.3 provides support for these expectations. As the plots in the rightmost column indicate, conservative state publics have certainly tended to vote Republican in recent decades. Since 1993, Republican control of state government has been correlated at 0.7 with mass economic conservatism and at 0.4 and 0.5 with cultural and racial conservatism, respectively. In the middle era (1965–1992), the same correlation with economic conservatism was a still-robust 0.6, but in the other two domains the relationship was essentially flat. Finally, before 1965 Republican control was only barely correlated with

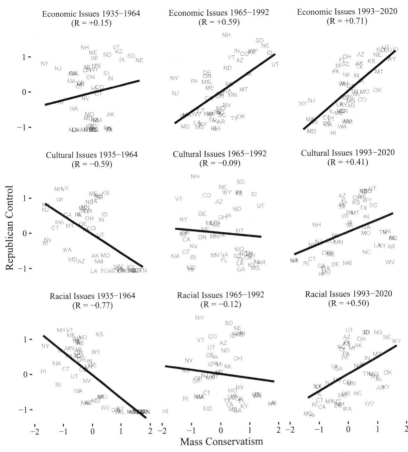

FIGURE 6.3. Mass conservatism and Republican control of state government by era and issue domain. All measures are standardized to have zero-mean, unit-variance within eras.

economic conservatism and had a strong *negative* relationship with cultural and racial conservatism.

This inverse relationship between conservatism and party control was due partly to the outlier status of southern states (see, for example, the lower-right corner of the "Racial Issues 1935–1964" panel). Removing the South from the calculations makes the pre-1965 relationships less negative and flips the cultural and racial ones positive in the 1965–1992 period. Even outside the South, however, the same qualitative pattern holds. Like Republican PID (see figure 3.6), Republican control of state government was once weakly if not negatively related to mass conservatism but over the past eight decades has come into strong alignment with it. This provides preliminary evidence that

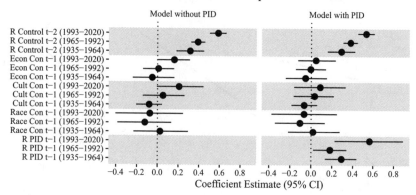

FIGURE 6.4. Dynamic panel model of party control of state government by era. The four mass opinion measures have been standardized to have zero-mean and unit variance. The data have been subsetted to years immediately following a state legislative election.

as the parties have diverged ideologically in recent decades, partisan selection has become more important.

To explore this suggestion more formally, we estimate two dynamic panel models of party control. In addition to the usual fixed effects and the two-year lag of the Republican control index, the first model includes our three measures of domain-specific mass conservatism. The second model includes these same predictors plus the Republican PID share in the mass public. All the variables (including state fixed effects) are interacted with era, enabling us to compare the drivers of party control at different points in time. Because all the opinion measures are estimates with associated uncertainty, we use a technique called the method of composition to adjust the coefficient estimates for measurement error.[23]

The results of the two models are reported in figure 6.4. The first things to notice are the era-specific coefficients for lagged Republican control. These coefficients have increased over time, from 0.32 before 1965 to 0.58 since 1993, indicating that partisan control of state government has become more temporally persistent within states. The result is that alternation in party control has become less frequent. Despite this upward trend, however, party control remains much less autocorrelated than policy ideology, whose lag coefficients in similar models typically range between 0.7 and 0.9.[24] In other words, party control does not "lock in" to the same degree as policy does but rather reverts more rapidly to its state-specific mean. As we will see later in this chapter, one reason for this mean reversion is that control of state government triggers a backlash in the public that advantages the out-party.

The next three sets of coefficients capture the degree to which mass conservatism predicts change in party control. As the confidence intervals indicate, the evidence that it does so is weak. In the model without PID, the only coefficient clearly distinguishable from zero is for mass cultural conservatism in the 1993–2020 period, though the coefficient for economic conservatism in the same era is marginally significant ($p = 0.09$). In these two domains, there is also a suggestive pattern of increasing coefficients over time. The magnitudes of these estimates suggest that flipping one arm of state government to the Republicans would require a four-SD increase in cultural conservatism and an eight-SD increase in economic conservatism (the opinion measures are standardized across state-years).

Even these fragile effects dissipate when we add a control for the Republican PID share in the mass public (figure 6.4, right panel). The addition of this variable complicates the interpretation of the mass conservatism coefficients, for if mass conservatism does affect party control it likely does so at least partly through an effect on mass PID. (Recall from chapter 3 that over the long term state partisanship has aligned with mass conservatism, especially on economic issues.) Nevertheless, it is clear that when it comes to short-term changes in party control, party identification is the most consistent and powerful predictor. In the post-1992 era, a two-SD change in mass PID would be sufficient on its own to flip the governorship or a legislative chamber.

In sum, the evidence that mass conservatism promotes the replacement of Democrats with Republicans is mixed at best. The evidence is strongest in the post-1992 era, suggesting that partisan selection may have become more important in recent decades. Still, the effect of mass partisanship swamps all measures of mass ideology, confirming its dominance as a driver of election outcomes. Given that over the past half a century mass partisanship has gradually aligned with mass conservatism (chapter 3), the latter may influence party control of state government indirectly over the long term. Over the short term, however, mass policy preferences are relatively unimportant determinants of shifts in partisan control.

6.4 Candidate Positioning and Electoral Success

One explanation for the weak relationship between mass conservatism and shifts in party control is that state parties adapt to their electorates. If voters reward moderate parties, then this adaptation would mask mass conservatism's effect on electoral outcomes.[25] Both selection and incentives can contribute to parties' ideological adaptation. First, voters may be more likely to (re)elect candidates with relatively moderate policy positions.

Through the selective attrition of extremists, general-election voters can shade both parties' cadre of officeholders toward the middle of the state's ideological spectrum. Second, the existence of such selection may incentivize candidates and incumbents to adopt moderate positions they would otherwise (for sincere or strategic reasons) eschew.[26] Thus, in principle, general-election voters can induce parties to adapt their position both by influencing which candidates get elected and by affecting the policy positions they adopt.

The existing empirical evidence suggests there are real, if modest, penalties for ideological extremism. In the US House, candidates who adopt relatively extreme policy positions are less likely to be elected,[27] and incumbents with extreme roll-call records are less likely to be reelected.[28] The penalties for extremism are not large, however, and they seem to have declined in recent decades.[29] There has been less research on other elected offices, but one recent study finds that although state legislators are punished for extreme roll-call records, the penalty is smaller than it is for US House members.[30]

We expand this empirical evidence by examining gubernatorial as well as state legislative candidates and employing a variety of ideological measures. The first measure, which is available for all offices we consider, is Adam Bonica's DW-DIME scores.[31] DW-DIME scores are derived from a machine-learning algorithm that uses campaign contributions to predict Congress members' DW-NOMINATE scores (a measure of the conservatism of their roll-call records).[32] These predictions are then used to project candidates for state offices onto the same scale. The second measure, which we created, is the contributed-weighted average of the DW-NOMINATE scores of the Congress members to which the candidate's donors also donated. It is thus similar to DW-DIME except that it uses only donations made during the primary campaign, mitigating the possibility of the electoral outcome influencing candidates' scores.[33] These average DW-NOMINATE scores are available only for gubernatorial candidates. Our third and final measure, available only for candidates who at some point served in the state legislature, is Boris Shor and Nolan McCarty's estimate of their ideal point based on their legislative voting record.[34] These scores are the closest analog to the measures used by previous scholars[35] to study whether voters hold incumbent members of Congress accountable for their roll-call votes. The resulting data set covers the years 1994–2018. We standardize all measures to have zero-mean and unit-variance across candidates and elections.

If voters punish ideologically extreme candidates, we should expect increases in the conservatism of either candidate (Democratic or Republican) to decrease Republican vote share.[36] To illustrate why this is so, consider a

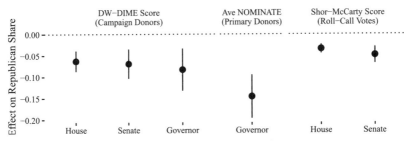

FIGURE 6.5. Effects of candidate conservatism on Republican vote share, 1994–2018.

unidimensional ideological spectrum on which the Democratic candidate is to the left of the Republican. If voters prefer the candidate closest to them in ideological space, then voters to the left of the midpoint between the candidates prefer the Democrat, and voters to the right of the midpoint prefer the Republican. A rightward move by either candidate moves the midpoint to the right, thus weakly increasing the proportion of voters on the left (Democratic) side of the midpoint.

We test this hypothesis by estimating a model of Republican vote share as a function of candidate conservatism.[37] To account for the confounding effect of durable district characteristics, such as their partisan lean, we include separate intercepts for constituency (state for governor, district-decade for state house and senate) along with region-year intercepts to account for region-specific time trends. The coefficient estimates can be interpreted as the difference in Republican share, relative to the constituency and region-year means, when either party nominates a candidate one standard deviation more conservative. It is important to keep in mind that, depending on the measure, the pooled standard deviation of conservatism is two to three times larger than the within-party SD. This means that a one-standard-deviation change in conservatism is roughly equivalent to moving from one ideological wing of a party to the other wing (e.g., from a liberal Democrat to a centrist Democrat).[38]

The results of this exercise are reported in figure 6.5. Republicans clearly suffer when either party nominates a relatively conservative candidate. According to the DW-DIME point estimates, a one-SD increase in candidate conservatism is associated with a decrease in Republican share of 6 (±2) percentage points in state house elections, 7 (±3) points in state senate elections, and 8 (±5) in gubernatorial elections. For governors, the estimate increases to 15 (±5) points when only primary donors are used to estimate conservatism,

indicating that the effect is not driven by the inclusion of postelection donations. Finally, the rightmost two estimates show that the results hold for
roll-call voting as well. A Republican state legislator whose roll-call record is
one standard deviation more conservative can expect to lose 3 (±1) points in
a state house election or 5 (±2) points in a senate election.

These estimates are consistent with a modest but real penalty for ideological extremism in state elections.[39] There is some suggestion that the penalty
might be increasing in the prominence of the office, but the estimates are
too imprecise for firm conclusions. What seems clear, however, is that both
incumbents and challengers have electoral incentives to cater ideologically
to their electorates. Candidates who take extreme positions receive fewer
votes than a more moderate candidate would have. Moreover, it is likely that
this extremism penalty was even larger before the 1990s, when state parties
were less polarized and more autonomous from their national brands and
there was probably more local news coverage of state politics. As chapter 5
demonstrated, however, at no point in the past eight decades did state parties moderate so completely as to converge on the same policy positions.
Rather, candidates and state parties have balanced the electoral benefits of
moderation against the centrifugal pull of primary voters and personal con-
victions. Due to these centrifugal forces, Democrats and Republicans representing comparable constituencies nevertheless take divergent positions,
and they implement different policies when they control state government.
This, then, raises a further question: Are state parties as a whole punished for
their deviations from the electoral center? This is the subject of the following
section.

6.5 Collective Accountability and Negative Feedback

Since the 1990s, party control of state government has become much more
temporally persistent (see figure 6.4) as well as more tightly aligned with the
partisan and ideological leanings of state publics. Yet, even in the twenty-first
century, the locally dominant party does routinely lose control of state offices,
especially the governorship. These losses often coincide with down years for
the national party, such as 2006 for Republicans and 2010 for Democrats. But
some have cut against the grain of both national tides and state partisanship,
often following bouts of extreme policymaking by the majority party.

The experience of Kansas in the 2010s provides a good example. True to
its solidly Republican leanings, Kansas began the decade by returning large
GOP majorities to the legislature and electing Republican governor Sam
Brownback in a landslide. The Tea Party–aligned Brownback spearheaded

the passage of an ambitious right-wing agenda, including a set of massive tax reductions that eviscerated the state's revenue base. This sharp rightward turn in policymaking sparked a vociferous backlash, including among some Republicans.[40] In 2014, an extremely good year for Republicans nationally, Brownback was only barely reelected, and in 2016 his party suffered substantial losses in the state legislature, even as Donald Trump carried the state by twenty points. By then Brownback was the least popular governor in the nation,[41] and in 2018 eight years of unified Republican control came to an end with the election of a Democratic governor. Even in ruby-red Kansas, voters' appetite for conservative policymaking had its limits.

Meanwhile, in Connecticut, Democrats faced a similar if less severe backlash. In 2010, Democrat Dannel Malloy captured the governorship while his party swept to a large majority in the state legislature. Governor Malloy and the Democratic majority proceeded to enact a long list of liberal policy changes: decriminalizing marijuana possession, strengthening gay rights, repealing the state's death penalty, and passing sweeping gun-control regulations. Although 2012 was a much better year for Democrats nationally than 2010, the party actually lost legislative seats in Connecticut. It continued to do so in subsequent elections until, by 2016, it retained only a narrow majority in the state house.

Similar examples can be found in just about every recent election cycle. In 2014, Republican Larry Hogan rode the popular backlash against a "rain tax" to the governorship of overwhelmingly Democratic Maryland.[42] In 2015, Democrat John Bel Edwards took advantage of a split among Republicans to capture the governorship of Louisiana. A Republican has served as governor of liberal Massachusetts since 2015 and Vermont since 2017. And in 2019, after a term of aggressively conservative policymaking under Republican Matt Bevin, Democrat Andy Beshear won the governorship of Kentucky. In all these cases, the minority party was able to exploit the perceived overreach of the majority party for electoral gain.

These examples suggest that state publics do notice and react to policy changes in their state. In principle, this reaction could go in either direction. On one hand, there is much evidence that public policies generate positive feedback: by changing the preferences, expectations, and resources of political actors, policies often generate and reinforce political support for themselves.[43] Specifically, the implementation of a new policy can convince some previously opposed citizens to support it instead. If this were broadly true, then we might expect an increase in policy conservatism to cause mass conservatism to increase as well, reinforcing or even intensifying public support for conservative policymaking.

On the other hand, unless mass conservatism responds perfectly to policy conservatism, we should generally observe negative feedback on the public's *relative* policy preferences. By relative preference, we mean the desire for policy *change*, for more or less government activity than is currently provided— what Stimson calls public policy "mood."[44] (Our concept of mass conservatism differs from policy mood in that it captures the public's "absolute" preferences over public policies and accordingly is measured using only survey questions that do not refer to the policy status quo.) As Wlezien has argued, public opinion typically responds "thermostatically" to policy change.[45] For example, when government expenditures on education increase, the public's support for more education spending generally decreases. This response is not due to a decrease in citizens' preferred level of spending but rather to the fact that fewer citizens' preferred level is greater than the new, higher level of actual expenditures.

These thermostatic dynamics have implications for elections as well. If electing Republicans makes policy more conservative and increases in policy conservatism decrease support for further rightward policy changes, then (assuming voters expect Republicans to continue moving policy to the right) Republican control of government should decrease voters' support for Republicans. In other words, at least some voters should engage in electoral *balancing*—voting against the party in power in order to achieve more moderate policies. Balancing helps explain why the president's party tends to lose US House seats in midterm elections[46] and why some voters split their tickets across offices.[47] It is also possible that some voters engage in anticipatory balancing: taking into account the likely outcome of one race (e.g., for presidency) when deciding how to cast their vote in others (e.g., the US House).[48] Anticipatory balancing does not require that voters hold incumbents accountable for actual policy outcomes. Rather, the mere expectation that Republicans will move policy to the right and Democrats will move it to the left may be sufficient to motivate balancing.

Previous research indicates that citizens respond thermostatically to policy changes at the state level as well. When state welfare or education spending goes up, the public becomes less supportive of further spending increases in the same domain.[49] Citizens also seem to incorporate these policy responses into their evaluations of state officials. For instance, when state policy conservatism increases over a legislative term, self-identified conservatives become much more likely to approve of the state legislature while liberals become much less likely to do so.[50] Taken together, this evidence suggests that state publics do notice broad changes in state policy and adjust their political attitudes according to their own policy preferences.

6.5.1 ELECTORAL FEEDBACK

Do these thermostatic reactions translate into electoral behavior? One way to answer this question is to examine how partisan control of government affects downstream elections. As noted above, balancing theory predicts that electing Republicans decreases future support for Republican candidates, all else equal. The ceteris paribus condition is important, for states do have enduring tendencies to elect state officials from one party or the other. As indicated by the relatively small coefficients on Republican control in figure 6.4, however, party control of state government is less temporally persistent than either mass partisanship or mass conservatism. In other words, party control has a stronger tendency to regress to the mean in state elections. This negative feedback process can be seen even more clearly if we again use the electoral RD design (for a description, see chapter 5, section 5.2) to isolate random variation in party control.

As a preliminary step, let us first examine whether and how the election of Republican state officials affects the conservatism of state publics. If our mass conservatism scores are successful in measuring the public's absolute preferences, we should not expect them to react negatively to policy changes the way that measures of relative preferences do. And indeed, the RD analyses provide no evidence of negative feedback on mass conservatism (figure 6.6, top row). At the same time, there is little sign of positive feedback either. For both the governorship and the state house, the estimated effect of Republican control is close to and statistically indistinguishable from zero. The experience of being governed by a given party does not seem to change voters' policy preferences, at least not in the short term.

Nevertheless, if we turn our attention to the remaining panels of figure 6.6, we see that voters do punish the incumbent party at the polls.[51] The second row of plots illustrates the state-level analogy to the presidential midterm slump: the effect of electing a Republican governor on the party's seat share in the state house (left) and senate (right). When a Republican barely wins the governorship, their party's seat share in each legislative chamber drops by about one percentage point in the next election. When a Democrat barely wins, Republicans gain two or three points. The differences between these outcomes (three points for the house, five points for the senate) are the chamber-specific penalties for controlling the governorship. If a party cared solely about maximizing its state legislative seats, it would prefer to (narrowly) lose the governorship rather than win it. A similar pattern holds for the effect of a Republican majority in the state house (figure 6.6, bottom left).[52] On average, when Republicans have won bare control of the state house, their

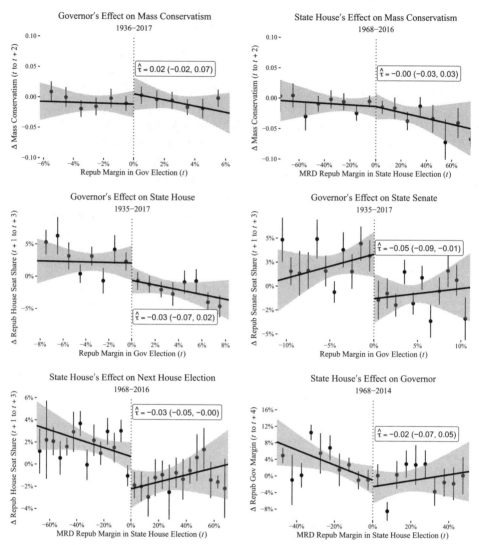

FIGURE 6.6. Feedback effects of party control. Left column shows effects of Republican control of the governorship; right column shows effects of control of the state house. Top row shows effects on the average of mass conservatism (economic and cultural), middle row effects on average legislative seat share (house and senate), and bottom row effects on gubernatorial margin.

legislative seat share has fallen by about two points in the next election; when they have fallen just short of control, they have stayed about even. Only for the state house's effect on the governorship (bottom right) is there no clear evidence of electoral feedback: when Republicans win bare control of the state house, they are about as likely to gain votes in the next gubernatorial election as they are when they fall just short.[53] One reason for the lack of an effect might be that in most states another house election intervenes before the next gubernatorial election so that by the time a governor's four-year term is up, voters have already had a chance to balance.

Subtleties notwithstanding, the overall pattern is clear: parties are punished electorally for controlling state legislative chambers and governorships. This is true even though individual officeholders enjoy a *personal* incumbency advantage. What explains this partisan disadvantage? Because the RD design compares races that are nearly equivalent in vote share and other characteristics, the answer is not parties' tendency to regress to the mean after a particularly strong showing. As we saw in figure 6.6, it is also not because party control changes voters' absolute policy preferences. One thing party control does affect, however, is the conservatism of state policies, which gives at least some voters reason to switch their votes to the opposition in an effort to induce policy moderation. Policy balancing is thus a likely explanation for the electoral reaction against the majority party.

The individual-level behaviors underlying these macro-level patterns are not entirely clear. For example, do voters notice whether the majority party has governed as moderates or extremists? The Republicans' experience in Kansas and other examples cited earlier suggest that large policy changes do make an impression. But the systematic evidence for this is rather weak. If we adjust for how much policy conservatism changed during a party's term of control, the estimated partisan penalty remains the same, suggesting that voters' reactions do not take into account how much policy actually changed. Most voters' balancing decisions may therefore be "crude" in the sense that they punish the majority party mechanically, without regard to how it has governed in the preceding term.[54]

Even if partisan balancing is crude, it still serves as an additional form of negative feedback on state politics. Together with the candidate-level extremism penalties documented earlier in the chapter, balancing reinforces the incremental nature of policy change in the states. Not only does each party's anticipation of electoral sanctions limit the magnitude of policy shifts, but the changes enacted by one party are often eroded or counteracted when the opposing party wins power. Moreover, if a party tries to enact rapid policy changes, this is likely to lead to larger future electoral losses, which will undermine the new policies. The negative policy feedback loop between policymaking and elections helps keep each state political system in a slowly evolving political equilibrium.

6.6 Summary

This chapter has documented the subtle but crucial role that elections play in linking state publics and their governments. Although state elections are

powerfully shaped by forces largely beyond the control of state-level politicians, there is still substantial scope for them to shape their electoral desti-
nies. In principle, elections can induce governments to represent their citizens via two main mechanisms: selection and incentives. The evidence that
mass policy preferences drive partisan shifts is fairly weak, suggesting that
partisan selection may not be a particularly effective mechanism of representation, at least over the short term. One reason for the weakness of selection,
however, may be the effectiveness with which elections incentivize state parties to adapt to their constituencies. Across all state offices, ideologically extreme candidates are punished at the polls. Moreover, state electorates seem
to hold state parties accountable for their policymaking, shifting support to
the opposition party in an effort to counterbalance excessive policy changes.
These phenomena provide prima facie evidence that state elections create
responsive governments. Whether this potential is realized is the subject of
the next two chapters.

Responsiveness:
The Public's Influence on State Policies

If democracy is working well, the outputs of political processes should be robustly related to citizens' preferences. But how, specifically, should we gauge the strength of this relationship? Scholars have proposed a number of different measures,[1] but in this book we focus on two in particular: *responsiveness* and *proximity*. The first measure, responsiveness, is the expected change in officials' positions or government policies associated with a one-unit change in citizens' preferences.[2] In a perfectly responsive democracy, a given change in citizens' preferences (e.g., from a ten-dollar minimum wage to an eleven-dollar one) would be followed by a policy change of the same magnitude (a one-dollar increase in the minimum wage). The second measure, proximity, is the closeness of the match between citizens' preferences and political outputs. When proximity is at its maximum, citizens get exactly what they want (e.g., there is no difference between the actual minimum wage and the public's preferred one).

Each of these measures captures an important component of democracy's normative appeal. Responsiveness indicates citizens' influence or power[3] over the government, whereas proximity captures something more like fine-grained control. Importantly, a political system can simultaneously perform well by one metric and poorly by the other.[4] If policies are biased (e.g., the actual minimum wage is always two dollars lower than what the public prefers), then policies will not be very proximate even if they are perfectly responsive.[5] Proximity can also be poor if policymaking is *overly* responsive.[6] If citizens' minimum-wage preferences range between ten and fifteen dollars but states cluster at extremes of five and twenty dollars, then states may be highly responsive without any state public getting the wage it wants.

This chapter and the next evaluate the quality of statehouse democracy according to these two measures. We begin in this chapter with an analysis of ideological responsiveness: the relationship between the general liberalism–conservatism of state publics and the liberalism–conservatism of government officials and policies. Our most important finding is that state governments are indeed responsive to public opinion. Not only do states with conservative publics have conservative officials and policies, but when public opinion is unusually conservative in a state, its policies change in a conservative direction. The latter is evidence of what we call *dynamic responsiveness*. Due to the limits of ideological scaling, however, this analysis allows us to say little about policy proximity or about related quantities such as ideological bias. We therefore reserve these topics for chapter 8, which examines representation on an issue-by-issue basis.

7.1 Operationalizing Responsiveness

If citizens collectively influence the government, then states where the public is more conservative should produce more conservative political outcomes. A simple way to operationalize the relationship between public preferences and government outputs is a bivariate regression,

$$(7.1) \qquad y_s = \alpha + \beta \bar{x}_s + \varepsilon_s,$$

where y_s is a measure of government outputs in state s and $\bar{x}_s$ is a measure of the preferences of the average citizen in the state. The slope parameter β captures states' responsiveness to citizens, while the intercept α is the expected output when $\bar{x}_s = 0$.

The substantive interpretation of these statistical quantities hinges on two demanding conditions. The first is whether government outputs, y_s, and the mass public's policy preferences, x_s, are measured on the same scale. That is, a value of, say, $y_s = 0$ means substantively the same thing as $\bar{x}_s = 0$. This "joint scaling" assumption can be problematic even when the concept being measured (e.g., the value of the minimum wage or legal recognition of same-sex marriage) is apparently straightforward,[7] but it is even more problematic in cases where both $\bar{x}_s$ and y_s are summary measures of conservatism derived from distinct policy items.[8] Without jointly scaled measures, we cannot say for certain whether responsiveness is proportionate nor at what value of β policymaking becomes overresponsive. Neither can we interpret the intercept α as an absolute measure of policymaking bias. We can, however, still make relative statements, comparing, for example, the strength of responsiveness at different points in time or the policymaking bias in different regions.

A second key condition, which we are in a better position to address in this chapter, is that variation in $\bar{x}_s$ is independent of other determinants of y_s. This condition imbues β with a causal interpretation—as the policy effect of a unit change in mass preferences, holding constant other factors not themselves affected by mass preferences. Due to data limitations, most previous studies have focused on the cross-sectional link between the mass public's policy preferences and governmental outputs. But a major problem with cross-sectional analyses is that it is very difficult to rule out the possibility that some third, unmeasured characteristic—states' political culture, for example—confounds the relationship between mass conservatism and policy conservatism or even the possibility that policy conservatism causes mass conservatism rather than the other way around.

Although we cannot conclusively rule out these sources of confounding, we attempt to limit them through a dynamic approach that leverages over-time variation in preferences and policymaking within each state. Specifically, our analysis of policy responsiveness later in this chapter employs a dynamic panel (DP) model similar to equation (5.1) in chapter 5:

$$(7.2) \qquad y_{st} = \alpha_s + \gamma_t + \rho_1 y_{s,t-1} + \rho_2 y_{s,t-2} + \beta \bar{x}_{st} + \varepsilon_{st},$$

where y_{st} is policy conservatism, $\bar{x}_{st}$ is mass conservatism, α_s and γ_t are state- and year-specific intercepts, and $y_{s,t-1}$ and $y_{s,t-2}$ are first- and second-order lags of policy conservatism. In the DP model, the dynamic responsiveness coefficient β captures the relationship between mass and policy conservatism within states over time, given each state's recent policy history and net of any year-specific changes common to all states. A positive value of β means that in years when a state public is more conservative than usual for that state, the state's policies tend to become more conservative in the following year. Such a relationship provides evidence that citizens influence the ideological direction of state policymaking.

7.2 Position Responsiveness

In order to influence government policies, citizens must first influence the positions of government officials. As we have noted, elections provide two main mechanisms for achieving this: by affecting which party wins election (*partisan selection*) and by influencing the positions taken by officials within each party (*partisan adaptation*).[9] If partisan selection were the only channel of responsiveness, we would expect the probability of electing Republicans to increase with a constituency's conservatism but no relationship between mass conservatism and officials' conservatism within each party. If partisan

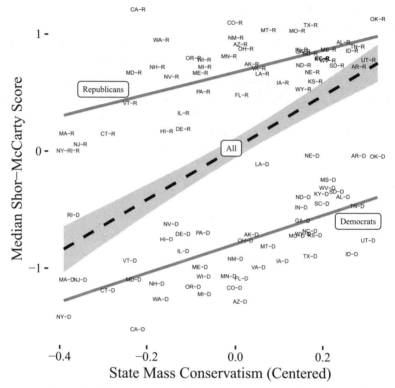

FIGURE 7.1. State legislators' responsiveness to the conservatism of state publics. The vertical axis indicates the median Shor-McCarty score of legislators in each party and state (averaged across chambers and years); the horizontal axis, the average of the economic and cultural conservatism of their state in the year of their first election (centered within year and then averaged across years). Solid lines indicate the relationship within parties, and the dashed line represents the relationship with the chamber median.

adaptation were the only channel, we would expect the reverse: responsiveness within each party but no relationship between mass conservatism and party control. Of course, if officials are entirely unresponsive, there should be no relationship at all between their positions and the preferences of the public.

Figures 7.1 and 7.2 help adjudicate among these competing expectations. Both figures plot the cross-sectional relationship between states' mass conservatism and the conservatism of elected officials in each party.[10] In figure 7.1, the dependent variable is the median Shor-McCarty ideal point in each party caucus, averaged across chambers and years.[11] As indicated by the separation between the two clouds of points, Democratic legislators are more liberal than same-state Republicans in every state, though the degree of polarization varies across states (e.g., low in Arkansas, high in California). Nevertheless, as the solid regression lines show, there is a clear positive relationship within each party. Democratic legislators are relatively liberal in liberal states and conservative in conservative states, and the same goes for Republicans, to the point where the median Democrat in Oklahoma is about as conservative as the median Republican in New York. Among governors (figure 7.2), there is even more ideological overlap between the parties. For example, Democrat Cecil Andrus, who managed to win four gubernatorial elections

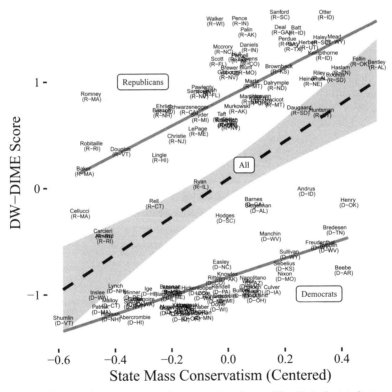

FIGURE 7.2. Governors' responsiveness to the conservatism of state publics. Vertical axis indicates governors' DW-DIME score; horizontal axis, the average of the economic and cultural conservatism of their state in the year of their first election (centered within year). Solid lines indicate the relationship within parties, and the dashed line represents the relationship across all governors.

in conservative Idaho, has a higher DW-DIME score than Republicans Donald Carcieri and Lincoln Almond, governors of liberal Rhode Island.[12] These within-party differences suggest that, whether through preemptive adaptation or the selective attrition of out-of-step candidates, the ideological stances of state officials are influenced by the conservatism of their electorates.

More indirectly, these figures also present evidence of partisan selection. The dashed regression lines labeled "All" capture the relationship between mass conservatism and the ideological positions of all officials, regardless of party. For legislators, this means the average of the Shor-McCarty medians in the state house and senate. For governors, it is simply the winner's DW-DIME score. Note that, especially for legislators, the dashed line is steeper than the solid lines such that in liberal states it is closer to the Democratic line and in conservative states closer to the Republican. This is because Democratic governors and especially legislators are more plentiful in liberal states, so they receive more weight in the overall average. Republicans' greater electoral success in conservative states thus intensifies the relationship between mass and elite ideology already present within each party.

This analysis thus supports the conclusion that state officials are ideologically responsive to their publics and that this responsiveness is driven by a combination of partisan selection and adaptation. We must be cautious about the credibility and generalizability of this conclusion, however, due to the limited time coverage of our measures of state officials' conservatism. Not only do these measures not extend before the 1990s, but neither is well suited to tracking change over time. For a fully dynamic perspective, we must turn instead to analysis of the responsiveness of state policymaking.

7.3 Policy Responsiveness

While the relationship between mass opinion and elected officials' positions is an important foundation of democracy, the effect of opinion on government policies is arguably the ultimate metric of representation. In the remainder of this chapter, we focus squarely on this relationship.

First, in the spirit of *Statehouse Democracy*, we examine the cross-state relationship between mass and policy conservatism. Following a long line of previous work in the state politics literature, we distinguish between the South and non-South in our analysis.[13] We also distinguish among three eras of state politics: 1935–1964, 1965–1992, and 1993–2020. As figure 7.3 shows, mass and policy conservatism have always been solidly correlated across non-southern states. Going back to the 1930s, non-southern states with liberal

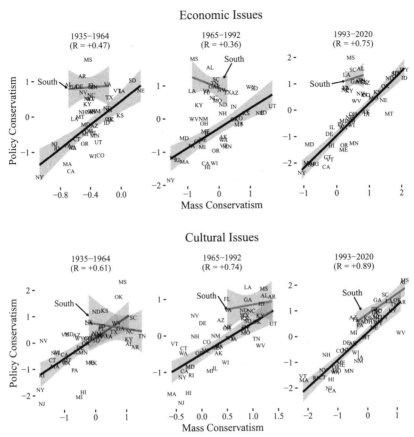

FIGURE 7.3. Cross-sectional relationship between mass and government policy conservatism by region, era, and issue domain. Measures are standardized across state-years. The South is defined as the eleven former Confederate states.

publics, such as New York, New Jersey, and Rhode Island, have had relatively liberal policies, economic as well as cultural. Conversely, conservative states like Nebraska (on economic issues) and West Virginia (on cultural issues) had similarly conservative policies. This relationship has strengthened over time, from a cross-state correlation around 0.65 in both domains before 1965 to nearly 0.9 since 1993.

The South stands out as a clear outlier from the rest of the nation. This is especially true on economic issues. Since at least the 1930s, the economic policies of southern states have been about a standard deviation more conservative than non-southern states with ideologically similar publics. For example, in the 1935–1964 period, the publics of Ohio and Florida both occupied positions near the middle of the cross-state ideological spectrum (around −0.4 in that era), but while Ohio's economic policy conservatism score was −0.4, Florida's was +0.9. This is understandable in light of the fact that in this period Florida and other southern states disenfranchised many of their more economically liberal residents, including nearly all of their Black citizens. What is more puzzling is the persistence of these regional differences over time. Even in the 1993–2020 period, southern states remained a distinctive bloc with conservative economic policies out of step with their more moderate publics. The South is much less distinctive on cultural issues. Although southern states have more conservative cultural policies than non-southern states with similar publics, this conservative intercept shift is smaller than in the economic domain. The cross-sectional relationship in the region between cultural policy and opinion has also increased considerably over time. Basically flat before 1965, the relationship is now almost as strong within the South as it is outside it. This suggests that on cultural but not economic issues, southern states have changed their policies in response to public demands.

More direct evidence of dynamic responsiveness—how state policy changes in response to public preferences—is provided by the results of the dynamic panel model described earlier in equation (7.2). As with the cross-sectional analysis in figure 7.3, we estimate this model within domains, using mass economic ideology to predict change in economic policies and mass cultural ideology to do the same for cultural policies. A positive coefficient on mass conservatism implies that when opinion is more liberal than usual in a state, policy tends to move leftward, and vice versa when it is more conservative than usual. To explore how responsiveness differs across moderators such as region and era, we estimate variations of our baseline model with these factors interacted with mass conservatism.

The results of our baseline dynamic panel specification are reported in columns (1) and (4) of table 7.1. As the coefficients in the first row indicate, when mass conservatism increases by one standard deviation in either domain, policy conservatism in the same domain is expected to increase by 0.08 SDs (where standard deviations are again defined across state-years). These dynamic responsiveness estimates are much smaller than the corresponding cross-sectional estimates, which (pooled across regions and years) are 0.52 on economic issues and 0.68 on cultural issues. The technical reason for this discrepancy is that the state-specific intercepts (fixed effects) and the lagged dependent variables in the model account for the bulk of the variation in state policy conservatism. The remaining variation explained by mass conservatism represents how much we would expect a state's policy to change in response to public opinion in just a single year.

TABLE 7.1 Dynamic responsiveness and its moderators

	Dependent Variable: Policy Conservatism (t)					
	Economic (1)	Economic (2)	Economic (3)	Cultural (4)	Cultural (5)	Cultural (6)
Mass Con.$_{t-1}$	**0.08**	**0.12**	**0.08**	**0.08**	0.06	**0.10**
	(0.02)	(0.03)	(0.02)	(0.03)	(0.04)	(0.03)
Mass Con.$_{t-1}$ × 1965–1992		**−0.09**			0.02	
		(0.04)			(0.08)	
Mass Con.$_{t-1}$ × 1936–1964		**−0.12**			−0.04	
		(0.05)			(0.06)	
Mass Con.$_{t-1}$ × South			−0.07			−0.03
			(0.05)			(0.07)
Policy Con.$_{t-1}$	**0.42**	**0.28**	**0.42**	**0.36**	**0.42**	**0.35**
	(0.03)	(0.04)	(0.03)	(0.02)	(0.03)	(0.03)
Policy Con.$_{t-2}$	**0.34**	**0.20**	**0.35**	**0.29**	**0.29**	**0.28**
	(0.03)	(0.04)	(0.03)	(0.02)	(0.04)	(0.03)
Policy Con.$_{t-1}$ × 1965–1992		−0.02			**−0.20**	
		(0.05)			(0.05)	
Policy Con.$_{t-1}$ × 1936–1964		−0.09			**−0.29**	
		(0.07)			(0.06)	
Policy Con.$_{t-2}$ × 1965–1992		−0.01			**−0.15**	
		(0.06)			(0.05)	
Policy Con.$_{t-2}$ × 1936–1964		−0.06			**−0.21**	
		(0.07)			(0.05)	
Policy Con.$_{t-1}$ × South			**−0.13**			−0.06
			(0.06)			(0.06)
Policy Con.$_{t-2}$ × South			**−0.12**			−0.04
			(0.06)			(0.06)
State Fixed Effects	yes	yes	yes	yes	yes	yes
Year Fixed Effects	yes	yes	yes	yes	yes	yes
State × Era Fixed Effects	no	yes	no	no	yes	no
Year × South Fixed Effects	no	no	yes	no	no	yes
Observations	4,284	4,284	4,284	4,284	4,284	4,284
R²	0.84	0.86	0.85	0.71	0.75	0.71

Note: All analyses cover the years 1937–2020. Standard errors, shown in parentheses, are clustered by state. Bold coefficients are statistically significant at the 10% level. Point estimates and standard errors take into account measurement error in mass conservatism and policy conservatism.

7.3.1 HETEROGENEITY: ERA AND REGION

Is dynamic responsiveness stronger under certain conditions than others? In other words, are there factors that moderate public opinion's influence on policy? The cross-sectional relationships in figure 7.3 provide hints of such heterogeneity, suggesting that responsiveness is stronger outside the South, at least on economic issues, and that it has generally strengthened over time. The DP model reveals similar patterns with respect to dynamic responsiveness.

Let us first consider how dynamic responsiveness has changed over time. Columns 2 and 5 of table 7.1 report the results of a model with mass conservatism interacted with era, with the most recent period (1993–2020) as the baseline category.[14] The main effect of mass conservatism (top row) thus represents dynamic responsiveness in years since 1993, while the coefficients in the next two rows capture the estimated difference in responsiveness between the 1993–2020 and 1965–1992 periods (second row) and between the 1993–2020 and 1936–1964 periods (third row). This exercise yields different results for the economic and cultural domains. On economics, dynamic responsiveness has increased markedly and monotonically over time. Indeed, before 1965, public opinion is estimated to have had essentially no effect on change in states' economic policies. In contrast, on cultural issues there has been no clear trend in responsiveness; the only difference across eras is in the lagged dependent variables, the coefficients of which indicate that cultural policy conservatism has become more temporally persistent over time (this is not true of economic conservatism).

Turning to heterogeneity by region (columns 3 and 6), we again find results that corroborate the patterns in figure 7.3. The coefficients in the first row of these columns capture responsiveness in non-southern states, which in both domains is as high or higher than the corresponding estimates from the baseline model (columns 1 and 4). The interaction effects in the fourth row (labeled "Mass Con.$_{t-1}$ × South") capture the difference in responsiveness between regions. Although neither is statistically distinguishable from zero, both suggest that dynamic responsiveness is weaker in southern states. On economic issues, the point estimate for southern states is close to zero, but on cultural issues regional differences are more modest. Although there are too few southern states for firm inferences, the apparent difference in responsiveness between the two domains is consistent with figure 7.3, which shows policy and mass conservatism in southern states to have aligned more tightly in the cultural domain than on economics.

In sum, the evidence suggests that on economic issues, public opinion exerts more influence on state policymaking now than in the past and that responsiveness has been consistently stronger outside the South. On cultural issues, the evidence of variation across time and region is substantially weaker. What explains these patterns? With respect to temporal heterogeneity, one possibility that should be considered is changes in measurement. Although our analysis accounts for differential measurement error in mass and policy conservatism, it does not account for the fact that these latent variables now account for a greater proportion of the observed variation in issue opinions and state policies than they did in earlier eras. The greater responsiveness evident in recent decades may therefore reflect the increasing dominance of a single ideological (and partisan) dimension of cross-state variation. Still, this increasing responsiveness is reassuring in light of the contemporary state-level democratic "deficits" and "backsliding" highlighted by previous work.[15] These are legitimate concerns, but as we discuss in more detail in chapter 9, there are reasons to believe that the quality of statehouse democracy was substantially lower earlier in the twentieth century.

Chief among these earlier deficits was the pre-1960s South's racially exclusionary one-party system. Though we defer a fuller discussion of the South until chapter 9, it is worth noting here that previous research has found few regional differences in states' responsiveness to their *electorates*—which, in the one-party South, were almost exclusively White.[16] The South's anomalous conservatism and lack of responsiveness might thus be attributable to the fact that our measure of mass preferences includes the whole public, not just voters. Also consistent with this explanation is the fact that southern policy representation is more distinctive on economics than on cultural issues, where the policy preferences of White and Black Americans have historically differed less within states (see, for example, figure 2.5 in chapter 2). What remains puzzling, however, is that regional differences in responsiveness have persisted far after the demise of Jim Crow and the reenfranchisement of Black southerners in the 1960s. Whether this persistence is attributable to simple status-quo bias or to southern states' continuing underrepresentation of their Black citizens, the legacy of the region's authoritarian past persists to this day.

7.3.2 MECHANISMS: TURNOVER VERSUS ADAPTATION

As we have noted, dynamic responsiveness to mass preferences can occur by two main mechanisms: partisan selection and partisan adaptation. Partisan selection is a two-step process. First, voters' conservatism must affect their probability of electing candidates of one party over another. Second, the newly elected officials must implement different policies than their opponents would have. In short, if greater conservatism in the public causes the election of more Republicans, and electing more Republicans causes policies to become more conservative, then partisan selection mediates the effect of opinion on policy. Adaptation, by contrast, is that portion of dynamic responsiveness not mediated by the selection of candidates of one party or another but rather due to each party responding directly to shifts in public sentiment. As figures 7.1 and 7.2 showed, the cross-sectional evidence suggests that parties and their candidates do adapt ideologically to state electorates,

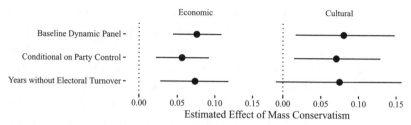

FIGURE 7.4. Adaptation versus selection as mechanisms for responsiveness.

taking liberal positions in liberal states and the opposite in conservative ones. But it is also true that Democratic and Republican officeholders diverge ideologically within states, raising the possibility that responsiveness can be accomplished via partisan selection as well. Which is the dominant mechanism of dynamic responsiveness is an empirical question.

Evaluating the relative importance of selection and adaptation to dynamic responsiveness involves three causal effects: the effect of mass conservatism on party control of government, the effect of party control on policy conservatism, and the effect of mass conservatism on policy conservatism with party control held constant. We have already investigated two of these three causal steps. In chapter 4, we found that electing Republicans rather than Democrats has strong effects on the conservatism of officials' policy positions and a smaller but still substantial effect on the conservatism of state policies. This has been true throughout the period we examine, though the effects are largest in the era since 1993. These findings thus provide solid support for the second step in partisan selection. However, in chapter 6, we found only mixed evidence that mass conservatism has a positive effect on Republican control of state offices, with the evidence again strongest in recent decades. The first step in the partisan selection mechanism thus appears to be on somewhat shaky ground.

Figure 7.4 presents further evidence for the weakness of partisan selection as a mechanism of responsiveness.[17] The top rows of this figure report estimates of mass conservatism's total effect on policy conservatism. The most important pattern, however, is that the mass conservatism coefficients barely budge when the Republican control index is added to the model (second row). Holding Republican control fixed in this way blocks the portion of the effect of mass conservatism that is mediated through the partisan control of government. This means that the mass conservatism coefficients now capture its direct (unmediated) effect rather than its total effect. In both cases, the indirect effect (the difference between the direct and total effects) is small, composing at most a quarter of the mass conservatism's influence on policy. The third row shows that we also see the same basic pattern of similarity if we compare dynamic responsiveness in years that follow an election, when party control could conceivably change, with years not following an election, when (with few exceptions) it will be constant.[18]

Given the imprecision of the mediation estimates and the strong assumptions required to interpret them causally, we should not focus too much on their exact magnitude. It is nevertheless striking how little support the mediation analyses provide for partisan selection as a mechanism of responsiveness. This is true not because party control has no policy effects—they are in fact quite large and robust—but rather because mass conservatism is only weakly related to shifts in party control. These results thus leave substantial scope for responsiveness in the absence of changes in party control. It is also worth noting that the final analysis, by examining nonelection years separately, implicitly holds constant each party's internal composition as well as the between-party balance of power. The fact that this analysis yields results very similar to those from controlling explicitly for party control suggests that within-party turnover does not account for much of dynamic responsiveness.[19] Thus, while we cannot determine exactly how important within-party turnover is, the evidence supports the hypothesis that the adaptation of reelection-motivated incumbents to shifts in public sentiment is an important, and perhaps the dominant, mechanism of responsiveness.

Despite the ambiguity of the evidence presented here, there are nevertheless reasons to suspect that partisan selection has recently grown in importance as a mechanism of state policy responsiveness. First, there is fairly solid evidence that this has occurred in Congress, where within-party responsiveness to constituency preferences peaked in the 1940s–1970s and declined thereafter.[20] Second, as chapters 3 and 4 showed, mass conservatism and party control have become aligned across states, while at the same time the policy effects of party control have increased. Conservative states are now generally controlled by Republicans and liberal states by Democrats. Moreover, not only have the policy differences between Republican and Democratic states increased but the variance in policy outcomes across states has as well.[21] The ultimate result is that conservative states now usually elect Republicans, who usually implement conservative policies. These changes may have occurred too recently to be reliably detected by our dynamic model, but it is possible that they will become more salient once we have another decade or two's worth of data.

7.3.3 CUMULATIVE RESPONSIVENESS

Policy responds to public opinion but does so incrementally. The estimates reported in table 7.1, which represent the immediate effect of public opinion

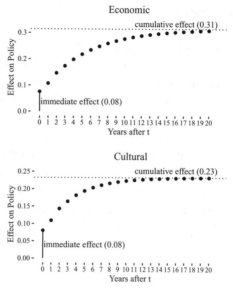

FIGURE 7.5. Cumulative effects on policy conservatism of a permanent one-unit increase in mass policy conservatism.

on the next year's policymaking, are an order of magnitude smaller than the cross-sectional slopes depicted in figure 7.3. The sluggishness of this response is the result of the policy conservatism's persistence over time. This same persistence, however, means that the effects of a one-time blip in mass conservatism will continue to be felt years in the future. As an extreme illustration, suppose that a state's public that had long been at its state-specific mean suddenly and for just a single year became one SD more culturally conservative. The dynamic estimates in table 7.1 imply that in the next year its cultural policy conservatism would increase to $\beta = 0.08$ above its previous level. The following year, its policy conservatism would decay to $\rho_1 \beta = 0.04$ above its long-run mean. The year after that it would be $\rho_1^2 \beta + \rho_2 \beta = 0.03$ above the mean, then $\rho_1^3 \beta + \rho_2^2 \beta = 0.01$, and so forth in future years as it gradually approached its long-run equilibrium again. In other words, due to the persistence of policy conservatism over time, the residue of a one-time shock to public opinion would continue to be observed years after the opinion shock itself had dissipated.

Alternatively, suppose that instead of changing for one year only, mass conservatism increased permanently from its previous equilibrium to a new equilibrium one unit higher (see figure 7.5). In the first year after this increase, the effect on policy conservatism would be β, the same as before. However, because mass conservatism remained permanently higher, it would continue to exert effects in subsequent years, though these effects would be increasingly offset by the mean reversion captured by the lag coefficients. In the second year after the opinion shift, policy conservatism would be $\rho_1\beta + \beta$ above its previous mean; in the third year, $\rho_1^2\beta + \rho_2\beta + \rho_1\beta + \beta$ above; and so forth until the mean-reverting effects of the lagged dependent variable counterbalanced the effect of mass opinion. The difference between the new equilibrium and the old (the cumulative effect or long-run multiplier) will be $\beta/(1 - \Sigma\rho_j)$.[22] The dynamic panel estimates imply that the long-run multiplier of mass conservatism is 0.31 for economic policies and 0.24 for cultural ones. In other words, the cumulative effect of public opinion is much larger than the immediate effect and in the same order of magnitude as the corresponding cross-sectional responsiveness estimates. Over the long term, the gradual accumulation of incremental policy responses to mass preferences is capable of producing the "awesome" cross-state correlation between opinion and policy documented by Erikson, Wright, and McIver.[23]

7.4 Summary

This chapter has examined one measure of the quality of democracy: policy responsiveness to mass preferences. Unlike most previous studies of representation, which are primarily cross-sectional,[24] we have adopted a dynamic perspective on responsiveness, examining how policy *changes* in response to mass opinion. When the temporal persistence of policy is accounted for, we find the immediate effect of both public opinion on individual issues and mass conservatism across many issues to be small relative to both the cross-state variation in policy conservatism and the powerful cross-sectional relationship between policy and opinion. If mass conservatism undergoes a durable shift, however, its effects will accumulate gradually over time until eventually policy conservatism reaches a new equilibrium. It is therefore possible for the mass public to cause large changes in policy conservatism, such as those exhibited by Idaho and Vermont in figure 4.2, but this process plays out incrementally over a long period of time.

Before the 1990s, state policymaking seems to have been more responsive in the cultural domain than on economics, but in recent decades this difference has dissipated as dynamic responsiveness on economic issues has increased markedly. Finally, contrary to the emphasis on selection in much recent scholarship on representation, we found little evidence that more than a quarter of mass conservatism's effect on policy is mediated through partisan control of state offices. This is not because policy is unaffected by party control but rather because the changes in parties' electoral fortunes are only

weakly related to mass conservatism. This suggests that the strategic adaptation of incumbents is not only an important mechanism of responsiveness
but perhaps the dominant one.

These results paint a largely positive portrait of democracy in the states.
The public does influence state policymaking, even if this influence takes
some time to be fully realized. However, as we noted at the beginning of this
chapter, responsiveness is not the only indicator of the quality of representation. In particular, responsiveness does not measure how close a match there
is between citizens' preferences and the policies they receive. To understand
this, we must make use of different data and a different measure, proximity,
which is the subject of the next chapter.

Proximity:
The Match between Preferences and Policies

As the previous chapter showed, state policymaking is responsive to mass preferences. Not only do liberal states have liberal policies, but when a state's public is more liberal than usual, its policies tend to become more liberal in the following year. This is what we should expect if citizens exert influence over the actions of their governments. Influence, however, is not the same as control. A person may influence the direction of a spring without being able to pull it to where he or she wants it to reach; the driver of a car with an overly sensitive steering wheel may find it difficult to keep it in the middle of the road rather than wobbling from left to right. Analogously, when citizens truly control the government, they are able to steer policymaking exactly where they want, resulting in policies that match public preferences.[1] Following Christopher Achen, we refer to the closeness of this match as policy *proximity*.[2]

Studies of policy proximity in US states have generally come to much more pessimistic conclusions than studies focusing on responsiveness. Previous research indicates that state policies match majority opinion only about half the time, a figure so low as to signal a severe "democratic deficit" in the states.[3] Gay rights provide a powerful illustration of this deficit.[4] As of 2019, a majority of every single state public supported laws banning antigay discrimination in employment, public accommodations, credit, and housing. In that year, however, only twenty-three states banned housing discrimination on the basis of sexual orientation, twenty-two states banned employment discrimination, and fifteen states banned credit discrimination. On all these policies, fewer than half of states matched the preferences of a majority of their citizens. Another example is climate change mitigation.[5] Polls show that most Americans think the government should pass laws that dramatically reduce fossil fuel usage in order to reduce greenhouse gas emissions.[6] Nevertheless, fewer than a third of states have implemented a cap on greenhouse gas emissions or acted to reduce emissions from cars and trucks.[7]

Building on previous research, particularly that of Jeffrey Lax and Justin Phillips, this chapter provides a systematic analysis of policy proximity in the states. Due to the difficulty of putting citizens and policies on a common ideological scale, we depart from chapter 7 and instead examine representation on a policy-by-policy basis. Doing so permits direct comparison of mass preferences and state policies, enabling us to calculate their proximity to each other as well as related quantities, such as policies' bias relative to public opinion.

Our results confirm the conventional wisdom in some ways but also offer important qualifications to it. State policies are indeed frequently out of step with public opinion. The average policy matches majority opinion only 59 percent of the time. One reason for this imperfect representation is that many issues exhibit a pronounced bias, with policy being systematically too liberal or (more often) too conservative relative to public opinion. More important than ideological bias, however, is bias toward the status quo.[8] Due to the difficulty of overturning existing policies and the incremental character of policy responsiveness, policies are least proximate to public opinion when an issue is new to the political (and polling) agenda. But proximity also tends to improve over time.[9] The longer an issue has been on the agenda, the more likely policy is to match public opinion, despite the fact that controversial issues tend to linger longer on the polling agenda than issues that have long been resolved one way or another. In our data, we find that by the time polling on a given issue ceases, the proportion of policies matching majority opinion rises to 64 percent.

Gay rights and climate change are again instructive examples. A few decades ago, not a single state prohibited antigay discrimination or funded programs to combat climate change—a status quo that matched the much more conservative state of public opinion at that time. Since then, both public opinion and state policy have liberalized on these issues, but policy has lagged behind. Thus, for most of the time that these issues have been politically salient, the public has been more liberal than state policies, with the result that conservative policies have often been mismatched with liberal opinion majorities. If present trends continue, however, we should expect these mismatches to become less frequent over time. They may eventually disappear entirely as these policies converge on a consensus, at which point pollsters and researchers will cease to ask about them in surveys, as has occurred on now-settled issues such as alcohol prohibition and female jury service.

Once again, then, a dynamic approach offers new perspectives on state politics. Proximity is not a static property of a given issue. Rather, issues tend to follow a common pattern over time. Before an issue is politically salient, states typically exhibit policy consensus: all states either have or do not have the policy. The policy status quo is usually conservative but not always so. When an issue appears on the political agenda, it often does so because opposition to the status quo has risen in the public. By the time pollsters start including the issue on surveys, policy proximity has already decreased relative to its earlier state of consensus and may continue to deteriorate for some time as opinion continues to shift. Belatedly, states begin aligning their policies with public opinion, with liberal states being the first to adopt liberal policies and conservative states first on conservative policies. Though there are important exceptions, most issues eventually reach a new equilibrium where policy is once again fairly proximate to public opinion. In sum, while policy proximity is often poor in the short term, over the long run the gradual accumulation of incremental responsiveness tends to align state policy with public opinion.

8.1 Data on Policy-Specific Representation

Evaluating policy-specific representation requires a different approach to measurement from that taken in earlier chapters. Rather than summarizing policy and opinion variation with broad ideological measures, we instead estimate mass preferences separately for each issue using the dynamic MRP model described in chapter 2. Furthermore, we restrict the data to issues where a state policy can be matched to a corresponding survey item that gauges public support for that policy. In our matched data set, the time series on each policy issue begins in the first year after the policy enters the state policy agenda (i.e., the first state adopts it) and there is publicly available polling on the policy. It then continues until either the policy exits the state policy agenda (i.e., Congress or the Supreme Court imposes a uniform policy on all states) or polling is no longer available.[10]

After imposing these restrictions, we are left with a total of seventy-two paired policies and survey items—more than double the number in any previous study of state policy representation. These policies are listed in table 8.1. The table also reports the time spans for which both policy data and opinion estimates are available (proximity span), the percentage of state-years in which the policy was in place, and average public support for the policy. The sample covers a diverse set of issues, but its composition depends heavily on data availability, especially with respect to survey items, so it cannot be considered representative of the universe of state policies or even of our larger policy data set.

TABLE 8.1 Policies in policy proximity data set

Policy	Proximity Span	% State-Years with Policy	% Public Support
Abortion Policies			
Emergency contraception	2005–2018	80	52
Counseling required	1992–2010	35	87
Abortion ban (pre-*Roe*)	1967–1973	74	15
Medicaid for abortion	1981–2020	31	36
Parental consent for abortion	1989–2020	40	77
Parental notification required	1983–2010	47	82
Partial-birth abortion ban	1996–2000	19	63
Ultrasounds required	2019–2020	30	53
Waiting period for abortion	1992–2020	44	76
Drug and Crime Policies			
Abolish death penalty	1941–2020	22	33
Decriminalization of marijuana	1973–2020	25	34
Medical marijuana	2001–2020	36	82
Smoking ban—restaurants	1995–2020	40	56
Alcohol prohibition laws	1936–2020	2	23
Education Policies			
Charter schools	1999–2020	81	77
Corporal punishment in schools	1954–2020	31	43
Moment of silence required	1985–2020	23	59
School vouchers	1992–2020	17	49
Ten Commandments in schools	1999–2020	12	69
Environmental Policies			
California car emissions standard	2002–2020	25	73
Endangered species act	2011–2014	94	66
Greenhouse gas cap	2006–2020	21	70
Renewable portfolio standard	2009–2020	74	68
Solar tax credit	2001–2020	64	77
Gambling Policies			
Casinos allowed	1951–2020	18	49
Lottery allowed	1964–2020	55	72
Gay Rights Policies			
Public accommodations discrimination ban	1977–2020	21	63
Civil unions	2000–2013	17	55
Job discrimination protections	1977–2020	29	63
Hate crimes ban—gays	2000–2018	54	74
Housing discrimination	1977–2020	21	63
Joint adoption for gay couples	1993–2014	16	44
Same-sex marriage	2000–2013	6	41
Sodomy ban	1977–2003	45	51

TABLE 8.1 (*continued*)

Policy	Proximity Span	% State-Years with Policy	% Public Support
Gun Policies			
Assault weapon ban	1989–2020	12	68
Background checks	1959–2020	24	81
Open carry law for guns	1996–2020	76	51
Waiting period for guns	1959–2020	22	81
Immigration Policies			
E-verify	2006–2018	26	82
English is official language	1995–2020	55	77
Health care for undocumented kids	2013–2020	12	24
Immigrant driver's licenses	2007–2012	6	22
In-state tuition for immigrants	2007–2020	31	43
Sanctuary states policy	2018–2020	78	48
Labor and Welfare Policies			
Age discrimination ban	2019–2020	96	83
Collective bargain—state workers	2012–2017	55	58
Collective bargain—teachers	1959–2020	54	71
Disability discrimination ban	1977–1990	81	90
Paid sick leave	2019–2020	67	63
Right to work	1955–2020	40	65
ACA Medicaid expansion	2014–2020	62	78
TANF work requirements	1996–2015	73	83
Civil Liberties and Health			
Hate crimes ban	2000–2018	87	74
Contraception insurance coverage	2018–2020	55	86
Pain and suffering limits in lawsuits	1975–2015	30	70
Physician-assisted suicide	1997–2020	6	60
State vaccination mandates	2016–2020	100	83
Racial Discrimination			
Ban on interracial marriage	1964–1967	35	55
Discrimination in public accommodations	1963–1963	63	55
Fair employment law	1948–2020	71	79
Fair housing in private housing	1964–1968	39	64
Transportation Regulations			
Mandatory car insurance	1938–2020	48	91
Mandatory seat belts	1984–2020	86	66
Motorcycle helmets required	2010–2020	40	80

continues

TABLE 8.1 (*continued*)

Policy	Proximity Span	% State-Years with Policy	% Public Support
Tax Policies			
Earned income tax credit	2019–2020	57	72
Income tax	2018–2020	82	55
Women's Rights			
Equal pay for women	1942–1972	39	88
Equal Rights Amendment ratified	1974–2020	61	84
Gender discrimination laws	1974–2020	87	84
Jury service for women	1936–1967	78	79
No-fault divorce	2018–2020	100	79
State equal rights law	1974–2020	43	84

Two forms of selection bias are particularly relevant. First, although the sample contains at least one opinion-policy pair in every year between 1936 and 2020, it is tilted toward more recent years. Three-quarters of observations are from 1983 onward, and half are from after 1999. Second, the sample of years covered by each policy is incomplete and unrepresentative due in large part to survey organizations' bias toward controversial issues.[11] For example, elective abortion was illegal in every state for most of the twentieth century, but it was not until 1967, as the movement to liberalize abortion laws gained momentum, that the first opinion polls appeared on the subject (table 8.1, third row). The timing of the end of public polling is nonrandom as well. Once they were no longer live political issues, polling on female jury service (ended 1967), antimiscegenation laws (also 1967), disability discrimination bans (1990), and antisodomy statutes (2003) all disappeared.

Due to pollsters' predilection for controversy, issues where the public is divided or policy is out of step with majority opinion are overrepresented in the data. The likely result is downward bias in our proximity estimates. On the other hand, polling also overrepresents politically salient issues, on which governments may be more responsive,[12] possibly leading to an overly rosy picture of representation. The net result of these selection biases is hard to assess, but readers should bear them in mind when interpreting the results of our analysis (as well as that of other scholars).

8.2 Policy Bias

We begin our empirical analysis with an examination of the relationship between public support for a policy and states' probability of adopting it. This exercise is similar to the analysis of ideological responsiveness in chapter 7, with the important difference that in the issue-specific analysis, mass preferences and public policies are measured on the same scale. As a consequence, we can interpret the intercept term (appropriately transformed) in a regression of policy on opinion as indexing the policy bias on a given issue.

Using a version of such a regression model suitable for binary outcomes, figure 8.1 plots the opinion–policy relationship across state-years for all seventy-two issues in our paired data set. The policies are coded so that larger values indicate (support for) the more conservative policy option. For example, in the case of gay adoption, zero indicates that homosexual couples are permitted to adopt children and one indicates that they are not. The gray crosshairs in each plot indicate 50 percent support and 50 percent probability of adoption, and the black curves are the model-predicted values across the observed range of public support.

The first thing to notice about figure 8.1 is that, consistent with the ideological responsiveness documented in chapter 7, state policy and issue-specific opinion are nearly always positively correlated. The strength of responsiveness does vary across issues. On some, such as gay marriage or ACA Medicaid expansion, the opinion–policy relationship is very steep. On others, such as whether states require schools to observe a moment of silence, it is much flatter. Only a few exceptional issues, such as charter schools and female jury service, exhibit a negative relationship. Overall, though, states seem to be highly responsive to their publics' issue-specific preferences.

As we have noted, however, responsiveness does not imply perfect representation. Ideally, policy responsiveness would be unbiased: it would pass through the intersection of the crosshairs at 50 percent public support and 50 percent adoption probability. There are a few policies where representation is approximately unbiased. These include renewable energy portfolio standards (row 4, column 4), mandatory seat belts (row 4, column 7), bans on racial discrimination in public accommodations (row 6, column 1), income taxes (row 6, column 2), Medicaid coverage for abortions (row 8, column 1), and TANF work requirements (row 9, column 7). Although policy responsiveness differs across these issues, on none of them is policymaking tilted systematically in one direction or another.

Many policies, however, do exhibit an ideological bias—that is, a tendency for state policies to be systematically more liberal or more conservative than public opinion. Consider the issue of mandatory auto insurance ("Auto Insur Req") in the upper-left corner of the figure. In nearly all state-years, support for the conservative policy option (not requiring drivers to carry auto insurance) is below 50 percent, while the predicted probability of not requiring

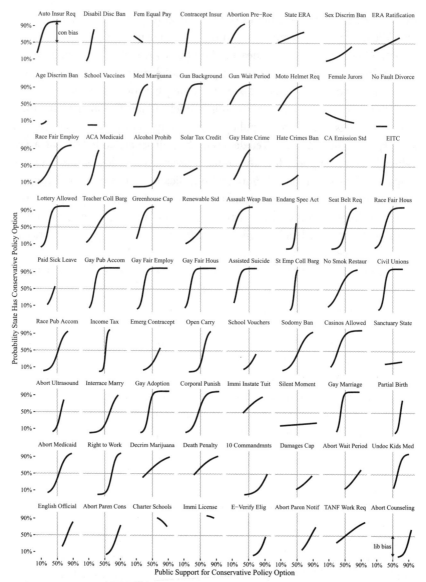

FIGURE 8.1. Issue-specific responsiveness. Unit of analysis is the state-year. Horizontal axis indicates public support for the conservative policy option on the issue in question. Vertical axis indicates the estimated probability of the conservative policy option being in place. Lines indicate predicted values from a logistic regression. Panels are ordered by the conservatism of issue-specific opinion.

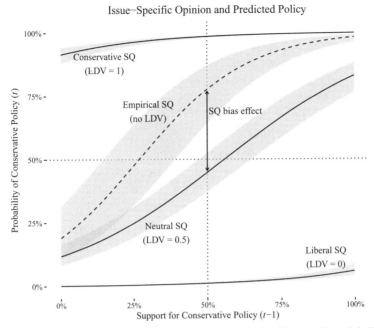

FIGURE 8.2. Random-effect logistic regression models of policy adoption. The dashed line labeled "Empirical SQ" is the predicted probability of a conservative policy given the level of public support, without controlling for the policy status quo. Lines labeled "Liberal SQ" and "Conservative SQ," respectively, indicate the predicted outcomes conditional on a liberal (0) and conservative (1) status quo. "Neutral SQ" is the model's prediction for a status quo value of 0.5. The difference between the empirical and neutral SQ predictions indicates how much of the ideological bias is due to the disproportionate prevalence of conservative status quos.

auto insurance is above 50 percent. According to the fitted curves, a state in which half the public supported mandatory auto insurance would have less than a 10 percent chance of requiring it. In short, policymaking on this issue exhibits a marked conservative bias. Other issues are biased in the opposite direction. Mandatory preabortion counseling ("Abort Counseling," lower-right corner), for example, is supported by a majority of the public in every state-year covered by our polling data, but most states still do not require it. If the fitted curve were extrapolated to the vertical crosshair line, it would predict an evenly split state to have less than a 10 percent chance of adopting the policy. Not until public support is 90 percent or higher does a state have better than even odds of adoption. This policy thus exhibits a strong liberal bias.

For a more holistic perspective on issue-specific policy representation, we fit several regression models of policy adoption.[13] The results of these models are plotted in figure 8.2. The dashed line on this figure represents the predicted probability of a conservative policy outcome without accounting for the status quo. Its marked upward slope indicates that issue-specific policy responsiveness is strong and close to proportional: when the public moves from 25 percent to 75 percent support, the probability of adoption increases by forty-six percentage points. But the predicted probabilities also highlight the generally conservative bias in state policymaking. When a state public is evenly split on an issue, policy is likely to be conservative about three-quarters of the time. This conservative bias in representation is consistent with figure 8.1, where about 56 percent of state policies are more conservative than one would expect based on public opinion.

In an important sense, however, the apparently conservative bias in representation is misleading. As we saw in the case of mandatory abortion counseling, there are also some issues with a liberal bias. Most of the instances of liberal policy bias are instances of conservative policy innovation—that is, where the status quo is liberal. In addition to many state abortion restrictions proposed in the wake of *Roe v. Wade* (1973), examples include right-to-work laws (sanctioned by the federal Taft-Hartley Act of 1947), requirements that employers verify employees' work authorization (E-Verify), English-as-official-language laws, and caps on pain-and-suffering damages in lawsuits.[14] These examples suggest that when the status quo favors liberals, conservatives face as many challenges to implementing policy changes popular with the public as liberals do.

For more systematic evidence on status-quo bias, we modify the regression model figure 8.2 by adding a lagged dependent variable (LDV)—that is, an indicator for the value of the policy in the preceding year. Whereas the model with no LDV reveals the unconditional association between opinion and policy (given state, year, and policy intercepts), the LDV model enables us to predict the policy outcome conditional on specific values of the status quo. Consistent with the policy persistence emphasized in previous chapters, whether a state has a given policy in a given year is very strongly predicted by whether it had that policy in the previous year.[15] As a consequence of this persistence, the probability of policy *changing* in a given year is very small, even when the public overwhelmingly favors the change. This is illustrated by solid lines in figure 8.2, which represent predicted probabilities from a logistic version of the model. If the status quo is conservative (top), then a decrease in public support from 75 percent to 25 percent increases the probability of a liberal policy change by only 3.5 percentage points (from 0.4 percent to 3.9 percent). When the status quo is liberal (bottom), an analogous opinion shift changes the probability of policy change by just 2 points.

This symmetry suggests that the conservative intercept shift evident in the unconditional predicted probabilities in figure 8.2 may be due not to ideological bias per se but rather to the fact that policy status quos are disproportionately conservative. One way to illustrate this in a regression of policy on opinion is by comparing the policy prediction at 50 percent support from the unconditional model with the analogous prediction from a model with lagged policy set to 0.5 (i.e., an equal mix of liberal and conservative status quos). The difference in these predictions represents the portion of the conservative bias in state policymaking attributable to the ideological skew in the distribution of status quos. As figure 8.2 shows, when we account for the status quo, the ideological bias almost completely disappears: when both citizens and status quos are evenly split, the probability of a conservative policy is just under 50 percent.

The ideological tilt of state policymaking is no less real for being attributable to status-quo bias. Because liberals seek policy change more often than conservatives, they face material disadvantages in achieving their policy goals. In fact, 72 percent of the policies where we have data on both policy and public opinion start with a conservative status quo that reformers seek to shift in a liberal direction.[16] The initially conservative status quo of state policy is true across a wide variety of domains, including those pertaining to workplace regulations, environmental protections, gay rights, and women's rights.

Nevertheless, in contemporary American politics conservatives do often seek change, sometimes radical change.[17] As Matt Grossmann has shown, however, right-wing efforts to radically retrench the size and scope of state government have been largely stymied, at least so far.[18] One important reason for this mixed record is that liberals and other defenders of government policies and programs holding over from earlier decades have benefited from the same status-quo bias that usually advantages conservatives.

8.3 Policy Proximity

Although bias is an important indicator of the quality of representation, a more holistic one is proximity.[19] Proximity itself can be operationalized in two main ways. One measure of proximity, which we label *agreement*, is the proportion of citizens who favor the policy actually in place in their state.[20] Agreement thus measures proximity to the average citizen. For example, if 56 percent of a state public favors prohibition but the state permits the sale of alcohol, then the agreement score for this state and policy is 1 − 0.56 = 44%. A second and more common measure, which we label *congruence*, is simply a binary indicator for whether the policy in place has majority support in the public.[21] Congruence measures proximity to the median citizen. By this measure, the prohibition example above would have a congruence score of zero (since less than half the population favors the state's policy). Congruence is a

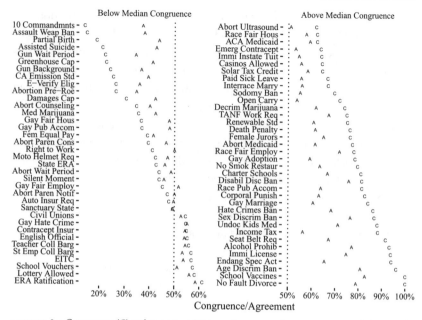

FIGURE 8.3. Congruence (C) and agreement (A) by policy, averaged across state-years. Policies in the left column are below the median level of congruence (61.5%); those in the right column are above the median.

dichotomous indicator of majority rule, while agreement provides a continuous measure of how many citizens' preferences are satisfied. Both measures, however, become continuous when averaged across policies, states, and/or years.

Figure 8.3 provides an initial cut at policy proximity, plotting the congruence and agreement levels of each policy (averaged across state-years where opinion and policy measures are available). The distribution of congruence across the seventy-two policies is centered around 60 percent but with large variation across policies. Levels of congruence range from a low of 14 percent for bans on posting the Ten Commandments in schools to a high of 100 percent for vaccination mandates and no-fault divorce. Agreement tends to be lower than congruence: for the average policy and state, policy matches the preferences of about 55 percent of citizens. The two measures are highly correlated ($R = 0.94$), but agreement has substantially lower variance. Even on the most incongruent issues, policy matches the preferences of at least a third of citizens, and for the most congruent agreement scores range as high as 83 percent.

While far from perfect, the overall level of congruence we find is meaningfully higher than the most comprehensive comparable study, Lax and

Phillips's examination of thirty-nine state policies.[22] According to their data, policies align with majority opinion only about half the time—ten percentage points lower than our estimate of around 60 percent.[23] On the other hand, our estimate is a bit lower than that found in Anne Rasmussen, Stefanie Reher, and Dimiter Toshkov's study of thirty-one European democracies, which found policies to be congruent about two-thirds of the time.[24] Given the variation across policies, conclusions about the average level of congruence are likely to be highly sensitive to the sample of policies (let alone countries), so it is difficult to compare across studies. Nevertheless, our larger sample size and diverse range of issue areas gives us some confidence that the democratic deficit in the states is not as dire as Lax and Phillips fear.

8.3.1 THE DYNAMICS OF POLICY PROXIMITY

The static perspective we have taken so far highlights variation across policies, but it conceals another important source of heterogeneity: time. Given that both mass opinion and public policies change over time, proximity is unlikely to be stable across the lifetime of an issue. This is especially true if, as chapter 7 showed, policymaking responds incrementally to public demands. While little previous research has explicitly examined how proximity changes over time, a few studies have touched on the subject. Noting that "it takes time for policy to move into congruence with opinion," Lax and Phillips report that policies that have been on the political agenda for more than a decade are modestly more congruent than newer issues.[25] Similarly, another recent study finds that congruence on seven immigration and health care policies increased ten percentage points between 2008 and 2014.[26] Do these suggestive patterns hold up in a larger sample of policies and over a much longer time span?

Building on Lax and Phillips's observation, we first examine whether policies that have been on the policy agenda longer exhibit higher levels of congruence. As figure 8.4 shows, this is indeed the case. The figure plots the relationship between policies' congruence (measured in the last year that opinion estimates are available) and their "age" (i.e., the number of years since their first appearance in our policy data set). The youngest policies are a mix of recent arrivals on the political agenda, such as Medicaid expansion under the 2010 Affordable Care Act, and ones that were only briefly relevant or salient, such as blanket prohibitions on elective abortion in the half decade before *Roe v. Wade* (1973) invalidated them. The oldest policies, such as the death penalty, income taxes, and waiting periods for handgun purchases, have divided states since the 1930s, if not earlier. As the fitted line indicates, congruence rises rapidly with policy age, especially in the first few decades.[27] New issues average

Congruence by Policy Age
(Last Year of Opinion Data)

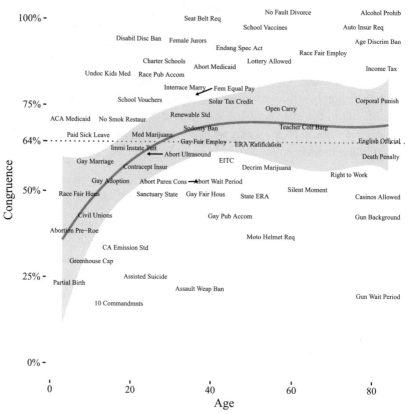

FIGURE 8.4. Congruence by policy age. The analysis is restricted to the last year for which opinion estimates on a given policy are available. The horizontal axis indicates how many years have elapsed since the
policy entered our policy data set; the vertical axis indicates the percentage of states where policy matches
majority opinion. The dotted line indicates the mean across policies. The smoothing line is based on a
cubic polynomial fit.

around 40 percent congruence, but by year fifteen congruence has passed
50 percent. Forty years in, congruence levels off at around 70 percent.

In principle, the correlation between policy age and congruence could be
driven not by increasing congruence over time within each policy but rather
by differences in the mix of policies across eras. In other words, it is possible
that policy representation was for some reason easier on issues that emerged
in the early to mid-twentieth century than it is for twenty-first-century policies. Cutting against this possibility is the fact that average congruence across
the last-year observations plotted in figure 8.4 is 64 percent—five points

higher than the average across policies when all years are included. This suggests that congruence tends to be lower earlier in a policy's political life span.

We can test this conjecture more directly by examining the relationship between policy age and congruence after centering both variables at their policy-specific means. This within-policy centering is equivalent to including policy-specific fixed effects in a regression model, and it has the same effect of accounting for any time-invariant attributes of policies—such as the year they appeared on the agenda—that might affect congruence. Figure 8.5 presents the results. The gray lines in this plot represent policy-specific linear trends in congruence over time, and the black line represents the average

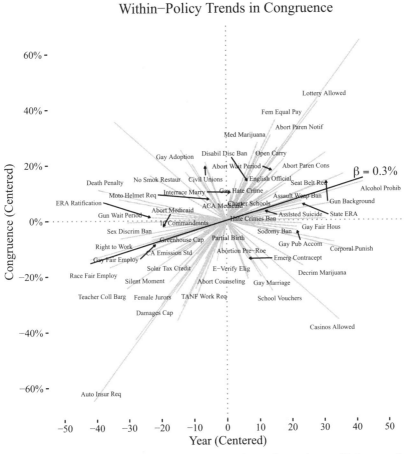

FIGURE 8.5. Within-policy trends in congruence. Solid gray lines indicate policy-specific linear trends; black line indicates the pooled average trend. Both year and congruence are centered at zero within policies. To avoid overlap, only fifty-five of seventy-two policies are labeled.

trend.[28] The slopes differ widely across policies. A substantial number, including gay adoption, school vouchers, and casinos, traverse the upper-left and lower-right quadrants, indicating declining congruence over time. Most policies, however, improve their congruence over time. On average, congruence increases by three percentage points each decade; over the course of eight decades, it would be predicted to improve by twenty-four points.

Again, selection bias likely attenuates this estimate. A policy such as same-sex civil unions, for example, was not polled until it became controversial, and, because it was federalized by the US Supreme Court, it exited our data set before states had fully responded to increases in public support. More generally, policies related to gay rights illustrate the nonlinear patterns in congruence generated when public opinion undergoes large and rapid change. In the 1980s, large majorities in nearly every state opposed extending full rights to homosexuals and same-sex couples, and state policies reflected these preferences almost perfectly. These issues thus exhibited high levels of agreement and near-universal congruence. Over the next several decades, public support for gay rights increased rapidly, decreasing agreement and congruence in the short term as policy lagged behind public opinion. Eventually, however, policymaking began to catch up, and by the 2010s policy proximity on gay rights was again on the upswing.

Our analyses also highlight a few issue areas where policy has been persistently out of step with public opinion. Some are cases where intense and well-organized interest groups are pitted against broad but less committed opinion majorities. Gun control is a prime example. Despite their long time on the agenda, gun policies such as assault weapon bans, prepurchase waiting periods, and background checks are among the most incongruent in our data set (see figure 8.4). All have supermajority support in the public but are opposed by powerful groups like the National Rifle Association and its highly engaged membership base.[29] Another incongruent cluster of policies includes moral issues such as abortion (e.g., bans on "partial birth" procedures) and religious expression in schools (e.g., allowing schools to post the Ten Commandments), on which policy has usually been more liberal than the public prefers. Incongruence on these issues probably stems less from asymmetries in organization or intensity than from the fact that those opposed to them have higher income and education levels and thus greater political influence.[30] These examples make it clear that persistently poor representation, while not the norm, definitely occurs on some issues, and these representational deficits are linked to political inequalities across social groups.

8.4 Summary

As the last two chapters have emphasized, representation is a dynamic process. State governments respond to their citizens' preferences, but they do so
incrementally rather than instantaneously. Strong bias toward the status quo
means that policy is difficult to change, and in the short term it is often out
of step with what the public demands. But representation tends to improve
over time. Among policies that have been on the agenda for more than three
decades, state policy is congruent with majority opinion 70 percent of the
time. On most issues, the democratic deficit documented by Lax and Phillips
is a short-term phenomenon. In the long run, public opinion tends to work
its will.

Even over the long term, however, state policy representation is far from
perfect. Not only are some policies persistently unresponsive, but these representational deficits seem to be symptomatic of unevenness in the quality of
American democracy more generally. It is to these "brown spots" in American democracy that we now turn our attention in the next chapter.

Deficits:
Gaps in American Democracy[1]

Thus far, we have painted a relatively positive picture of American democracy. Contrary to more pessimistic accounts, we have argued that public inattention, partisanship, and other challenges do not prevent state governments from responding to their citizens. The policy preferences of state publics do influence state policymaking, albeit sluggishly, and policy proximity, though often poor on newer issues, tends to improve over time. According to this evidence, state-level democracy is surprisingly healthy.

This generally optimistic conclusion, however, glosses over important differences in representation across social groups and geographic units. As Guillermo O'Donnell has observed, many nominally democratic countries contain "brown spots" where governance is less democratic or even authoritarian.[2] The United States is no exception. Its undemocratic features were most glaring early in its history, when Black Americans were overwhelmingly subject to chattel slavery, Native Americans were denied full citizenship, women lacked basic civic and legal rights, and with few exceptions only propertied White men could vote.[3] Over the subsequent two centuries, constitutional amendments, legal changes, and informal institutional evolution have rectified many of these undemocratic features.[4] Yet democratization in America has been neither smooth nor unidirectional. Indeed, as Richard Valelly notes, the United States is unique among Western nations for having enfranchised and then disenfranchised a major social group (southern Black men) through nominally democratic means.[5] Nor is American democratization necessarily complete today, as recent debates over economic inequality, democratic backsliding, voter suppression, and the carceral state attest.[6] Rather, brown spots in American democracy persist to this day, resulting in variation in the quality of democracy across space and along demographic lines.[7]

In this chapter, we examine three such undemocratic features—the Jim Crow South, legislative malapportionment, and partisan gerrymandering—and assess their effects on the quality of representation. Each of these phenomena has magnified the political "voice" of some Americans while disempowering others, thus distorting the linkages between citizens and state-level officials. While they are surely not the only sources of democratic deficits in the American states, these three phenomena were among the most durable and significant. Moreover, they have varied enough across states and years in the era we cover to permit evaluation of their effects.

None of these three phenomena can be reduced to a single policy or formal institution. The Jim Crow South was maintained by an interlocking bundle of formal and informal institutions, no single component of which was fully responsible for the political exclusion of Black (along with many White) southerners.[8] These included Whites-only party primaries, poll taxes, literacy tests, and discretion-laden "understanding" clauses as well as extralegal intimindation and violence.[9] These devices then led to a vicious cycle that further disempowered Black southerners by reducing their political influence, diminishing their incentives to attempt to weather the sea of obstacles between them and the ballot box.[10] Legislative malapportionment, which until the court-led "reapportionment revolution" of the 1960s prevailed in states across the nation, was the joint consequence of formal rules that endowed elected officials with the power to draw district lines and the informal practice of apportioning citizens unequally across districts.[11] Similarly, partisan gerrymandering, which has become particularly salient in the past couple of decades, results from political control of districting combined with elected officials' efforts to maximize the electoral prospects of their party.[12]

Our empirical analyses show that these distortions had significant implications for policy representation. During Jim Crow, the policies of southern states were far less congruent with the preferences of their Black residents than those of their White residents, while in non-southern states the racial gap was much smaller. By the twenty-first century, the racial gap in policy congruence had closed almost completely in both regions, though overall congruence remained higher outside the South. Similarly, after the reapportionment revolution, representation improved dramatically in the states that had previously been the most malapportioned. Finally, in an analysis of the post-1972 period, we find that states with legislative districts gerrymandered to favor one party overrepresent the views of adherents of the favored party.

All three forms of representational distortion not only bias policy representation toward particular groups but also worsen it for the public as a whole.

9.1 The Jim Crow South

Well into the second half of the twentieth century, the eleven states that had
seceded before the Civil War remained a racial and political order sharply
distinct from the rest of the United States.[13] While racial segregation was
mandated in six additional states,[14] only the former Confederate states combined near-total disenfranchisement of their Black citizens with near-perfect
domination by the Democratic Party. At the same time, direct primaries did
partially substitute for the region's lack of interparty electoral competition,
and there is evidence that this competition induced southern members of
Congress[15] and state governments[16] to represent the all-White electorate. The
South's exclusionary one-party system thus exhibited a mix of democratic
and authoritarian features.[17]

More to the point, these authoritarian features were targeted at a distinct
group: Black southerners. The combination of literacy tests, poll taxes, the
exclusionary White primary, and extralegal violence by Whites made formal
political participation all but impossible for Black southerners. The left panel
of figure 9.1 shows the percentage of voting-age Black southerners registered
to vote in the mid-twentieth century.[18] In 1947, despite the Supreme Court's
recent invalidation of Whites-only primaries, no southern state had a Black
voter registration rate over 25 percent. In Alabama and Mississippi, only 1 percent of Black citizens were registered, and in Louisiana just 2 percent were.
The highest Black registration rates were concentrated in southern states with
relatively few Blacks, such as Arkansas, Tennessee, and Texas.[19] Across the
region, only 12 percent of Black southerners were registered to vote in 1947.

The situation gradually improved over the next decade, but by 1960 the
registration rate for Black southerners was still just 28 percent, and fewer
than a fifth of Black southerners actually voted.[20] The right panel of figure 9.1
shows that voting-age Blacks were also substantially less likely to be registered to vote than voting-age Whites.[21] In 1952, Black southerners registered
to vote at about 40 percent the rate of Whites, and in 1960, they were still less
than half as likely to be registered.

Only after the 1960s, when the federal government finally intervened
forcefully enough to dismantle legal suffrage barriers in the South, could the
South reasonably be considered a genuine democracy.[22] In the wake of this
intervention, registration rates increased for both races. Moreover, Black reg-

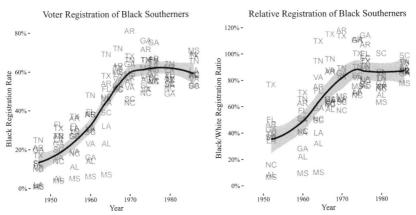

FIGURE 9.1. The left panel shows the percentage of voting-age Black southerners registered to vote between 1947 and 1986. The right panel shows the ratio of Black to White registration rates in southern states between 1952 and 1986.

istration rates in the South finally began to approach those of White southerners. By 1967, Blacks were registered to vote at about 75 percent the rate of Whites. The proportion of Blacks registered to vote continued to increase through the mid-1970s. The bottom panel of figure 9.1 shows that by the early 1980s, the relative registration rates of Blacks and Whites approached (but did not reach) parity. Turnout rates of Blacks and Whites in the South also closed significantly by the 1984 presidential elections and continued to narrow in subsequent elections.[23] By 2012, turnout rates of southern Whites and Blacks were nearly equal.[24]

There is debate, however, over the degree to which the formal democratization of the South has translated into tangible gains for Black southerners. One early review of scholarship on the civil rights movement notes that, in areas ranging from politics to education to public accommodations to poverty, scholars have been "more likely to stress what it failed to achieve."[25] More recent research has been more positive, finding that the dismantlement of Jim Crow led not only to a surge in Black political participation[26] and office holding[27] but also material gains in terms of government spending and economic outcomes.[28] At the same time, Black southerners, who are overwhelmingly Democrats, have been on the losing end of the region's realignment toward the Republicans, who now dominate nearly every southern state.[29] It is therefore possible that on net the voting rights revolution has not significantly improved southern states' policy representation of their Black citizens. In the next section, we evaluate this question empirically by comparing racial and regional differences in representation before and after the Second Reconstruction.

9.1.1 RACIAL DISPARITIES IN REPRESENTATION

If policy representation is a valid indicator of the quality of democracy, we should expect such representation to be poor in circumstances where we know that democracy is compromised. Since Black southerners were largely disenfranchised before the mid-1960s, state policymaking should have been less responsive to their preferences than to those of White southerners. Many scholars have argued, however, that poll taxes, lack of electoral competition, and other authoritarian features of southern politics undermined the representation of nonelite White southerners as well.[30] Insofar as this was true, we should expect policy representation to have been worse across the board in the South relative to outside it. Finally, if the Second Reconstruction really did succeed in democratizing the South, we should expect these racial and regional disparities in representation to have narrowed since the 1960s.

We evaluate this expectation by examining changes in state policies' proximity to the preferences of Black and non-Black (primarily White) residents of southern and non-southern states. Recall that agreement is the proportion of the public—or in this case, of each racial subpublic—that supports the state's policy choice. Congruence is a coarser measure focused directly on majority rule: a state policy is congruent if and only if its proximity is above 50 percent. Both measures are designed to capture how well state policies match public preferences (for more details, see chapter 8).

Figure 9.2 tracks state policies' match with the preferences of Black and non-Black Americans over time, separately for each region. The left panel plots agreement and the right one congruence. As the smoothing lines indicate, in the first half of the period the policies of southern states matched the preferences of their non-Black (read: White) citizens much more closely than those of their Black ones. For example, before 1970, southern state policies were congruent with 48 percent of White opinion majorities in the typical year versus just 37 percent of Black opinion majorities. The contemporaneous racial gap outside the South was about half the size: 6 percent as compared to the South's 11 percent. Since 1970, the racial gap has narrowed in both regions, to 3 percent outside the South and 4.5 percent within it. Agreement has shown a similar pattern of representational convergence in both regions, with racial differences in the South again starting from a higher point but exhibiting a larger decline. In short, although the racial gap has narrowed in both regions since the Second Reconstruction, it has done so more in the South despite the fact that southern states' representation of their White citizens has also improved.

This analysis thus provides clear evidence of Jim Crow's damaging effect on the representation of Black southerners. Moreover, there are several

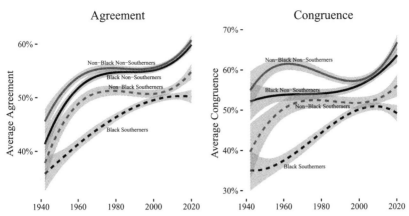

FIGURE 9.2. Proximity by race and region, 1942–2020. Lines indicate cubic polynomial fits, averaged across issues.

reasons to think that the data understate the representational damage. First, due to the paucity of polling, the sample of issues includes few civil rights or other explicitly racial state policies. Since the opinion gap between Black and non-Black Americans, especially southerners, was far larger on racial than nonracial issues, their inclusion in the sample would almost certainly magnify the racial gap in representation. Second, southern states, where Black Americans were disproportionately concentrated, exhibited lower proximity and congruence overall than non-southern states. (Recall from chapter 7 that southern states exhibit a conservative policy bias relative to non-southern states.) Consequently, comparing Black southerners to others in the same region does not account for the fact that non-Black southerners were worse represented than non-southerners of both races. This regional disparity is consistent with V. O. Key Jr.'s classic argument that the South's exclusionary one-party system undermined the representation of White as well as Black citizens.[31]

There is, in sum, substantial evidence that the nondemocratic features of the pre-1965 South damaged state policy representation in the region. This was especially true for Black southerners, who were the primary victims of segregation and disenfranchisement, but White southerners seem to have suffered as well. The South's racial gap in representation did not disappear after 1965, but it did gradually narrow.

Some important caveats are in order, however. First, the trend toward convergence in the South appears to have stalled around the year 2000, after which policies' proximity to Black preferences plateaued or even declined. One possible reason is that the early twenty-first century is when Democrats

finally lost their grip on southern state governments, ceding control to state
Republican parties with very few Black supporters. In response, the policies
of many southern states lurched to the right, away from the preferences of
most of their Black citizens.

A second caveat is that our focus on the presence or absence of formal
policies is poorly suited to capturing differences in how policy is implemented
or applied. To take a stark example, many New Deal–era welfare policies were
largely controlled at the local level, and as a result officials in the Jim Crow
South were able to apply or manipulate such policies in racially discrimina-
tory ways.[32] Thus the fact that Black southerners largely supported welfare
policies in principle does not adequately reflect the ways they suffered from
them in practice. Our legalistic focus also understates the degree to which putatively positive or race-neutral government activities, such as policing, can
serve as instruments of government coercion and control in race- and class-
subjugated communities.[33]

Third and finally, the Black/non-Black dichotomy we employ, while reasonable when examining the Jim Crow South, ignores other racial and ethnic
cleavages. For example, while voting rates among Black and White Americans have approached parity, turnout among Hispanics and Asian Americans
remains much lower.[34] As a result, it is likely that non-Black racial minorities also receive poorer policy representation than do White Americans.[35]
For all these reasons, we should not mistake the progress toward representational equality we document as a sign that American democracy is no longer
marred by racial disparities in political voice.

9.2 Legislative Malapportionment

Jim Crow was the most egregious undemocratic feature of American politics
in the period we cover, but it was not the only one. Another, dismantled by
judicial intervention around the same time, was the malapportionment of
state legislatures. Malapportionment occurs when legislative districts vary in
population size. As a consequence, the preferences of voters in smaller districts get more weight than those of voters in larger districts. Thus, unlike
suffrage restrictions such as those in the Jim Crow South, which distort the
relationship between the citizenry and the electorate, malapportionment dis-
torts the correspondence between votes and legislative seats.[36]

The most prominent instance of malapportionment in the United States is
the US Senate, where each state receives two senators regardless of its population size.[37] But malapportionment was once common in state legislatures
as well, due in part to the practice of apportioning districts to counties or

towns with only loose regard for their populations. The distortions caused by this practice were exacerbated by state legislatures' reluctance to redraw district lines to account for population growth. Some, such as Tennessee, refused to do so for half a century or more, with the result that cities and their suburbs were often severely underrepresented. The city of Memphis, for example, received the same representation in the Tennessee state assembly as rural districts one-tenth as large. In 1961, the US Supreme Court heard a lawsuit challenging the constitutionality of Tennessee legislative districts, and in *Baker v. Carr* (1962) and successor decisions the Court ruled that legislative districts had to be approximately equal in population. By the 1972 elections, this "one-person, one-vote" standard had been successfully imposed on all state legislatures.[38]

Although *Baker v. Carr* originated in a southern state, malapportionment was not confined to the South but instead cut across regional lines. The national scope of the problem as well as its large variation across states can be seen in figure 9.3. This figure plots a simple measure of the severity of malapportionment: the share of the state population covered by the smallest 50 percent of legislative districts.[39] In an equally apportioned legislature, the figure is 50 percent (i.e., half of districts cover half the population). However, if districts are highly unequal, a majority can be constructed with far less than half the population. For example, in the mid-1950s a majority of the California state senate could be achieved with districts covering 12 percent of the population; in Connecticut, a majority in the state house required less than 10 percent of the population.[40] At the other extreme, legislatures in some states, such as Massachusetts and Oregon, approached the equipopulous benchmark of 50 percent. As these examples suggest and figure 9.3 confirms, regional differences in malapportionment were not large. Figure 9.3 also shows that malapportionment actually worsened between the 1930s and 1950s before improving markedly in the 1960s thanks to judicial intervention.

Malapportionment systematically enhanced the political influence of certain interests while devaluing others. In particular, it led to the overrepresentation of rural voters at the expense of suburban and urban ones.[41] One consequence was that state spending was disproportionately directed to overrepresented areas—an imbalance largely eliminated by court-ordered reapportionment.[42] The partisan and ideological consequences of malapportionment were more nuanced and contingent. Outside the South, where rural areas generally leaned Republican, the imposition of a one-person, one-vote standard seems to have led to the election of more Democrats.[43] Rural areas were also more ideologically conservative than cities, but suburbs, which were also underrepresented under malapportionment, were often the most

Malapportionment, 1930s–1960s

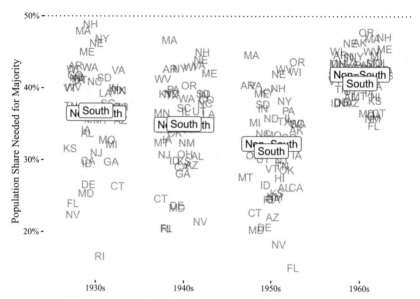

FIGURE 9.3. Malapportionment of state legislatures by decade. The vertical axis indicates the share of the state population covered by the smallest 50 percent of legislative districts, averaged across legislative chambers. The horizontal line at 50 percent represents the benchmark for equipopulous districts.

Policy Effects of Left Shift in Legislature

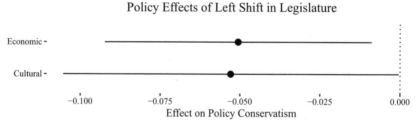

FIGURE 9.4. Policy effects of a leftward shift in the state legislature after *Baker v. Carr* (1962). Analysis covers the years 1957–1980. The dynamic panel model includes state and year FEs and lagged policy conservatism.

conservative, especially on economic issues.[44] Consequently, the ideological effects of malapportionment, though more often conservative than liberal, varied considerably across states.

As part of their study of the effects of the reapportionment revolution, Stephen Ansolabehere and James Snyder identify twenty-seven states where implementation of the one-person, one-vote standard had the effect of shifting the electorate of the median district to the left. The legislatures of Oregon, Wisconsin, and New York, for example, experienced such a shift, but

Idaho, Alabama, and Kentucky did not. To assess the effects of this shock to constituency preferences, we estimate a dynamic panel model of policy conservatism with an indicator for the left shift after 1962. As figure 9.5 reports, legislatures that reapportionment caused to shift leftward saw a decline in their economic and cultural policy conservatism relative to other states.[45] The magnitude of this short-term effect is on par with the effects of party control in models reported in chapter 5.

Did the shift to equipopulous districts improve policy representation overall? The evidence suggests that it did. In addition to equalizing state spending across districts, the one-person, one-vote standard seems to have brought state policies into closer proximity to citizens' preferences. Consider figure 9.5. The horizontal axis arrays states by their distance from equipopulation before *Baker v. Carr*—that is, 50 percent minus the minimum population share needed for a legislative majority (see figure 9.3). The vertical axis of figure 9.5 indicates how much congruence (left) and agreement (right) increased after the 1962 decision. As the figure shows, policy congruence and (especially) agreement increased the most in states where malapportionment was worst pre-*Baker*. Massachusetts, where districts were already close to equal in population, experienced little improvement in representation, whereas in neighboring Rhode Island, where a majority could be elected with less than a quarter of the population, congruence increased by four percentage points and agreement by seven. Note that because malapportionment was just as prevalent outside the South as within it, these improvements in representation manifested equally strongly across regions.

In sum, malapportionment impaired state policy representation. Because geographic areas were unequally represented in the legislature, government

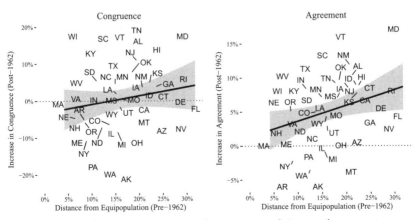

FIGURE 9.5. Effect of one-person, one-vote on policy proximity. Analysis covers the years 1936–2020.

was more responsive to some citizens than others. This is true not only for the distribution of government spending, as previous work has demonstrated, but also for the match between state policies and citizens' preferences. While not as momentous a revolution as those in civil and voting rights, the elimination of malapportionment rectified a marked democratic deficit in the states.

9.3 Partisan Gerrymandering

By the 1972 elections, all states had established equipopulous districts that complied with the Supreme Court's new one-person, one-vote standard.[46] This ended the extreme biases of malapportionment, but legislative maps continued to often favor one party over the other. Political geography provides part of the explanation. As Jonathan Rodden shows, Democrats' spatial concentration in cities has given Republicans a persistent advantage in the districting process of many states, especially in state senates.[47] But another powerful contributing factor was that politicians continued to draw legislative districts that maximized their own party's electoral prospects.[48] Although partisan gerrymandering is as old as the nation itself, recent technological advances and partisan polarization have supercharged politicians' capacity and incentives to engage in it.

It is not always easy to distinguish partisan gerrymandering from "unintentional" gerrymandering stemming from the spatial distribution of party support,[49] but we can measure the net partisan bias of a given legislative map. Our preferred measure of partisan bias, the *efficiency gap* (EG), follows naturally from the intended effects of partisan gerrymandering.[50] Unlike other forms of gerrymandering, such as those designed to protect incumbents of both parties, the goal of partisan gerrymandering is to maximize one party's seat share given its vote share. This is achieved by concentrating the party's opponents in a few lopsided districts ("packing") while dispersing its supporters so that they compose narrow but reliable majorities in as many districts as possible ("cracking"). Packing and cracking ensure that the supporters of the favored party are spread more efficiently (with respect to maximizing seat share) than those of the opposing party, whose votes are disproportionately wasted. The EG, which can be calculated from aggregate legislative election returns, is the ratio of wasted Republican votes to wasted Democratic ones.[51] It therefore indicates the degree to which a district map favors the Democratic Party. When the statewide legislative vote share is evenly divided between the parties, the EG is simply the size of the Democratic majority in the legislature (i.e., the percentage of seats held by Democrats minus 50 percent).

Partisan bias in state legislative districts has varied substantially over time as well as across regions of the country.[52] As the top panel of figure 9.6 shows, partisan bias was most prevalent in the era of malapportionment (1940s–1960s), when state officials had the most leeway in redistricting. Peaking at an average absolute magnitude of 10 percent, it began declining in the 1970s with the implementation of the one-person, one-vote standard and reached a low around 7 percent in the early twenty-first century.[53] The net direction of bias has shifted somewhat as well, favoring Democrats in the 1970s–2000s and Republicans before and after (figure 9.6, bottom).

These trends have differed somewhat across regions. In the 1940s, midwestern states had a severe pro-Republican bias, and southern states had a modest pro-Democratic one. The West and Northeast were closer to balanced.[54] The bias of midwestern maps attenuated over the next few decades, but they continued to favor Republicans into the twenty-first century. The South's pro-Democratic bias peaked in the 1970s as Republicans gained support in the electorate but made little headway in state legislatures, and the region's maps continued to favor Democrats until Republicans consolidated control in the 2010s.[55] Northeastern and western states have continued to show little net bias toward one party or the other, though this is due in part to offsetting biases within those regions.[56]

The 2010 redistricting cycle brought a marked uptick in the aggressiveness and sophistication of partisan gerrymandering, especially on the Republican side. In the 2010 elections, the GOP made large gains in state legislatures and governorship, allowing it to dominate the 2011–2012 districting process in many states. At the same time, the heightened policy stakes and partisan acrimony of twenty-first-century American politics increased Republicans' willingness to use their power to maximize their party's electoral prospects.[57]

In no state were these dynamics starker than in Wisconsin. Going into the 2010 elections, Democrats controlled the Wisconsin governorship and both chambers of the state legislature. This was by no means unusual: Democrats had enjoyed legislative majorities in sixteen of the preceding thirty years. In 2010, however, Wisconsin Republicans rode the national electoral tides and captured unified control of the state government.[58] This gave them an unfettered hand in redrawing state legislative lines to account for population changes recorded by the 2010 US Census. Republicans used the opportunity to implement a redistricting plan that gave them a 9 percent wasted-vote advantage in the state senate and a 12 percent advantage in the state house, rendering their majority virtually immune from electoral challenge.[59] After several decades of regular alternation in party control, and despite winning

Magnitude of Partisan Districting Bias

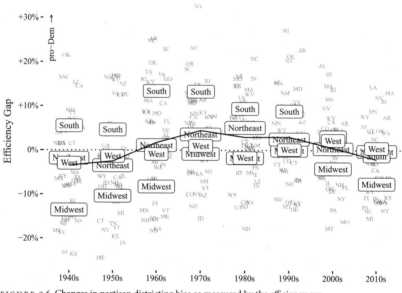

Direction of Partisan Districting Bias

FIGURE 9.6. Changes in partisan districting bias as measured by the efficiency gap.

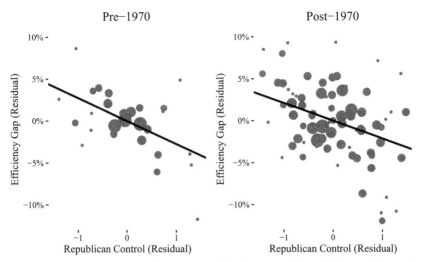

FIGURE 9.7. Effect of party control of government on the efficiency gap before and after 1970. Horizontal axes indicate the residualized number of elected branches (executive, state house, and state senate) controlled by Republicans, net of state and decade fixed effects, in redistricting years. Vertical axes indicate the residualized efficiency gap in the succeeding decade. Points are bin means, with size proportional to number of observations.

only a minority of legislative votes cast in both 2012 and 2018, Republicans maintained substantial legislative majorities for the entire 2010–2020 period.

Wisconsin is not the only state where control of redistricting enabled politicians to draw maps that locked in their hold on power. As a large body of research has shown, control of the redistricting process enables politicians to draw maps that favor their party in subsequent elections.[60] Figure 9.7 illustrates these effects of partisan control.[61] Before 1970, each additional branch of government Republicans controlled yielded a four percentage point decrease in the EG (left panel). After 1970, the estimated effect is two percentage points (right panel).[62] Thus, the introduction of the one-person, one-vote standard seems to have dampened party control's effect on the EG, but it did not eliminate state officials' willingness and capacity to draw districts that advantage their own party in subsequent elections.

Do these distortions of the correspondence between votes and seats affect representation more broadly?[63] There is good reason to expect them to. Because it packs supporters of one party in a few districts while spreading supporters of the other more evenly, partisan gerrymandering skews the cross-district distribution of mass preferences. As a result, in Democratic gerrymanders the median voter in the median district is more liberal than the statewide median, and in Republican ones the median of medians is more conservative.[64] Thus, even if every state legislator faithfully represented the

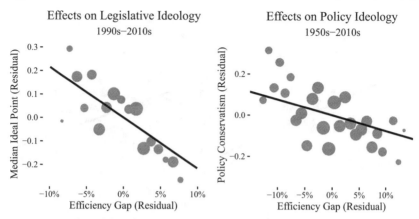

FIGURE 9.8. Effects of the efficiency gap on legislative conservatism (*left*) and policy conservatism (*right*). Horizontal axes indicate the residualized efficiency gap (net of state and decade fixed effects). Vertical axis in the left panel indicates the median Shor-McCarty ideal point, averaged across legislative chambers and also residualized. Vertical axis on the right indicates residualized policy conservatism (economic and cultural policies combined). Points are bin means, with size proportional to number of observations.

median voter in her or his district, partisan gerrymandering would shift the pivotal voters in the legislature in the ideological direction of the advantaged party. As we saw in chapter 5, however, Democratic and Republican candidates do not converge on the median vote but rather diverge within districts.[65] This divergence magnifies the representational effects of gerrymandering. Not only does it skew the median district away from the statewide median, but the legislator who represents that district is likely to be even more extreme.[66]

If this reasoning is sound, states with negative (i.e., pro-Republican) efficiency gaps should have more conservative legislatures and policies than states with positive EGs. Figure 9.8 presents evidence that this is the case. It plots the relationship between the EG in a given state-decade and the legislative conservatism (left) and policy conservatism (right) in the same state-decade. Both the EG and the outcome measures have been residualized by state and decade so that the slopes in the figures are the same as would be estimated in a model with state and decade fixed effects. The results suggest that if the EG shifts ten percentage points in a pro-Democratic direction, legislative conservatism decreases by 0.2 and policy conservatism decreases by 0.08.[67]

Partisan gerrymandering thus biases state governance in the ideological direction of the advantaged party. Does this bias degrade policy representation?

The answer appears to be yes. When and where the efficiency gap is larger, the match between state policies and mass preferences is poorer. Figure 9.9 shows this relationship visually, again using residualized versions of the independent and dependent variables. For each 10-point increase in absolute efficiency gap, congruence decreases by 2 points (left panel) and agreement decreases by 1.5 points (right).

Wisconsin again provides a compelling illustration of the representational consequences of partisan gerrymandering. When Republicans captured the state government in 2010, they were aided by a modestly pro-Republican efficiency gap (−5% in the state senate and −6% in the state house). The party took advantage of its newfound control to press an aggressively conservative agenda, restricting abortion access, passing a right-to-work law, and weakening collective bargaining for state workers. Republicans also refused to expand Medicaid under the Affordable Care Act, making Wisconsin the only state east of the Mississippi and north of the Mason-Dixon line not to do so.[68] As we saw in chapter 2 (figure 2.5), this refusal flew in the face of the Wisconsin public's supermajority support for expansion. Critics have attacked the policies Republicans did pass for being similarly out of step with public opinion.[69] The backlash against these policies helped Democrats make electoral gains in subsequent elections, but they were unable to break through the Republican gerrymander of 2011–2012, which nearly doubled the GOP's advantage

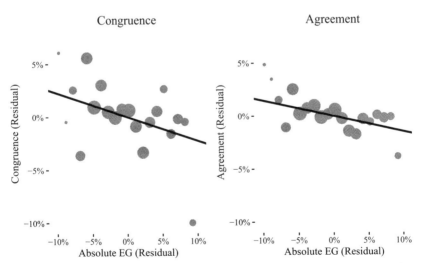

FIGURE 9.9. Policy proximity and the efficiency gap. Horizontal axes indicate the residualized absolute efficiency gap (net of state and decade fixed effects). Vertical axes indicate residualized congruence (*left*) and agreement (*right*). Points are bin means, with size proportional to number of observations.

in wasted votes. In short, gerrymandering not only enabled Republicans in Wisconsin to pass unpopular policies but also derailed the negative electoral feedback that militates against large and unpopular policy changes.

9.4 Summary

This chapter has reviewed three of the twentieth century's most salient and durable deficits in state-level democracy: the Jim Crow South, legislative malapportionment, and partisan gerrymandering. Each of these undemocratic brown spots advantaged certain interests over others: White southerners over Black southerners, rural Americans over urbanites and suburbanites, and the party in control of redistricting over the party out of power. These biases damaged the overall quality of representation, degrading the match between state policies and the public's preferences. In the case of Jim Crow and malapportionment, representation improved when the federal government intervened to impose more democratic standards. Partisan gerrymandering, however, is still very much alive, and its effects have only increased in recent decades as party control has grown in importance. This raises two questions: Can state-level democracy still be improved? And, if so, what institutional reforms would be most effective at doing so? The next chapter attempts to provide some answers.

Reforms:
Improving American Democracy

Throughout their history, Americans have experimented with reforms designed to improve democratic performance.[1] The age of Jackson brought universal White male suffrage and the direct election of judges and other officials.[2] During Reconstruction, slavery was abolished and Black men were enfranchised.[3] Populists and Progressives later won votes for women, the secret ballot, nonpartisan elections, campaign finance regulations, and various forms of direct democracy. Twentieth-century reformers fought poll taxes, literacy tests, and the White primary and sought a secure place in the political economy for organized labor. As "laboratories of democracy," states pioneered almost all these reforms, and scholars of state politics have engaged in vibrant debate over which if any of them actually enhance popular control of government.[4]

Whatever their intentions, the effects of putatively democratic reforms have often been uneven and ambiguous. Expanded suffrage for White men in the antebellum era went hand in hand with new restrictions for women and racial minorities.[5] The secret ballot also served as a de facto literacy test.[6] Nonpartisan elections helped economic elites secure control over local politics.[7] And the pro-union labor regime instituted during the New Deal quickly gave rise to a conservative reaction against the perceived power and corruption of "union bosses."[8] More prosaically, many highly touted reforms have failed to have any obvious effects at all on the workings of American politics.

As this history suggests, simply branding a reform as democratic does not make it so. In this chapter, we take a systematic look at the political effects of a number of reforms that were primarily implemented over the past few decades. We concentrate on this more recent period mainly for reasons of data availability. Several of our analyses rely on public opinion data, which is substantially richer in recent decades than in the mid-twentieth century. Because our analytic strategy relies on change within states over time, we cannot examine the effects of reforms adopted mainly or entirely in earlier eras, such as poll taxes and literacy tests. One advantage of our recent focus, however, is that most of the reforms we examine are still live political issues, allowing us to contribute to ongoing policy debates.

We examine reforms in four categories: citizen governance, voting, money in politics, and unions.[9] The citizen governance category includes three reforms designed to empower citizens relative to professional politicians: nonpartisan districting commissions, direct democracy, and term limits. Voting reforms include election-day registration, absentee voting, early voting, and voter identification (ID) laws. Money in politics includes individual contribution limits and bans on corporate contributions. Finally, union-related reforms include right-to-work laws, which weaken unions, and collective bargaining for public employees, which strengthens them. We estimate the effects of each of these reforms on five outcomes: voter turnout, partisan control of government, policy ideology, policy responsiveness, and policy proximity.

Very few reforms have detectable effects on any of these outcomes. In fact, only two of the ninety-nine effects we estimate (the effects of direct democracy and right-to-work laws on cultural policy conservatism) are unambiguously distinguishable from zero. There is suggestive evidence for the effects of several other reforms, usually but not always in the direction one would expect. In most cases, the null results are not due to effects being small but precisely estimated. Rather, many estimates have wide confidence intervals, indicating that the statistical evidence does not rule out large positive effects. It would therefore be inappropriate to interpret these results as refuting the arguments in favor of these reforms. Overall, however, this analysis indicates the dearth of affirmative statistical evidence that any widely implemented institutional reforms have major effects on state-level democracy.

10.1 Background on Institutional Reforms

10.1.1 CITIZEN GOVERNANCE

Before analyzing the effects of these reforms, we first provide some substantive background on them. We begin with reforms designed to foster *citizen governance*: districting commissions, direct democracy, and term limits. Although they are disparate in focus and ideological valence, we lump these reforms together because all three are designed to weaken professional politicians and include ordinary citizens in the governmental process.

Districting commissions are designed to reduce the prominence of partisan and other political considerations in the drawing of legislative districts.[10] There are two types of districting commissions: bipartisan and nonpartisan. On bipartisan commissions, the commissioners are appointed by politicians but include equal numbers of Democrats and Republicans. In some states, the tie-breaking commissioner is chosen by the other commissioners. In others, the tie-breaker is chosen by the state's Supreme Court. On nonpartisan commissions, the commissioners are selected to be representative of the state's population with no majority for either party. Politicians are typically prohibited from serving on these commissions. As of 2013, eight states had implemented maps drawn by either type of commission: New Jersey (implemented 1973), Pennsylvania (1973), Montana (1975), Hawai'i (1983), Washington (1993), Idaho (2003), Arizona (2003), and California (2013).[11] Since then, several more states have done so, including Michigan, Colorado, and Virginia, though these went into effect too recently to include in our analysis.

Though different, both bipartisan and nonpartisan districting commissions are designed to limit the degree to which one party can skew districts in its favor. When drawing districts, commissions are also usually required to take into account certain nonpartisan criteria, such as compactness and respect for communities of interest. These constraints on both the membership of commissions and the criteria for drawing districts should reduce the influence of partisanship in the drawing of district lines.[12] This should manifest itself in at least two ways. First, in states with redistricting commissions, the relationship between votes and seats should be less biased.[13] Second, since commissions are more insulated from political control, the direction of partisan districting bias should depend less on which party is in power during redistricting years.

To see whether commissions have their intended effect on districting, we estimate two-way fixed-effects models of the efficiency gap in the first post-reapportionment year in each decade, 1970s–2010s. We find only partial support for these expectations. As the first column of table 10.1 shows, given state and decade intercepts, the absolute size of the EG is no smaller in state-decades where districts were drawn by commission.[14] The absolute EG is also unaffected by the number of government branches Democrats controlled during redistricting, suggesting that over the past half a century neither party has been disproportionately prone to gerrymandering. The second column, however, indicates that commissions do effect a large reduction in the influence of party control on the *direction* of districting bias. In states without commissions, each branch controlled by Democrats is associated with a 3 percent (pro-Democratic) increase in the efficiency gap (row 2). In states

TABLE 10.1 Effect of districting commissions on districting bias, 1970s–2010s

	Abs(Efficiency Gap) (1)	Efficiency Gap (2)
Districting Commission	0.001	0.012
	(0.009)	(0.015)
Dem. Control$_{t-1}$ (centered at 1.5)	0.001	0.032
	(0.003)	(0.008)
Dem. Control$_{t-1}$ × Commission		−0.025
		(0.008)
Year Fixed Effects	yes	yes
Decade Fixed Effects	yes	yes
Observations	171	171
R^2	0.436	0.695

Note: Analysis includes only the first year following decadal reapportionment.
Standard errors are shown in parentheses.

with commissions, however, this partisan advantage drops by 2.5 percentage points, to near zero (row 3). As designed, commissions do seem to break the dominant party's ability to draw districts more favorable to themselves. Whether this affects representation more generally remains to be seen.

The second citizen governance reform we examine is direct democracy—specifically, the initiative and referendum.[15] These institutions enable citizens to circumvent their representatives and vote on policy proposals directly.[16] To influence policymaking, they need not be exercised overtly. The mere threat of direct democracy may lead officials to change their behavior in order to preempt future ballot measures,[17] and the results of initiatives or referenda may inform officials of voters' preferences.[18] Despite strong theoretical reasons to think that direct democracy improves—or at least affects—representation, the empirical evidence is mixed.[19]

The third citizen government reform we examine, term limits, prohibits state legislators from serving more than a set number of terms. Term limits are often justified with reference to the ideal of a "citizen-legislator": an amateur serving out of civic duty rather than a professional for whom politics is a career.[20] By fostering rotation in office, term limits may lead to representatives who better reflect their constituents' (current) preferences. Critics have argued, however, that they also result in less experienced legislators with weaker capacity and incentives to attend to public opinion.[21] There have been few empirical studies of the effect of term limits on representation, but one recent study finds that cross-sectional responsiveness is stronger in states with term limits.[22]

10.1.2 VOTING

The next set of institutions we examine are reforms designed to regulate the
process of *voting* (as opposed to suffrage eligibility per se). Four such reforms
have been widely implemented in recent decades: election-day (ED) registration, no-excuse absentee voting, early voting, and voter ID.[23] A number of
studies have found that ED registration increases turnout.[24] Studies of absentee and early voting have been more mixed, but there are reasons to expect
these reforms to increase turnout as well.[25] Although there has been little research of the subject, it is reasonable to suspect these turnout effects to have
downstream consequences for representation.

Voter ID laws have been the subject of the most controversy. Our focus
is on laws that require photo identification.[26] The ostensible goal of voter ID
is to ensure the integrity of elections by reducing voter fraud. But the reality
is that voter fraud is virtually nonexistent.[27] Consequently, many critics argue
that voter identification laws are really designed to deter minority voters and
help Republican candidates.[28] Regardless of their intent, voter identification requirements create a new burden on voters. Some studies have found that they
modestly reduce turnout,[29] while other studies find mixed effects on turnout,[30]
perhaps due to the countermobilization efforts of political campaigns. Despite
the large literature on the effect of voter ID laws on turnout, there have been
no comprehensive studies of the effect of these laws on political representation.

10.1.3 MONEY IN POLITICS

We examine two reforms designed to limit the influence of *money in politics*: individual limits on campaign contributions and bans on corporate contributions.[31] To the extent that financial contributions affect the outcome of
elections or otherwise induce politicians to give disproportionate weight to
the preferences of contributors, limiting them may have important representational consequences.[32] Several previous studies have examined the direct
effect of campaign finance limits on elections,[33] state legislators' ideology,[34]
and state policy,[35] but no previous study has examined the effect of campaign
finance rules on representation.[36]

10.1.4 LABOR UNIONS

The final set of reforms we examine are two designed to affect the power of *labor unions*: right-to-work laws and collective bargaining for state employees.

Though seemingly focused on economic relations between employers and employees, these laws have important repercussions for politics due to unions' unique role in facilitating collective action by and on behalf of workers.[37] Right-to-work laws prohibit union security agreements: agreements between unions and employers that require employees to join or contribute to unions as a condition of employment. States began passing such laws in the wake of the 1935 National Labor Relations Act (NRLA), which guaranteed private-sector workers the right to form unions and bargain collectively for wages and benefits, especially after they were explicitly sanctioned by the 1947 Taft-Hartley amendments to the NRLA.[38] Right-to-work laws proliferated first in southern, Plains, and Mountain West states, but thanks to renewed activism on the right, they have spread more recently to former union strongholds such as Michigan, Wisconsin, Indiana, and West Virginia.[39] By 2020, there were twenty-seven right-to-work states.

Right-to-work laws led to modest decreases in union membership.[40] They also led to more significant decreases in unions' political power. For one thing, union-affiliated Whites are more likely to identify as Democrats,[41] so reductions in union membership cost Democrats voters. In addition, right-to-work laws diminished the resources that unions could devote to political campaigns.[42] As a result of both these factors, one study recently found that right-to-work laws diminished Democratic presidential vote shares by 3.5 percentage points. It finds similar effects in Senate, House, and gubernatorial races as well as on state legislative control. And it finds that this reduction in the political power of labor's Democratic allies in state government moves state policies in a more conservative direction.[43]

A notable omission of the NRLA is that it did not guarantee collective bargaining rights to government employees.[44] In the early 1960s, however, state governments gradually started passing laws expanding limited collective bargaining rights to public-sector workers.[45] In 1960, only about 2 percent of state and local public-sector workers had the right to bargain collectively. By 2010, the share of public-sector workers with collective bargaining rights had grown to 63 percent.[46] In recent years, though, a number of conservative states have scaled back public-sector workers' collective bargaining rights due to coordinated efforts from conservative interest groups.[47]

The establishment of collective bargaining laws led to an increase in union membership and collective bargaining agreements.[48] It also increased unions' capacity for political mobilization.[49] It might be expected that collective bargaining laws would shift state policies to the left by increasing the power of labor. However, one recent study finds no evidence that introducing collective bargaining rights led to increases in the average level of resources devoted to education.[50]

10.2 The Effects of Institutional Reforms

We now turn to estimating the effects of the eleven reforms just described. As noted, we consider five kinds of outcomes: voter turnout, party control, policy ideology, policy responsiveness, and policy proximity. Since these analyses follow a similar structure, we describe our general approach first before discussing the specific results.

Aside from policy responsiveness, all of the quantities we are interested in are captured by the reform's direct effect on the outcome. To estimate these causal effects, we use the R package PanelMatch to implement a nonparametric generalization of a difference-in-differences estimator.[51] This approach matches each treated observation (e.g., a state that adopts a particular institutional reform, such as redistricting commissions) from a given state in a particular year with control observations from other states in the same year that have a similar treatment and covariate history. We match states with and without the reform on lagged outcomes, the partisan composition of their state government, and the mass public's ideological preferences on both the economic and social domains. Our estimate of the causal effect of the reform is the average difference in outcomes between the matched treated and control states. To provide sufficient time for the effects of the reform to propagate through the political system, we estimate effects eight years (or, in the case of turnout, two presidential elections) after the reform was implemented.

Our analysis of policy responsiveness differs from the others in that the quantity of interest is how mass conservatism's dynamic effect on policy conservatism *interacts* with a given reform. Since this cannot easily be accommodated by a difference-in-differences analysis, we instead return to the dynamic panel model from chapter 7, modified to include an interaction between mass conservatism and the reform in question. It should be noted that estimates from this analysis do not have as clear a causal interpretation as the matched panel estimates; they are best interpreted as descriptive statements of how responsiveness differs between states with and without the reform.

Finally, analyzing so many effects at once dramatically increases the probability of spurious results. We therefore adjust all the *p* values in this chapter to control the false discovery rate (FDR) within each of the five outcomes.[52] Doing so ensures that the expected proportion of falsely rejected hypotheses, which would otherwise greatly exceed the nominal level (i.e., $\alpha = 0.05$),

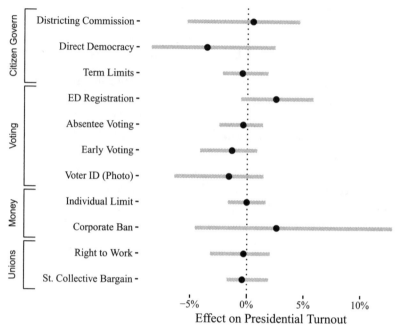

FIGURE 10.1. Effects of various institutional reforms on voter turnout, two presidential elections after implementation. After (and before) FDR correction, none of the estimates is statistically significant.

does not do so. Applying this correction causes a few effects that would be judged statistically significant on their own to become insignificant. These effects can be identified from the confidence intervals in the figures that follow, which we have left unadjusted.

We begin by considering reforms' effects on turnout in presidential elections (figure 10.1). Reforms designed to make voting easier, such as ED registration and no-excuse absentee voting, should be expected to increase turnout, while reforms that make it more difficult, such as voter ID, should be expected to decrease it. We have no clear expectations for the effects of nonvoting reforms. As it happens, none of the estimated effects are statistically distinguishable from zero, with or without FDR correction. The effect estimates for ED registration and voter ID are at least in the expected directions. The confidence intervals indicate that the effect of ED registration could be as high as 6 percent, and that of voter ID could be as low as −6 percent. But overall, there is no firm evidence that any of these reforms affects voter turnout.

The second set of outcomes we examine are related to party control of state government. One, labeled "H" in figure 10.2, is the Republican seat share in the state house, and the other, labeled "B," is the number of branches (house, senate, executive) controlled by Republicans. Although the debate over some reforms, such as districting commissions and voter ID, has become quite partisan, there is little indication that these reforms provide an electoral advantage to one party or the other.[53] One possible exception to this rule is right-to-work laws.[54] Though these effects do not survive FDR correction, the estimates suggest that the implementation of right-to-work laws cost Democrats 3.6 (CI: 0–11) percentage points in state house share and 5.6 (CI: 0–14) points in the share of institutions they control. Given their close alliance in most states, it makes sense that weakening unions would hurt Democrats as well.[55] However, despite public-sector unions' strong support for Democrats, there is no evidence that implementing collective bargaining for state employees damages Republican prospects.[56]

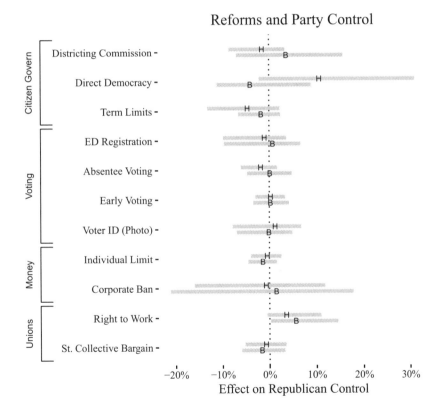

FIGURE 10.2. Effects of various institutional reforms on Republican control of state offices, eight years after implementation. After FDR correction, none of the estimates is statistically significant.

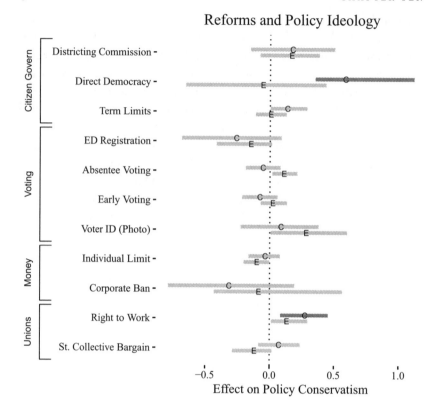

FIGURE 10.3. Effects of various institutional reforms on state policy conservatism, eight years after implementation. After FDR correction, only the cultural domain estimates for direct democracy and right to work are statistically significant.

Third, we estimate reforms' effects on state policy, again distinguishing between the economic and cultural domains ("E" and "C" in figure 10.3).[57] The two clearest effects are on cultural policy conservatism of right-to-work laws and direct democracy. Consistent with its apparently positive effects on Republican control of state government, right to work is estimated to increase cultural policy conservatism by 0.3 standard deviations (CI: 0.1–0.5). The corresponding estimate for economic policy is 0.1 SDs (CI: 0.0–0.3), though it does not survive FDR correction. Disempowering labor unions does seem to cause more conservative policymaking, though somewhat surprisingly this effect is not concentrated on the economic issues that compose unions' core concerns.

The estimated effects of direct democracy are even larger: a remarkable 0.6 SDs (CI: 0.4–1.1) increase in cultural policy conservatism.[58] Though perhaps implausibly large, it is not surprising that these effects should be most salient on cultural issues, where the educational and class gradient in political attitudes likely predisposes officeholders to take more liberal positions than their copartisans in the public.[59] For example, there is a long history of conservative activists using ballot measures to enact anti-LGBT policies or overturn pro-LGBT ones.[60] There is little indication that direct democracy affects economic policies similarly.[61] This could perhaps be due to offsetting effects. In some cases, such as California's 1978 "tax revolt," direct democracy may enable more conservative policymaking, but on others, such as the 2018 referendum that overturned Missouri's right-to-work law, it may do the opposite.[62]

Several other estimates do not survive FDR correction but nevertheless provide suggestive evidence of effects on policy conservatism. In particular, term limits may increase policy conservatism in the cultural domain, absentee voting and voter ID may do so in the economic domain, and ED registration and individual contribution limits may decrease economic policy conservatism. All these estimates are theoretically plausible, but again, given the number of tests we conduct, it would not be surprising to obtain a few spurious results.

We now turn to our fourth outcome, policy responsiveness. As noted, we depart from our approach for the other outcomes and use a dynamic panel model to estimate how mass conservatism's effect on policy conservatism interacts with each reform. A positive interaction indicates that policy change in response to mass preferences tends to be larger in states with the reform. The normative implications of greater responsiveness are not obvious. Without jointly scaled measures, we cannot rule out the possibility that policymaking is overresponsive.[63] Given the incremental nature of dynamic responsiveness, we are skeptical of the empirical prevalence of overresponsiveness. Nevertheless, it is worth bearing in mind that an increase in policy responsiveness does not necessarily imply that policy is closer to citizens' preferences.[64]

Regardless, previous scholarship has found little evidence of institutional effects on responsiveness at either the state or the municipal level.[65] Our findings are similar. None of the interaction coefficients reported in figure 10.4 survive FDR correction.[66] The most suggestive results are for state-employee collective bargaining, which may increase responsiveness in both domains, though it is hard to think of a plausible mechanism for this effect. Otherwise, there is little evidence of reforms that moderate the dynamic relationship between opinion and policy.

We end with reforms' effects on policy proximity—arguably the ultimate measure of the quality of representation (figure 10.5). Once again, none of the estimated effects are statistically significant once corrected to control the FDR. A few of the unadjusted estimates are significant, all with agreement as the outcome measure (these estimates are much more precise than those for congruence). Term limits, voter ID, and individual contribution limits are all estimated to decrease policy agreement by a bit less than a percentage point. By contrast, bans on corporate contribution are estimated to increase agreement by about a point. Average agreement scores range across states from a low of 46 percent in Mississippi to a high of 64 percent in Massachusetts, so these effect sizes are nontrivial but modest. It is noteworthy, however, how little evidence there is for reforms that *improve* policy proximity. In addition

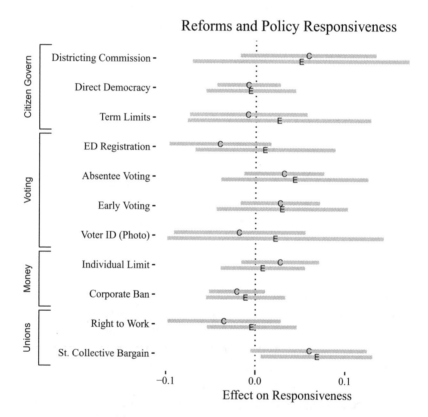

C   Cultural Domain   E   Economic Domain

FIGURE 10.4. Effects of various institutional reforms on dynamic responsiveness. Each estimate corresponds to the coefficient on the reform's interaction with mass conservatism in dynamic panel model of policy conservatism. After FDR correction, none of the estimates is statistically significant.

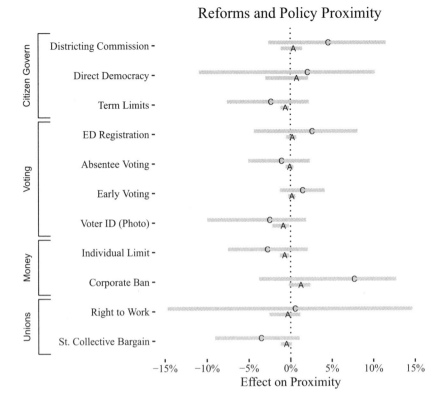

FIGURE 10.5. Effects of various institutional reforms on measures of policy proximity, eight years after implementation. After FDR correction, none of the estimates is statistically significant.

to corporate contribution bans, the only reforms for which substantial positive effects are even consistent with the data are districting commissions, direct democracy, ED registration, and early voting, but even these inferences are quite speculative. As with the other outcomes, it is hard to point to a putatively democratic reform that plausibly improves or even materially affects representation.[67]

10.3 Summary

This chapter has provided a systematic analysis of the effects of eleven putatively democratic reforms. Aside from the conservative policy impact of direct democracy and right-to-work laws, we found remarkably little evidence that these reforms affect political outcomes and even less that they improve the quality of democracy. Indeed, there is as much evidence that the reforms damage representation as there is that they improve it. Because we have sacrificed depth for breadth in this analysis, these findings should not be taken as the last word on any one of these reforms, some of which have been subject to more intensive investigations that have come to conclusions different from ours. Moreover, even in the absence of compelling evidence of their effects on representation, many of these reforms have good arguments in their favor. For example, given the evidence that districting commissions reduce distortions in the relationship between votes and seats (table 10.1), one might favor them as a matter of procedural fairness, independent of affirmative evidence of their downstream effects. Similarly, liberal Americans have good reasons to be concerned about the ways that direct democracy and right-to-work laws push state policies to the right, notwithstanding their lack of a clear impact on policy responsiveness or proximity.

Nevertheless, this chapter sends a cautionary message. Many of the reforms it examines have been the subject of grandiose claims and bitter political battles. These battles may well be worth fighting, but it should be with the clear-eyed understanding that none of these reforms is likely to radically transform state-level democracy. History tells us that fundamental transformations are possible. The disenfranchisement of Black southerners and many poor White ones at the turn of the twentieth century had massive effects on state policies, especially for Blacks, and its reversal in the Second Reconstruction was similarly transformative.[68] The reforms we have considered in this chapter pale relative to such revolutionary changes. The lesson is not that American democracy cannot be improved or even that existing reforms will not do so. Rather, it is that the empirical record on reforms that have been adopted widely enough to be evaluated provides little affirmative basis for believing that they will live up to the hopes of their most optimistic boosters.

11

Conclusion

Political science has a venerable tradition of skepticism regarding ordinary Americans' influence on, let alone control over, their governments. Recent exemplars of this pessimistic tradition include empirical studies, such as Jeffrey Lax and Justin Phillips's on state policy representation and Steven Rogers's on accountability in state elections, as well as ambitious syntheses, such as Martin Gilens's *Affluence and Influence* and Christopher Achen and Larry Bartels's *Democracy for Realists.*[1] This impressive body of scholarship poses a compelling and discomfiting challenge to what Achen and Bartels call the "folk theory" of democracy, which holds that elections reliably and unproblematically translate the will of the people into government policy.

This book has been a sustained attempt to address these challenges empirically and, to a substantial extent, rebut them. This has required both an unprecedented wealth of data and a distinctive approach to analyzing it. A key feature of our empirical strategy has been its focus on the relationship between citizens' policy preferences—the "starting point" of liberal democratic theory[2]—with what is arguably the end point of the political process: government policies. That is, unlike many empirical studies of representation, we have treated outcomes such as election results and roll-call votes as potential mediators of policy representation rather than as the ultimate phenomena of interest. Among other things, this focus on policies has revealed states to be more ideologically stable than election returns suggest and has shown partisan differences to be much less prominent than they are on legislative roll calls.

A second distinctive feature of our approach has been its emphasis on aggregation. This aggregation has come in two main forms. First, we have aggregated data on individual policies and survey items into summary measures of conservatism within broad issue domains. Second, rather than analyzing preferences and attitudes of individual citizens, we have focused on the aggregate characteristics of collectivities—namely, state publics. By strengthening the ideological "signal" relative to issue-specific noise, this double aggregation clarifies the structure underlying state policies and (especially) mass preferences and mitigates the instability and incoherence of issue-specific indicators. In combination with our model-based approach to measurement, it also is what permits us to compare ideological patterns in all fifty states across more than eight decades.

This brings us to our third distinctive contribution: our analysis of time-series as well as cross-sectional variation. Although many studies of representation have examined one or the other of these dimensions of variation, exceedingly few have analyzed them in combination, especially over such a long time span. Our dynamic perspective has several benefits. From a methodological point of view, it has enabled us to employ statistical models, particularly dynamic panel models, that provide a stronger basis for causal inference than would be possible with cross-sectional or time-series data alone. More substantively, it has allowed us to examine how representation unfolds over time, over both the short and the long term, and even how policy outputs feed back into the political process. Finally, our nearly century-long perspective has highlighted the fact that the character of state politics is not static but rather is strongly shaped by states' developmental trajectories and historical context.

Our distinctive approach has revealed new perspectives on state politics that both resonate with and challenge existing accounts. In line with more pessimistic views of American politics, we find that state policy responsiveness is often disappointingly sluggish and piecemeal. Due in large part to the difficulty of overturning existing policies, even large shifts in public opinion and partisan electoral fortunes frequently echo only faintly in states' policy profiles, at least in the short term. Moreover, the probability that a politically salient state policy is congruent with majority opinion is, in the short term, not much better than chance.

A central theme of this book, however, is that a snapshot perspective on representation captures only part of the story. Policy responsiveness may be incremental in the short term, but over the long term many small changes cumulate into large differences. According to our statistical estimates, it may take decades before the effects of ideological shifts in the mass public are fully felt. Nevertheless, the long-run result is a powerful correlation between opinion and policy and, for older issues, substantially greater congruence with majority preferences. In this respect, our results vindicate Robert Erikson,

Gerald Wright, and John McIver's *Statehouse Democracy*, whose finding of a strong cross-sectional correlation between mass and policy liberalism can be explained as the equilibrium outcome of the dynamic processes we document.[3]

In other respects, however, this book has also revealed the limitations of any single model of state politics, *Statehouse Democracy* included. Many of the puzzles that Erikson, Wright, and McIver so elegantly resolved no longer exist. Relying on data from around 1980, near the end of a period of unusually decentralized and depolarized politics, these authors highlighted the almost nonexistent relationship between states' partisan and ideological orientations as well as the large ideological variation across states within each party. These observations undergird their depiction of state parties as highly responsive to state median voters and state publics as equally responsive to the positions of the parties in their state.

Our data confirm their conclusions but reveal them to be unusual relative to state politics before and especially after. Since the 1980s, mass policy preferences in different domains have become strongly aligned with each other as well as with partisan preferences and electoral outcomes. Indeed, Democratic and Republican identifiers now diverge strongly within states while exhibiting little ideological variation across states. State policies, though already more aligned than mass preferences, followed a similar trajectory. Moreover, the causal effects of party control on state policies, which probably reached their nadir in the 1970s and 1980s, have grown sharply in the subsequent decades. As indicated by the large policy shifts in Wisconsin after the Republican takeover of 2010 and in Virginia after the Democratic one of 2019, it is no longer plausible to claim, even to a first approximation, that pressures to converge on the median voter cause the two parties to enact similar policies when they control state government.[4]

At the same time, however, *Statehouse Democracy*'s emphasis on parties' responsiveness to their electorates retains a great deal of truth. Even the increased partisan effects on policy evident in recent years pale relative to the policy differences across states. As noted earlier, one of the advantages of focusing on policy outcomes rather than, say, roll-call votes is that the latter tend to exaggerate differences between parties and downplay areas of relative consensus. Indeed, we find little evidence that partisan turnover is the primary mechanism by which mass preferences influence state policies—largely because, net of partisanship, mass policy preferences are weakly related to electoral shifts. Rather, it appears that due to the electoral incentives we document in chapter 6, politicians in each party feel strong pressure to adapt preemptively to public opinion. The paradoxical consequence is that although electoral competition is key to incentivizing responsiveness, fairly little of the public's influence over state policymaking is exerted through the actual outcome of elections. Though consistent with much research emphasizing politicians' anticipation of voter sanctions,[5] this conclusion is strikingly at odds with the prominent view that "citizens affect public policy—insofar as they affect it at all—almost entirely by voting out one partisan team and replacing it with another."[6]

11.1 Normative Implications

How, then, should we evaluate the quality of democracy in the states and, by extension, in America at large? On the whole, our findings are reassuring, though not entirely so. We find that, in broad strokes and over the long term, the public exerts a powerful influence over the general direction of state policymaking. Such responsiveness is often considered the sine qua non of democracy,[7] if not its very definition,[8] and without evidence of it we would have good reason to doubt that American democracy is functioning as it ought to. Of course, influence does not necessarily imply fine-grained control, and indeed we find that in the short run policies are often out of step with majority opinion. But again, policy proximity tends to increase the longer a policy is on the agenda. Moreover, policies with lopsided support tend to fall off the political (and polling) agenda, biasing the survey data toward controversial policies more likely to be incongruent. In sum, even by the demanding standard of popular control, state-level democracy seems to function better than pessimistic accounts suggest.

There are, however, grounds for concern as well. For one thing, the time lag between opinion change and policy response is not unproblematic. Opponents of, say, antisodomy laws or legal abortion may find only small comfort in the knowledge that the injustices they seek to rectify will be overturned a generation hence. The normative reassurance we offer is also limited by our near-exclusive focus on the *average* citizen. As a consequence, our finding that states respond dynamically to their publics does not rule out unequal responsiveness to citizens in different income or racial groups, as a number of other studies have found.[9]

Moreover—and not unrelatedly—our evidence suggests that the quality of democracy is uneven across states. Like the "brown spots" identified by Guillermo O'Donnell in many nominally democratic countries, states in the American South in particular seem to represent their citizens less well than do states in other regions.[10] The policies of southern states are more conservative than those of non-southern states with comparable publics, and the match between policies and public opinion is lower. Given the persistence of policies over time, this representational deficit is likely at least partly due to the hangover from its long history of authoritarianism and racial oppression through the mid-twentieth century,[11] which the decades since its transition to democracy have only partially erased.

This relatively sanguine explanation, however, is not fully satisfying. Though the statistical evidence is not conclusive, policy responsiveness seems to be lower to this day in the South, at least on economic issues. This is unsurprising, for there are good reasons to suspect that the extension of formal political equality to African Americans and other racial minorities in the South did not instantly endow them with political influence equal to that of White southerners. Southern Blacks' turnout in presidential elections did not converge with that of southern Whites until the early twenty-first century, and turnout among Latino southerners remains almost twenty points below the regional average.[12] For their part, southern Whites continue to display higher levels of antagonism toward Blacks than do Whites elsewhere in the country.[13]

Just as important, perhaps, is the extent of racial polarization in much of the region. Especially in Deep South states such as Alabama and Mississippi, the population roughly clusters around two modes: a smaller liberal one (mostly Black) and a larger conservative one (nearly all White). Due to this unusually skewed distribution, the median citizen—arguably the most relevant quantity from a theoretical point of view[14]—is actually substantially to the right of the average. The effects of this discrepancy are magnified by the discrepancy's interaction with the two-party system. The Republican Party, itself dominated by Whites, now dominates nearly every southern state, while Democrats are confined to semipermanent minority status.[15] Though states like Virginia are exceptions, most southern states have shifted from being governed by "conservative Democrats elected by whites to conservative Republicans elected by whites."[16] As a result, we find that Blacks continue to receive weaker representation than Whites in southern states.

Finally, it is worth noting that the institutional legacy of the Jim Crow South lives on in sometimes subtle ways. In some cases, these legacies are policies themselves, the most important of which are not merely "sticky" but also offer permanent institutional advantages for certain political actors and coalitions.[17] A chief example is state right-to-work laws, which prohibit employment contracts that require employees to join or contribute to a union. As we and others have argued, such laws persistently disadvantage unions, Democrats, and liberal policymaking. Every state in the former Confederacy has a right-to-work law, and all except Louisiana adopted it before the voting rights revolution of the 1960s.[18] These laws thus further entrenched the South's low-wage and thinly unionized labor market just as it was about to extend political and civil rights to all of its citizens, reinforcing a political-economic trajectory that was difficult to reverse.[19]

In sum, the normative implications of our empirical conclusions are mostly positive but by no means entirely so. The dynamic responsiveness we document indicates that US states satisfy what is arguably the most important substantive criterion of democracy: popular influence over the government. While far from perfect, this responsiveness nevertheless flies in the face of the most pessimistic accounts of American democracy. Moreover, there are good reasons to believe that these optimistic conclusions can also be extended to the US federal government, which is both less constrained than state governments and more attended to by ordinary citizens.[20] At the same time, these are very much "on average" claims: averaging across policies, the typical state responds over the long term to the conservatism of the average citizen. On some issues, such as gun control, policymaking may be dominated by intense and organized minorities rather than the mass public. Some citizens, such as minorities and the poor, likely have less influence over the government than others. And in some states, such as those in the South, policies may be less responsive and more biased than elsewhere. In short, our conclusion that states are on the whole responsive to their citizens does not imply that American democracy is perfectly or uniformly responsive to its citizens.

11.2 Prospects for Reform

In chapter 9, we examined the effects of eleven state-level reforms on five aspects of the political process. Only two effects were robust enough to really trust: both direct democracy and right-to-work laws increase the conservatism of state policies, mainly in the cultural domain. Although these consequences may please conservatives, the evidence we present provides little basis for defending them on ideologically neutral grounds. Neither reform seems to affect how much influence citizens have over policymaking (responsiveness) nor the match between policies and citizens' preferences (proximity). In the case of direct democracy, there are strong theoretical arguments, as well as a good deal of empirical evidence from other sources, for positive representational effects, especially on policies where citizens and elected officials have sharply diverging interests, such as term limits.[21] Similar arguments have been made for the other reforms we examine; we just don't find convincing evidence that they systematically improve democratic performance.

Personally, we are more optimistic about reforms designed to limit partisan bias in legislative maps, such as nonpartisan districting commissions. As chapter 9 shows, when one party is advantaged in the translation of votes to seats, representation suffers. The goal of partisan gerrymandering is to maximize the advantage of the party in control. As chapter 10 shows, districting commissions limit the dominant party's ability to gerrymander: when states implement them, the effect of party control on partisan districting bias almost disappears. There is thus good circumstantial evidence suggesting that districting commissions would improve democracy, even if the direct evidence on representational effects is inconclusive.

An important reason that the effects of districting commissions and other reforms are so uncertain is lack of variation across and especially within states. Only fourteen states use some sort of commission to draw state legislative districts, and only four of these—Hawai'i, Washington, Idaho, and Arizona—implemented the reform between 1976 and 2012. Similarly, all but five states with the direct initiative adopted it by 1924, a decade before the first national opinion polls.[22] More precise causal estimates may simply not be possible until more time has passed and more states have had a chance to try these reforms. In our view, the proper attitude toward democratic reforms is a mix of openness and skepticism. Americans should continue to experiment with ways to make democracy work better while at the same time continuing to critically evaluate reforms rather than taking their efficacy on faith.

11.3 Whither State Politics?

As we have emphasized throughout, state politics is dynamic, not static. What is true of its operation at one point in time may not be true of others. Thus any given portrait of state politics, including this one, will almost certainly become outdated as time passes. It therefore behooves us to consider how future trends might change the character of state politics.

With respect to state politics, the most important developments over the past half a century have been the ideological polarization of the parties and the nationalization of American politics.[23] Though distinct phenomena, these trends have interacted with and reinforced each other in powerful ways. As national elites from the two parties have increasingly clustered around opposing poles on cultural and racial as well as economic issues, their ideological "brands" have become increasingly clear, reducing the scope for state parties to develop distinctive subnational reputations. At the same time, as the media and voters themselves have focused increasing attention on national politics at the expense of state and local politics, the electoral rewards of subnational partisan differentiation have diminished. These developments have substantially attenuated state-level politicians' ability and incentives to adapt themselves to their state electorates.

Even today, however, these developments are far from complete. In particular, minority-party candidates for governor—from Maryland Republican Larry Hogan to Kansas Democrat Laura Kelly—still regularly win elections by projecting a moderate image and, often, by taking advantage of scandal or policy overreach by the dominant party. Given that (gerrymandering aside) state legislative elections closely track the public's party loyalties, the minority party's ability to compete for the governorship provides an important check on one-party domination in the states.

If political attention and attitudes continue to nationalize, however, such victories will likely become rarer and rarer. Moreover, if the parties continue to polarize within states, policy differences between "red" and "blue" states will grow more and more distinct, possibly worsening representation in all states.[24] Under such conditions, alternative accountability mechanisms such as primary elections[25] and direct democracy,[26] both birthed in an earlier era of widespread one-party dominance, might become more important mechanisms of representation.

Another threat to the health of democracy in the states is the continuing demise of local news.[27] Across the country, newspapers are laying off journalists and reducing their coverage of state and local politics. In some places, they are even closing or reducing the numbers of days that they publish print editions.[28] The decline in news coverage of state politics has likely contributed to lower levels of knowledge about state and local officeholders and candidates.[29] This decline in knowledge about local candidates makes it harder to hold candidates accountable.[30] This is likely to lead to less split-ticket voting in gubernatorial races.[31] It is possible this will reduce the incentives for politicians to take moderate issue positions and will thus reduce policy responsiveness.[32]

On the other hand, what if these trends have already reached their apogee or countervailing trends intervene? It is possible, for example, that a relatively staid Biden presidency in the wake of the more exciting Obama and Trump ones will redirect attention away from national politics. An increase in the salience of policies largely determined at the state and local level, such as criminal justice and policing, might have a similar effect. Likewise, if left-wing interest groups and activists begin to match conservatives' recently heightened focus on state-level politics and policies,[33] public attention might follow. It is also possible that new sources of local news coverage will emerge. Finally, it should be noted that the nationalization of American politics has taken place within a particular constitutional regime in which the national government's power has been relatively untrammeled. As the persistent constitutional controversy over the Affordable Care Act indicates, however, this expansive view of federal power is under serious attack from conservatives; if these attacks succeed, the locus of policymaking (and political conflict) on issues such as health care and abortion will shift to the states.

A final caveat is in order. Our analysis has been predicated on the assumption that, aside from the South before the 1970s, state elections have been free, fair, and inclusive. In fact, it is our conviction that variations in the precise form of democratic institutions—at least those that have been tried in the United States—matter little relative to the fundamental distinction between democracy and authoritarianism. As much as it would be comforting to believe that the United States has irrevocably transitioned to democracy, democratization is always reversible. Indeed, the nation underwent just such a reversal after the failure of Reconstruction in the late nineteenth century.[34] As scholars like Steven Levitsky and Daniel Ziblatt warn, it could happen again, and with incidents such as the effort to block certification of the 2020 presidential election, in some respects it already has.[35] American democracy cannot be taken for granted but must be actively protected and sustained.

11.4 Implications for Future Research

Even if it succeeds in its ambitious mission, this book hardly represents the final word on state politics. Let us therefore suggest some promising avenues for future research. First, it bears reemphasizing what has been largely absent from our account: interest groups.[36] Although scholars such as Virginia Gray and David Lowery have shown the constellation of organized interests to be a critical factor in state politics,[37] producing dynamic measures of this construct proved impossible given the data at our disposal. It is entirely possible, however, that future research will find a way around this problem. One potentially promising data source for this and other measures is state and local newspapers, which, if mined with text-as-data methods, may yield a wealth of useful information—not least on the media itself, another feature of state politics we largely neglect.[38]

As scholars develop new measures, we hope they do not lose sight of the importance of making those measures *dynamic*. Dynamic measures are crucial not only to understanding change over time but also for credible causal inference, as we hope we have shown. That said, there are certainly opportunities to make these inferences still more credible using stronger causal research designs. Particularly valuable would be designs that leverage as-if-random variation in the policy preferences of state electorates, which would establish more firmly that the opinion–policy covariation we document is not confounded by other causes. Even the best-identified design, however, is of little use if the estimates it yields are too noisy to be informative. This again points to the importance of measurement—in particular, to the importance of measuring outcomes of interest as precisely as possible. Given the ever-expanding availability of data and the increasing sophistication of research methods, we are sure that future research will bring many new insights about democracy in the American states.

Acknowledgments

We began this project soon after we both arrived at MIT in 2012, so it has been a long time in the making, and we could not have completed it without the advice and assistance of many people.

As readers will see, the book incorporates material from collaborative research with several other scholars: James Dunham, Yiqing Xu, Chris Tausanovitch, and Nicholas Stephanopoulos, the first two of whom were graduate students at MIT. We also drew more indirectly on our collaborations with Michael Dougal, Eric Schickler, Tom O'Grady, Justin de Benedictis-Kessner, John Sides, Lynn Vavreck, Parrish Bergquist, Leah Stokes, Elissa Berwick, Clara Vanderweerdt, Hiroto Katsumata, Teppei Yamamoto, Adam Berinsky, Sara Chatfield, Erin Hartman, Jas Sekhon, and Mallory Wang. Going back further in time, we are grateful for the training and mentorship we received from our PhD advisers, Eric Schickler and Jonathan Rodden, as well as from Kevin Quinn and Simon Jackman, who introduced us to Bayesian measurement models.

We also owe a deep debt to the many research assistants who contributed to this project, without whom it would not have been possible. Particular credit goes to our research support associate Melissa Meek, whose management of the data collection for this project went far beyond the call of duty. Melissa's predecessors and successors Stephen Brown, Rob Pressel, Kathryn Treder, Anna Weissman, Laurel Bliss, and Camilla Alarcon (who proofread a draft of the manuscript with admirable care) also contributed to various stages of the project. We also benefited from the help of graduate students Meg Goldberg (MIT), Alex Copulsky (MIT), and Alex Kertz (George Washington) as well as that of undergraduate research assistants too numerous to name but no less essential. We are also grateful for the financial support from

MIT and GW that underwrote this research assistance and other aspects of the project.

Later, during the long process of writing and revising this book manuscript, we also received help from many quarters. We received feedback on versions of this project from audiences at MIT, GW, the University of Illinois, Washington University in St. Louis, Texas A&M, Georgetown, Columbia, the University of Chicago, Ohio State, Princeton, Dartmouth, Northwestern, Harvard, Rochester, Berkeley, and Yale. An amazing group of scholars agreed to participate in our book conference, including Chris Tausanovitch, Justin Phillips, Andrea Campbell, and Dave Hopkins. In addition, Robert Erikson, Thad Kousser, and Daniel Hopkins generously provided us with extensive feedback and suggestions on drafts of this manuscript. Jonathan Obert and Emily Zackin helped with brainstorming and editing at various points, and a number of our colleagues at MIT and GW provided helpful advice, especially Charles Stewart, Chris Capozzola, Eric Lawrence, Sarah Binder, and Danny Hayes. Finally, we are very grateful to our series editor Adam Berinsky for prodding us to write this book, and to Chuck Myers and Sara Doskow at University of Chicago Press for shepherding it to publication.

Finally, each of us is deeply grateful for the love, support, and patience of our families. Chris couldn't have done this project without Carolyn, Eli, and Mira, his parents Allen and Shirley Anne, and his parents-in-law Susan and Allen, and Devin feels the same about Sara, Milo, and Hazel, his parents George and Michelle, and his mother-in-law Polly.

Notes

Chapter 1

1. Novak, *The People's Welfare*, 155; Gerstle, *Liberty and Coercion*, chap. 2.

2. Teaford, *The Rise of the States*, chaps. 2–5.

3. Teaford, *Rise of the States*, chaps. 6–7; Cebul, Tani, and Williams, "Clio and the Compound Republic."

4. Valelly, *The Two Reconstructions*; Derthick, *Keeping the Compound Republic*, 17–23; Gerstle, *Liberty and Coercion*, chap. 9.

5. Lichtenstein, *State of the Union*; Kreitzer, "Politics and Morality in State Abortion Policy."

6. Sears and Citrin, *Tax Revolt*; Gais and Weaver, *State Policy Choices under Welfare Reform*; Hertel-Fernandez, *State Capture*.

7. Grossmann, *Red State Blues*.

8. Erikson, Wright, and McIver, *Statehouse Democracy*.

9. On policy responsiveness more generally, see Page and Shapiro, "Effects of Public Opinion on Policy"; Erikson, MacKuen, and Stimson, *The Macro Polity*; Soroka and Wlezien, *Degrees of Democracy*; Tausanovitch and Warshaw, "Representation in Municipal Government."

10. Erikson, Wright, and McIver, *Statehouse Democracy*, 80.

11. Erikson, Wright, and McIver, *Statehouse Democracy*, 92; see also Achen, "Measuring Representation"; Matsusaka, "Problems with a Methodology Used to Evaluate the Voter Initiative."

12. Lax and Phillips, "The Democratic Deficit in the States"; see also Matsusaka, "Popular Control of Public Policy."

13. Bartels, *Unequal Democracy*; Hajnal, *Dangerously Divided*; Rigby and Wright, "Whose Statehouse Democracy"; Schlozman, Brady, and Verba, *Unequal and Unrepresented*.

14. But see Erikson, Wright, and McIver, *Statehouse Democracy*, chap. 9.

15. Ansolabehere and Snyder, *The End of Inequality*; Mickey, *Paths Out of Dixie*.

16. Daniel Hopkins, *The Increasingly United States*; Hayes and Lawless, *News Hole*.

17. Erikson, Wright, and McIver, "Public Opinion in the States: A Quarter Century of Change and Stability"; David Hopkins, *Red Fighting Blue*; Grumbach, "From Backwaters to Major Policymakers."

18. Rogers, "Electoral Accountability for State Legislative Roll Calls and Ideological Representation."

19. Levitsky and Ziblatt, *How Democracies Die*, 2; Grumbach, *Laboratories against Democracy*.

20. Michener, *Fragmented Democracy*.

21. Rocco, Keller, and Kelly, "State Politics and the Uneven Fate of Medicaid Expansion."

22. These figures are based on our own dynamic multilevel regression and poststratification model of state-level support for the Medicaid expansion among citizens with an opinion, based on national polling data. State-specific polls have also found supermajority support. The Marquette Law School Poll, for example, found in 2019 that 71 percent of Wisconsinites with an opinion favored the Medicaid expansion; Marquette Law School Poll, "New Marquette Law School Poll Finds Some Issues Less Divisive amid Continuing Partisan Divide."

23. Kaiser Family Foundation, "Status of State Medicaid Expansion Decisions: Interactive Map."

24. In Alaska, the incumbent Republican governor was replaced by an independent. Maine's Medicaid expansion was originally approved by initiative in 2017, but the Republican governor refused to implement it, so implementation was delayed until a Democrat replaced him in 2019; Rocco, Keller, and Kelly, "State Politics and the Uneven Fate of Medicaid Expansion," online appendix, Table A2.

25. On veto points in the lawmaking process, see Krehbiel, *Pivotal Politics*. On the importance and scarcity of lawmakers' time, see R. Hall, *Participation in Congress*.

26. On budgetary incrementalism, see Wildavsky, *The Politics of the Budgetary Process*. Large, discontinuous changes are more common within individual policy subsystems, such as nuclear power; Baumgartner and Jones, "Agenda Dynamics and Policy Subsystems." But because policy punctuations are usually staggered across policy areas, change to a state's overall policy profile is still typically incremental.

27. Stimson, MacKuen, and Erikson, "Dynamic Representation."

28. Monroe, "Public Opinion and Public Policy, 1980–1993."

29. Our evidence about the small effects of most institutional reforms echoes findings in comparative politics. Rasmussen, Reher, and Toshkov's study of thirty-one European democracies finds that institutional variation has little influence on the opinion–policy link; Rasmussen, Reher, and Toshkov, "Opinion-Policy Nexus."

30. Achen and Bartels, *Democracy for Realists*.

31. For example, Dahl, *Polyarchy*; on the prevalence of elections in authoritarian regimes, see Levitsky and Way, "Elections without Democracy."

32. Achen and Bartels, *Democracy for Realists*; see also Mann and Ornstein, *It's Even Worse Than It Looks*.

33. In this respect, we are most similar to the literature on policy diffusion, which examines how and why states differ in their uptake of new policies; Walker, "The Diffusion of Innovations among the American States." This research, however, tends to be less interested in the ideological orientation of state policies and the role of mass preferences than it is in specific policy details and in factors such as geographical proximity, interstate competition, and emulation of successful policies; see, for example, Karch, "Emerging Issues and Future Directions in State Policy Diffusion Research." Integrating the largely disconnected literatures of state policy diffusion and state policy responsiveness is a promising avenue of future research. For a recent attempt to do so, see LaCombe and Boehmke, "The Initiative Process and Policy Innovation in the American States."

34. Stimson, MacKuen, and Erikson, "Dynamic Representation," 543.

Chapter 2

1. See Converse, "The Nature of Belief Systems in Mass Publics"; Poole and Rosenthal, *Ideology and Congress*.

2. McLean and Sorens, "The Changing Ideological Politics of U.S. State Firearms Regulation."

3. Lewis and Tausanovitch, "When Does Joint Scaling Allow for Direct Comparisons of Preferences?"; Broockman, "Approaches to Studying Policy Representation"; Jessee, "(How) Can We Estimate the Ideology of Citizens and Political Elites on the Same Scale?"

4. Walker, "The Diffusion of Innovations among the American States"; Boehmke and Skinner, "State Policy Innovativeness Revisited."

5. Hofferbert, "The Relation between Public Policy and Some Structural and Environmental Variables in the American States"; Klingman and Lammers, "The 'General Policy Liberalism' Factor in American State Politics"; Wright, Erikson, and McIver, "Public Opinion and Policy Liberalism in the American States"; Gray et al., "Public Opinion, Public Policy, and Organized Interests in the American States."

6. Ansolabehere, Rodden, and Snyder, "The Strength of Issues."

7. Achen, "Mass Political Attitudes and the Survey Response"; Zaller and Feldman, "A Simple Theory of the Survey Response."

8. Converse, "Popular Representation and the Distribution of Information."

9. Page and Shapiro, *The Rational Public*, 19–23.

10. Sorens, Muedini, and Ruger, "US State and Local Public Policies in 2006"; cf. Sharkansky and Hofferbert, "Dimensions of State Politics, Economics, and Public Policy"; Hopkins and Weber, "Dimensions of Public Policies in the American States."

11. For further details, see Caughey and Warshaw, "The Dynamics of State Policy Liberalism, 1936–2014," 902–3.

12. For example, Bartels, "Democracy with Attitudes."

13. Our usage of *preferences* is thus similar to what Bartels calls *attitudes*; see Bartels, "Democracy with Attitudes," 52.

14. Converse, "Nature of Belief Systems."

15. Tversky and Kahneman, "The Framing of Decisions and the Psychology of Choice."

16. Rasinski, "The Effect of Question Wording on Public Support for Government Spending," 391.

17. Schuman, "Ordinary Questions, Survey Questions, and Policy Questions."

18. Berry, Fording, and Hanson, "An Annual Cost of Living Index for the American States, 1960–1995."

19. For an overview, see Caughey et al., *Target Estimation and Adjustment Weighting for Survey Nonresponse and Sampling Bias*.

20. An additional complication is that pollsters often sought to make their samples representative of the *electorate* rather than the whole adult population. On quota sampling generally, see Berinsky, "American Public Opinion in the 1930s and 1940s."

21. For an exception, see Norrander, "Measuring State Public Opinion with the Senate National Election Study"; for overviews, see Cohen, *Public Opinion in State Politics*; Caughey and Warshaw, "Public Opinion in Subnational Politics."

22. This is true, for example, of multistage area samples such as the ANES, which is designed to be representative at the regional rather than state level; see Stoker and Bowers, "Designing Multi-Level Studies."

23. For example, Wright, Erikson, and McIver, "Measuring State Partisanship and Ideology with Survey Data."

24. Gelman and Little, "Poststratification into Many Categories Using Hierarchical Logistic Regression"; Park, Gelman, and Bafumi, "Bayesian Multilevel Estimation with Poststratification."

25. Lax and Phillips, "How Should We Estimate Public Opinion in the States?"; Warshaw and Rodden, "How Should We Measure District-Level Public Opinion on Individual Issues?"; but see Buttice and Highton, "How Does Multilevel Regression and Poststratification Perform with Conventional National Surveys?"; Caughey and Warshaw, "Public Opinion in Subnational Politics."

26. For example, Lax and Phillips, "Democratic Deficit."

27. Broockman, "Approaches to Studying Policy Representation."

28. More precisely, each of their discrimination parameters is estimated to be close to the geometric mean discrimination across items.

29. Another reason we plot the unmodeled estimates in figure 2.6 is that the dynamic MRP model used in figure 2.5 includes the mass conservatism scales as predictors, and so plotting the modeled estimates runs the risk of overstating the correlation between mass conservatism and issue-specific opinion.

30. For slightly different implementations of dynamic MRP models for individual issues, see Pacheco, "Using national surveys to measure dynamic US state public opinion"; Shirley and Gelman. "Hierarchical models for estimating state and demographic trends in US death penalty public opinion."

31. For example, wage and price controls during the Nixon administration; Cowie, *Stayin' Alive*, 151–52.

32. Given the standard identification restrictions for ordered probit models, within-group variation can be ignored in the single-issue model because it is absorbed into the threshold parameters.

33. Mislevy, "Item Response Models for Grouped Data," 277.

34. Specifically, we assume that θ_i, the conservatism of individual citizens i in group g, is distributed normally with mean $\bar{\theta}_{gt}$ and standard deviation σ_{θ_t}.

35. For details on the group-level ordinal IRT model, see Caughey, O'Grady, and Warshaw, "Policy Ideology in European Mass Publics, 1981–2016."

36. Recall that $\alpha_{qtK} = \infty$; thus the second term is $\Phi(-\infty) = 0$.

37. Although β_q^2 also appears in the denominator as well as the numerator, the derivative of π_{gqkt} with respect to $\bar{\theta}_{gt}$ is still strictly increasing in the absolute value of β_q.

38. Quinn, "Bayesian Factor Analysis for Mixed Ordinal and Continuous Responses."

Chapter 3

1. This chapter is based partly on joint work with James Dunham. See Caughey, Dunham, and Warshaw, "The Ideological Nationalization of Partisan Subconstituencies in the American States."

2. Beck, "What Was Liberalism in the 1950s?," 240.

3. On the parties' ambiguous stances on civil rights in the 1950s, see Carmines and Stimson, *Issue Evolution*, chap. 2; Schickler, *Racial Realignment*, chaps. 9–10.

4. It is probably no coincidence that Anthony Downs's pioneering *An Economic Theory of Democracy* (1957), which argued that parties competing along a single ideological dimension will converge on the position of the median voter, was published just after this election.

5. Angus Campbell et al., *The American Voter*; Converse, "Nature of Belief Systems."

6. For a comparison of elite and mass polarization, see Hill and Tausanovitch, "A Disconnect in Representation?"

7. We borrow this term from Abramowitz, *The Great Alignment*.

8. The ANES has fielded some panel surveys, but the longest of these spans only half a decade. The cluster-sampled design of the ANES is not designed to yield representative samples from each state. Even if the samples were representative, they would be too small for reliable inference (the typical margin of error for state-level percentages is about ±15%).

9. This is consistent with Layman and Carsey's contention that partisan realignment has extended partisan cleavages into new domains without displacing old ones. See Layman and Carsey, "Party Polarization and 'Conflict Extension'"; cf. Schattschneider, *The Semisovereign People*.

10. This is consistent with Wright and Birkhead's findings with respect to partisanship and symbolic ideology. See Wright and Birkhead, "The Macro Sort of the State Electorates."

11. Daniel Hopkins, *Increasingly United States*.

12. Green, Palmquist, and Schickler, *Partisan Hearts and Minds*, 77.

13. Sears and Funk, "Evidence of the Long-Term Persistence of Adults' Political Predispositions."

14. Stoker and Jennings, "Of Time and the Development of Partisan Polarization," 263.

15. Layman and Carsey, "Party Polarization and Party Structuring of Policy Attitudes"; Highton and Kam, "The Long-Term Dynamics of Partisanship and Issue Orientations."

16. MacKuen, Erikson, and Stimson, "Macropartisanship."

17. Note that unlike figure 3.1, these analyses are based on state-level estimates of partisanship rather than individual-level data.

18. White southerners began to abandon their Democratic partisanship once it became clear that the party of their forebears was no longer more committed to the defense of White supremacy than were the Republicans; see Green, Palmquist, and Schickler, *Partisan Hearts and Minds*, chap. 6. As two-party competition reemerged in the region, upper-class White southerners tended to switch to the Republican Party before lower-class ones did; see Shafer and Johnston, *The End of Southern Exceptionalism*. See also Kuziemko and Washington, "Why Did the Democrats Lose the South? Bringing New Data to an Old Debate."

19. The growth of Independents to a position of rough parity with Democrats and Republicans did not indicate wholesale dealignment of the electorate. As Keith et al. note, most Independents "lean" toward one party, and their political behavior is often indistinguishable from weak party identifiers. This is not to say that the rise of Independents has been inconsequential. As Klar and Krupnikov argue, Independents' reluctance to identify with either party, even if they routinely support one over the other, is symptomatic of a broader disenchantment with parties generally and disengagement from important forms of political behavior. See Keith et al., "The Partisan Affinities of Independent 'Leaners'"; Klar and Krupnikov, *Independent Politics*.

20. The correlation between the second and third periods is 0.63, lower than between the first and second. The greater partisan instability in the latter portion of this period is consistent with Highton and Kam's finding that at the individual level, the stability of PID relative to issue orientations declined in the last quarter of the twentieth century; Highton and Kam, "Long-Term Dynamics."

21. Converse, "Nature of Belief Systems."

22. Achen and Bartels, *Democracy for Realists*.

23. Abortion is often cited as an exception; see, for example, Killian and Wilcox, "Do Abortion Attitudes Lead to Party Switching?"

24. Page and Shapiro, *The Rational Public*. See also Rodden, *Why Cities Lose*, which shows largely parallel trends in mass ideology between urban, suburban, and rural areas.

25. Stimson, *Public Opinion in America*.

26. Wlezien, "The Public as Thermostat: Dynamics of Preferences for Spending"; see also Atkinson et al., *The Dynamics of Public Opinion*.

27. Caughey, O'Grady, and Warshaw, "Policy Ideology in European Mass Publics."

28. The brief uptick in racial conservatism before 1950 was driven entirely by a seventeen-point decline between 1942 and 1948 in support for integrating the US military—one of only two racial items to bridge pre- and post-1947.

29. On the persistence of White southerners' racial conservatism, see Valentino and Sears, "Old Times There Are Not Forgotten."

30. Burnham, "Party Systems and the Political Process."

31. Layman and Carsey, "Party Polarization and 'Conflict Extension.'"

32. Layman and Carsey, "Party Polarization and Party Structuring"; Layman et al., "Activists and Conflict Extension in American Party Politics."

33. Caughey, Dougal, and Schickler, "Policy and Performance in the New Deal Realignment."

34. Wright and Birkhead, "Macro Sort"; see also Erikson, Wright, and McIver, "Public Opinion in the States."

35. The analyses in this section were originally reported in Caughey, Dunham, and Warshaw, "Ideological Nationalization."

36. By the late 1930s, Democrats outside the South were already more racially liberal than same-state Republicans; see Schickler, "New Deal Liberalism and Racial Liberalism in the Mass Public, 1937–1968."

37. Without this assumption, we could not distinguish changes in mass conservatism from changes in how well conservatism predicts item-specific survey responses.

38. Within each year, we used analysis of variance to decompose variation in conservatism across subconstituencies into between-party and within-party components. The proportion of variation explained by party is the between-party sum of squares divided by the total sum of squares.

39. Schickler, *Racial Realignment*; Black and Black, *The Rise of Southern Republicans*.

40. Wilson, *The Amateur Democrat*; Rosenfeld, *The Polarizers*.

41. Daniel Hopkins, *Increasingly United States*; Hayes and Lawless, *News Hole*.

Chapter 4

1. Idaho's brief experiment with a sales tax was rejected by popular referendum in 1936; see Idaho Secretary of State, Election Division, "Idaho Initiative History."

2. Weatherby and Stapilus, *Governing Idaho*, 46.

3. Pearson, "Saying Yes to Taxes."

4. In constant 2012 dollars, normalized by state differences in cost of living.

5. Bryan, *Yankee Politics in Rural Vermont*, 123.

6. The percentage of Vermonters who had been born in other states increased from 27 percent in 1960 to 54 percent in 2000, and fewer than 20 percent of these newcomers were born in states outside the Northeast; see Aisch, Gebeloff, and Quealy, "Where We Came From and Where We Went, State by State."

7. Vermont was one of the most malapportioned states in the country in the 1940s and 1950s; David and Eisenberg, *Devaluation of the Urban and Suburban Vote*. Due to gains in representation for urban and suburban voters, the establishment of equipopulous districts in Vermont led to a leftward shift in the median district in the state; Ansolabehere and Snyder, *End of Inequality*, 301.

8. Weatherby and Stapilus, *Governing Idaho*, 55–56.

9. Bloom, *How States Shaped Postwar America*, 21; Saxon, "Deane Chandler Davis."

10. Bryan, *Yankee Politics in Rural Vermont*, 119–20; Saxon, "Deane Chandler Davis."

11. Weatherby and Stapilus, *Governing Idaho*, 198–99.

12. Weatherby and Stapilus, *Governing Idaho*, 183–84.

13. Witt and Moncrief, "Religion and Roll Call Voting in Idaho"; Weatherby and Stapilus, *Governing Idaho*, 205–7.

14. Goodnough, "Gay Rights Groups Celebrate Victories in Marriage Push."

15. See Baumgartner and Jones, *Agendas and Instability in American Politics*.

16. For intuition on why an evolving-difficulty model fits the data better than a constant-difficulty model, imagine a data set with just two policies: legal abortion and same-sex marriage. Suppose that for both policies, states' probability of adoption is predicted perfectly by their policy ideology. For abortion, each state's probability is constant across time, but for same-sex marriage it increases over time from near zero to near one. Legal abortion poses no problem for the constant-difficulty model, but no single difficulty value for same-sex marriage will fit the data well. A low difficulty value will overestimate adoption early on, when few states have done so, and a high value will understate adoption later on. The evolving-difficulty model avoids this problem by allowing the difficulty parameter to be high in years when the adoption probability is low and low when the probability is high.

17. For opposing views of Republicans' success in shrinking state governments, see Hertel-Fernandez, *State Capture*; Grossmann, *Red State Blues*.

18. See Grumbach, "From Backwaters to Major Policymakers."

19. For the distinction between extremity and consistency, see Broockman, "Approaches to Studying Policy Representation."

20. Jennings, "Some Policy Consequences of the Long Revolution and Bifactional Rivalry in Louisiana"; Mayhew, *Placing Parties in American Politics*, 268, 279.

21. Erikson, Wright, and McIver, "Political Parties, Public Opinion, and State Policy in the United States."

22. For example, Dye, *Politics, Economics, and the Public*.

23. Specifically, the party control index indicates how many of the following Republicans control: the governorship, the state house, and the state senate.

Chapter 5

1. This chapter is based partly on joint work with Chris Tausanovitch and Yiqing Xu. Caughey, Tausanovitch, and Warshaw, "Partisan Gerrymandering and the Political Process"; Caughey, Warshaw, and Xu, "Incremental Democracy."

2. Cain, "Sunday Q&A with James B. Alcorn, State Board of Elections Chairman"; Vozzella, "A Rare, Random Drawing Helped Republicans Win a Tied Virginia Election but It May Not End There"; Gabriel, "Virginia Official Pulls Republican's Name from Bowl to Pick Winner of Tied Race."

3. Scott, "What Virginia's Drawing-Bowl Tiebreaker Means for the State's Medicaid Expansion."

4. "How an Election in 1991 Led to Virginia's 2018 Medicaid Vote."

5. Goodnough, "After Years of Trying, Virginia Finally Will Expand Medicaid." Kousser, Lewis, and Masket document a similar ideological adaptation to the right among California state legislators after the surprising success of California's 2003 recall election against Democrat Gray Davis; see Kousser, Lewis, and Masket, "Ideological Adaptation?"

6. Roemer, *Political Competition*; Grofman, "Downs and Two-Party Convergence."

7. Gerring, *Party Ideologies in America, 1828–1996*.

8. Poole and Rosenthal, "The Polarization of American Politics"; Erikson, Wright, and McIver, "Political Parties, Public Opinion, and State Policy"; Shor and McCarty, "The Ideological Mapping of American Legislatures."

9. For example, Alesina, Londregan, and Rosenthal, "A Model of the Political Economy of the United States."

10. McCarty, Poole, and Rosenthal, *Polarized America*.

11. Noel, *Political Ideologies and Political Parties in America*.

12. Hill and Tausanovitch, "A Disconnect in Representation?"

13. For example, Adams and Merrill, "Candidate and Party Strategies in Two-Stage Elections Beginning with a Primary."

14. For example, Cadigan and Janeba, "A Citizen-Candidate Model with Sequential Elections"; Thomsen, "Ideological Moderates Won't Run."

15. Jacobson, "The Electoral Origins of Polarized Politics."

16. Other factors, too, have probably contributed to an increase in partisan effects on policy. For example, policy effects in state legislatures should depend on the degree to which the majority party can use its control to skew policy outcomes away from the median legislator in the chamber; for example, Cox, Kousser, and McCubbins, "Party Power or Preferences?" Over the past half a century, there is a variety of evidence that the two parties in Congress have leveraged their greater homogeneity into strong formal mechanisms of party discipline and control, enhancing the majority's influence over policymaking; Aldrich and Rohde, "The Consequences of Party Organization in the House." Given that state legislatures have polarized, too, it is plausible that party power has increased there as well; Shor and McCarty, "Ideological Mapping"; but see Mooney, "Measuring State House Speakers' Formal Powers, 1981–2010," who finds no evidence that the formal powers of state speakers have increased since 1981.

17. See the literature reviewed in Caughey, Warshaw, and Xu, "Incremental Democracy."

18. Pettersson-Lidbom, "Do Parties Matter for Economic Outcomes?"; D. Lee, "Randomized Experiments from Non-random Selection in US House Elections."

19. Hyytinen et al., "When Does Regression Discontinuity Design Work?"

20. But see Caughey and Sekhon, "Elections and the Regression Discontinuity Design."

21. We say "typically" because it is possible for election outcomes to affect policy through other channels, such as by electing candidates with differing levels of competence, though this would be unlikely to produce large ideological differences in policymaking.

22. Bonica, "Inferring Roll-Call Scores from Campaign Contributions Using Supervised Machine Learning." We obtain nearly identical results if we instead employ Aldrich-McKelvey scores, a survey-based measure of citizens' perceptions of the governor's conservatism; Ramey, "Vox Populi, Vox Dei?"

23. All our RD analyses use the R package rdrobust to select regression bandwidths and estimate treatment effects and robust confidence intervals. Calonico et al., *rdrobust: Robust Data Driven Statistical Inference in Regression-Discontinuity Designs*.

24. Shor and McCarty, "Ideological Mapping."

25. Feigenbaum, Fouirnaies, and Hall, "The Majority-Party Disadvantage."

26. For details, see Caughey, Tausanovitch, and Warshaw, "Partisan Gerrymandering."

27. Krehbiel, *Pivotal Politics.*

28. Erikson, Wright, and McIver, "Political Parties, Public Opinion, and State Policy," 737.

29. Caughey, Dunham, and Warshaw, "Ideological Nationalization"; see also Poole and Rosenthal, "The Polarization of American Politics."

30. Henderson, "Issue Distancing in Congressional Elections."

31. F. Lee, *Beyond Ideology.*

32. Nearly identical results are obtained if we estimate the effect on a one-dimensional measure of policy conservatism that pools policies from the two domains. They are also the same if, instead taking the first difference, we adjust for lagged policy conservatism using the method of Calonico et al., "Regression Discontinuity Designs Using Covariates."

33. Jacobson, "Electoral Origins."

34. McCarty, Poole, and Rosenthal attribute over three-quarters of contemporary congressional polarization to "intradistrict divergence" and less than a quarter to "sorting" of Democratic and Republican members into ideologically congenial districts; McCarty, Poole, and Rosenthal, "Does Gerrymandering Cause Polarization?"

35. Grumbach, "From Backwaters to Major Policymakers."

36. More generally, see Michener, *Fragmented Democracy.*

37. Cf. Poole and Rosenthal, "The Polarization of American Politics," 1061.

38. Caughey, Warshaw, and Xu, "Incremental Democracy," 1355.

39. *Time,* "The Lonely One"; Usher, "The Lausche Era, 1945–1957"; A. Chen, *The Fifth Freedom,* 165, 273.

40. Fausset, "North Carolina, in Political Flux, Battles for Its Identity."

Chapter 6

1. See Ladd, "The 1994 Congressional Elections."

2. Stimson, *Public Opinion in America.*

3. *New York Times,* "The 1994 Elections," B9.

4. *New York Times,* "The 1994 Elections," B11.

5. "Ben Nelson (D)," in *The Almanac of American Politics.*

6. *New York Times,* "The 1994 Elections," B9.

7. Alesina, Londregan, and Rosenthal, "A Model of the Political Economy of the United States"; Bafumi, Erikson, and Wlezien, "Balancing, Generic Polls and Midterm Congressional Elections."

8. *New York Times,* "The 1994 Elections," B11. The generally greater success of Democratic incumbents in the adverse environment may be attributable not only to the usual sources of the incumbency advantage but also to the fact that they could back up their (popular) campaign positions with their demonstrated record in office, making their positions more credible than those of challengers. On campaign promises and commitment problems, see Alesina, "Credibility and Policy Convergence in a Two-Party System with Rational Voters."

9. Manin, Przeworski, and Stokes, "Elections and Representation."

10. Fearon, "Electoral Accountability and the Control of Politicians."

11. For example, Besley and Coate, "An Economic Model of Representative Democracy."

12. Snyder and Ting, "Roll Calls, Party Labels, and Elections."

13. Fearon, "Electoral Accountability and the Control of Politicians"; Ashworth, "Electoral Accountability."

14. Jennings and Zeigler, "The Salience of American State Politics"; Daniel Hopkins, *Increasingly United States.*

15. Rogers, "National Forces in State Legislative Elections"; Rogers, "Electoral Accountability."

16. For a very similar figure, see Rogers, "National Forces."

17. Berry, Berkman, and Schneiderman, "Legislative Professionalism and Incumbent Reelection"; Rogers, "National Forces"; Benedictis-Kessner and Warshaw, "Accountability for the Local Economy at All Levels of Government in United States Elections."

18. The Republican control index indicates how many of the three main institutions of state government—the governorship, state house, and state senate—are controlled by the Republican Party.

19. Hopkins, *The Increasingly United States*; Rogers, "National Forces"; Rogers, "Electoral Accountability." See also Tausanovitch, "Why Are Subnational Governments Responsive?"

20. MacKuen, Erikson, and Stimson, "Macropartisanship."

21. Achen and Bartels, *Democracy for Realists.*

22. A regression of the Republican control index on state mass Republicanism and national change in Republican US House share has an R^2 of 0.49. If separate intercepts for each election year are substituted in the place of change in House share, the variance explained increases to 0.56.

23. Treier and Jackman, "Democracy as a Latent Variable," 215–16.

24. These are in models that do not propagate uncertainty in the policy ideology scores. As chapter 8 notes, individual policies are even more persistent across time than policy ideology scores.

25. Erikson, Wright, and McIver, "Political Parties, Public Opinion, and State Policy."

26. Snyder and Ting, "Roll Calls, Party Labels, and Elections."

27. Ansolabehere, Snyder, and Stewart, "Candidate Positioning in U.S. House Elections"; A. Hall, "What Happens When Extremists Win Primaries?"

28. Canes-Wrone, Brady, and Cogan, "Out of Step, Out of Office: Electoral Accountability and House Members' Voting."

29. Wilkins, "Is Polarization Hurting the Re-election Prospects of US House Incumbents?"; Bonica and Cox, "Ideological Extremists in the US Congress"; Tausanovitch and Warshaw, "Does the Ideological Proximity between Candidates and Voters Affect Voting in US House Elections?"

30. Rogers, "Electoral Accountability."

31. Bonica, "Inferring Roll-Call Scores." We use these scores instead of Bonica's better-known CF scores because the latter do not discriminate as well within party; Bonica, "Mapping the Ideological Marketplace"; Tausanovitch and Warshaw, "Estimating Candidates' Political Orientation in a Polarized Congress."

32. Poole and Rosenthal, *Ideology and Congress.*

33. For a similar measure, see A. Hall, "What Happens"; Hall and Snyder, "Candidate Ideology and Electoral Success."

34. Shor and McCarty, "Ideological Mapping."

35. Canes-Wrone, Brady, and Cogan, "Out of Step, Out of Office: Electoral Accountability and House Members' Voting."

36. Erikson, Wright, and McIver, "Political Parties, Public Opinion, and State Policy," 744.

37. We pool Democratic and Republican candidates in the same model, resulting in two observations per constituency-election. This "double-counting" does not artificially decrease our uncertainty estimates because we cluster standard errors by state or district-decade. The results are very similar if we instead use the midpoint between the candidates' ideological scores. The advantage of the double-observation approach is that we do not have to drop elections where one candidate's score is missing.

38. More precisely, it is equivalent to moving from about the fifteenth percentile of a party's ideological distribution to the eighty-fifth percentile.

39. It is possible that these apparent effects are due to parties' tendency to nominate relatively moderate candidates in races where they already have a better chance of winning, but evidence from US House elections suggests that they are at least partly causal; see A. Hall, "What Happens"; Hall and Thompson, "Who Punishes Extremist Nominees?"

40. Shorman, "The Brownback Legacy."

41. Carpenter, "New Poll Ranks Gov. Sam Brownback as Nation's Least Popular Governor."

42. Yglesias, "How Did Democrats Lose Maryland?"

43. Pierson, "When Effect Becomes Cause"; Andrea Campbell, "Policy Makes Mass Politics"; but see Patashnik and Zelizer, "The Struggle to Remake Politics."

44. Stimson, *Public Opinion in America.*

45. Wlezien, "The Public as Thermostat"; Soroka and Wlezien, *Degrees of Democracy.*

46. Erikson, "The Puzzle of Midterm Loss," 1014.

47. Fiorina, "The Reagan Years: Turning to the Right or Groping for the Middle?"

48. Alesina and Rosenthal, *Partisan Politics, Divided Government, and the Economy*; Mebane, "Coordination, Moderation, and Institutional Balancing in American Presidential and House Elections."

49. Pacheco, "The Thermostatic Model of Responsiveness in the American States."

50. Langehennig, Zamadics, and Wolak, "State Policy Outcomes and State Legislative Approval"; see also Flavin, "Policy Representation and Evaluations of State Government."

51. Our analyses here replicate those of Folke and Snyder, "Gubernatorial Midterm Slumps"; Feigenbaum, Fouirnaies, and Hall, "Majority-Party Disadvantage"; see also Erikson, Folke, and Snyder, "A Gubernatorial Helping Hand?"

52. As in chapter 5, we use a multidimensional regression-discontinuity (MRD) design to estimate the effects of legislative control.

53. We do not examine the governor's effect on the next governor's election because any negative feedback to party control is masked by the governor's personal incumbency advantage. This is also true for state legislative majorities, but in that case the effect of personal incumbency is much smaller because the seats that distinguish a narrow Republican from a narrow Democratic majority compose a very small proportion of the party's total number of seats. For evidence that the partisan incumbency advantage is small or possibly negative, see Fowler and Hall, "Disentangling the Personal and Partisan Incumbency Advantages."

54. Folke and Snyder, "Gubernatorial Midterm Slumps."

Chapter 7

1. For example, Achen, "Measuring Representation"; Huber and Powell, "Congruence between Citizens and Policymakers in Two Visions of Liberal Democracy."

2. Cf. Achen, "Measuring Representation."

3. In the sense of Dahl, "The Concept of Power."

4. Matsusaka, "Problems with a Methodology."

5. For example, Simonovits, Guess, and Nagler, "Responsiveness without Representation."

6. Bafumi and Herron, "Leapfrog Representation and Extremism"; Lax and Phillips, "Democratic Deficit."

7. Hill and Huber, "On the Meaning of Survey Reports of Roll-Call 'Votes.'"

8. Lewis and Tausanovitch, "When Does Joint Scaling"; Jessee, "(How) Can We Estimate."

9. Partisan adaptation itself can occur via two mechanisms: through the selective attrition of officials within each party or through candidates' preemptive adaptation in anticipation of electoral sanctions.

10. For similar figures, see Erikson, Wright, and McIver, "Political Parties, Public Opinion, and State Policy"; Ansolabehere, Snyder, and Stewart, "Candidate Positioning."

11. For a description of the Shor-McCarty scores of state legislators' ideological preferences, see Shor and McCarty, "Ideological Mapping."

12. For a description of DW-DIME scores, see Bonica, "Inferring Roll-Call Scores."

13. In this chapter, we define the South as the eleven former Confederate states, not including Kentucky and Oklahoma. We do so because the political systems of the core southern states were qualitatively different from those of border states, particularly with regard to their lack of partisan competition before the 1960s; see, for example, Key, *Southern Politics in State and Nation.*

14. In this model the state FEs and lagged dependent variables are also interacted with era.

15. Lax and Phillips, "Democratic Deficit"; Grumbach, "Laboratories of Democratic Backsliding."

16. Caughey, *The Unsolid South*; Olson and Snyder, "Dyadic Representation in the American North and South."

17. We do not control for mass Republicanism in these models because doing so would force us to drop years before 1946. However, if we do so the results are similar, with the main difference being that the coefficients for mass cultural conservatism before 1970 are attenuated to statistical insignificance.

18. The results are also similar if we estimate the indirect effect by multiplying the effects of mass conservatism on Republican control and Republican control on policy conservatism.

19. If it did, we would expect the effect of mass conservatism in years following an election to be substantially larger than the effect in all years conditional on party control.

20. Ansolabehere, Snyder, and Stewart, "Candidate Positioning."

21. See also Grumbach, "From Backwaters to Major Policymakers."

22. Franses, "Distributed Lags"; De Boef and Keele, "Taking Time Seriously."

23. Erikson, Wright, and McIver, *Statehouse Democracy*, 80.

24. But see Stimson, MacKuen, and Erikson, "Dynamic Representation"; Soroka and Wlezien, *Degrees of Democracy*; Pacheco, "Thermostatic Model."

Chapter 8

1. Achen, "Measuring Representation"; Matsusaka, "Popular Control"; Lax and Phillips, "Democratic Deficit"; Burstein, *American Public Opinion, Advocacy, and Policy in Congress.*

2. Achen, "Measuring Representation."

3. Lax and Phillips, "Democratic Deficit"; see also Matsusaka, "Popular Control"; but see Hare and Monogan, "The Democratic Deficit on Salient Issues: Immigration and Healthcare in the States."

4. Lax and Phillips, "Gay Rights in the States: Public Opinion and Policy Responsiveness."

5. On climate-related public opinion and policies, see Sekar, "Misrepresented: Understanding the Gap between US Public Opinion and Policy on Climate Change"; Stokes, *Short Circuiting Policy*.

6. For instance, a March 2019 Gallup poll indicated that 60 percent of Americans support policies to "dramatically reduce the use of fossil fuels such as gas, oil and coal in the US within the next 10 or 20 years, in order to reduce greenhouse gas emissions."

7. For a recent review of climate change policies in the states, see Bromley-Trujillo and Holman, *Climate Change Policymaking in the States*.

8. For example, Monroe, "Public Opinion and Public Policy, 1980–1993."

9. Lax and Phillips, "Democratic Deficit," 156–57.

10. On many policy issues, we found that there was no recently available public polling. As a result, we have conducted several original surveys over the past few years to assess public opinion on a number of state policies.

11. Burstein, "The Impact of Public Opinion on Public Policy," 38.

12. Hare and Monogan, "The Democratic Deficit on Salient Issues."

13. Like the plots in figure 8.1, the models predict whether a state has the conservative option on a given policy as a function of public support for that option, plus "random effects" (REs) for state, year, and policy. The REs function similarly to the fixed effects we employ in other models but have the benefit of being centered at 0, making the model's intercept more interpretable. If we also center the issue-specific support at 0.5, the intercept corresponds to the expected policy outcome when opinion is evenly split—that is, the ideological bias.

14. For the diffusion of abortion restrictions after Roe, see Kreitzer, "Politics and Morality in State Abortion Policy."

15. In linear versions of these models, the LDV coefficient on lagged policy is around 0.95, indicating very strong persistence across years.

16. It is important to note, however, that our public opinion data tends to be heavily weighted toward the present. By the time our opinion data is available, many policies with initially conservative policy status quos had trended toward liberal adoption. For instance, when our study begins in 1936, Colorado was the only state that had departed from the original status quo of no protections for older workers against workplace discrimination and adopted a ban on age discrimination. By 2019, though, when public opinion on age discrimination is available for the first time, nearly all states had bans on age discrimination; Neumark, "Age Discrimination Legislation in the United States"; Lahey, "State Age Protection Laws and the Age Discrimination in Employment Act." As a result of this recency bias in the availability of public opinion, in the first year that opinion and policy data are available for each issue, policy is conservative about 56 percent of the time.

17. See, for example, Hertel-Fernandez, *State Capture*.

18. Grossmann, *Red State Blues*.

19. Bias is one potential cause of poor proximity, but it is not the only one. As Lax and Phillips note, proximity can also suffer if governments are *over*responsive to the general ideological leanings of the public; Lax and Phillips, "Democratic Deficit"; see also Erikson, Wright, and McIver, *Statehouse Democracy*, 93; Bafumi and Herron, "Leapfrog Representation."

20. Formally, if $y_{ps} \in \{0,1\}$ indicates whether state s has policy p, x_{pi} indicates whether citizen i favors that policy, and N_s is the number of citizens in s, then agreement$_{ps} \equiv N_s^{-1} \sum_{i \in s}^{N_s} \mathbf{1}_{\{y_{ps} = x_{pi}\}}$. This quantity is equivalent to 1 minus the mean squared difference between y_{ps} and x_{pi}, which

is the measure of proximity proposed by Achen, "Measuring Representation," 484. We take the term "agreement" from Anonymous, "The Limits of Representation," which apparently derived this formula independently and whose authorship we have been unable to determine.

21. Formally, congruence$_{ps} \equiv \mathbf{1}_{|\text{agreement}_{ps} > 0.5|}$. This is the measure of proximity used in Lax and Phillips, "Democratic Deficit" and Matsusaka, "Popular Control" as well as studies of congressional representation such as Broockman, "Approaches to Studying Policy Representation" and Krimmel, Lax, and Phillips, "Gay Rights in Congress."

22. Lax and Phillips, "Democratic Deficit."

23. Our congruence estimate is closer to that found by Matsusaka in his study of ten state policies (59 percent); Matsusaka. "Popular Control."

24. Rasmussen, Reher, and Toshkov, "Opinion-Policy Nexus."

25. Lax and Phillips, "Democratic Deficit," 157.

26. Hare and Monogan, "The Democratic Deficit on Salient Issues"; see also Bisbee, "BARP."

27. Agreement follows a similar pattern.

28. Unlike figure 8.4, there is no obvious evidence of nonlinearity over time.

29. Lacombe, "The Political Weaponization of Gun Owners"; Hill, *Frustrated Majorities*.

30. Gilens and Page, "Testing Theories of American Politics."

Chapter 9

1. This chapter is based in part on joint work with Chris Tausanovitch and Nicholas Stephanopoulos. Caughey, Tausanovitch, and Warshaw, "Partisan Gerrymandering"; Stephanopoulos and Warshaw, "The Impact of Partisan Gerrymandering on Political Parties."

2. O'Donnell, "On the State, Democratization and Some Conceptual Problems," 1359.

3. Berlin, *Many Thousands Gone*; Smith, *Civic Ideals*; Wortman, *From Colonial Times to the New Deal*; Keyssar, *The Right to Vote*.

4. For an overview, see Dahl, *How Democratic Is the American Constitution?*, 26–31.

5. Valelly, *Two Reconstructions*, 1–2; see also Bateman, *Disenfranchising Democracy*; King et al., *Democratization in America*.

6. Anderson, *One Person, No Vote*; Gilens, *Affluence and Influence*; Levitsky and Ziblatt, *How Democracies Die*; Weaver and Prowse, "Racial Authoritarianism in U.S. Democracy"; Grumbach, "Laboratories of Democratic Backsliding."

7. For more on inequalities in representation, see, for example, Bartels, *Unequal Democracy*; Gilens, "Inequality and Democratic Responsiveness"; Hajnal, *Dangerously Divided*; Rigby and Wright, "Whose Statehouse Democracy"; Schaffner, Rhodes, and La Raja, *Hometown Inequality*; Brunner, Ross, and Washington, "Does Less Income Mean Less Representation"?; Erikson, "Income Inequality and Policy Responsiveness."

8. Mickey, *Paths Out of Dixie*, 54–58.

9. Brown-Dean et al., *50 Years of the Voting Rights Act*; for a compelling quantitative analysis of the racially disparate effects of various suffrage restrictions and of the important role of local discretion, see Keele, Cubbison, and White, "Suppressing Black Votes."

10. Fraga, *The Turnout Gap*, 85–86.

11. Cox and Katz, *Elbridge Gerry's Salamander*.

12. McGhee, "Partisan Gerrymandering and Political Science."

13. Key, *Southern Politics*.

14. Farhang and Katznelson, "The Southern Imposition," 1n1.

15. Caughey, *Unsolid South.*

16. Olson and Snyder, "Dyadic Representation."

17. Mickey, *Paths Out of Dixie.*

18. The data in figure 9.1 are based on administrative data on voter registration shown in United States Commission on Civil Rights, *Hearings Before the United States Commission on Civil Rights*, 243, table 1; James, "The Transformation of Local State and Class Structures and Resistance to the Civil Rights Movement in the South," 460–61, table 6.1 and 6.2; and various volumes of the Census Bureau's Statistical Abstracts series. Administrative registration data during this period was imperfect, but Stanley obtains similar estimates from survey data; see Stanley, *Voter Mobilization and the Politics of Race*, 151–54 and table 24.

19. See also Fraga, *Turnout Gap*, 85–86.

20. See earlier sources for registration trends; for voting trends, see Fraga, *Turnout Gap*, 43.

21. For a similar figure, Alt, "The Impact of the Voting Rights Act on Black and White Voter Registration in the South," figure 12.2. The data for Arkansas in the 1970s differed across sources so we removed it from the time series. Registration data for Whites were interpolated backward from 1960 based on figure 1 in Brown-Dean et al., *50 Years*, and figure 1 in Keele, Cubbison, and White, "Suppressing Black Votes."

22. Mickey, *Paths Out of Dixie.*

23. Estimates of historical turnout are based on self-reported turnout rates in the American National Election Studies (ANES) and Current Population Surveys (CPS) table 25 in Stanley, *Voter Mobilization*, 155 and figure 2 in Brown-Dean et al., *50 Years*, 10. Note, though, that self-reported turnout reports on surveys are often inaccurate, especially for more politically engaged people; see Ansolabehere and Hersh, "Validation."

24. Fraga, *Turnout Gap*, 47, 110.

25. Fairclough, "Historians and the Civil Rights Movement," 397.

26. Alt, "Impact of the Voting Rights Act"; Brown-Dean et al., *50 Years*.

27. For more on the surge in Black office holding after the VRA, see Handley and Grofman, "The Impact of the Voting Rights Act on Minority Representation"; but see Hajnal, *Dangerously Divided*, 109, who finds that Black voters continue to face substantial disadvantages in electing the candidates of their choice.

28. Cascio and Washington, "Valuing the Vote"; Wright, *Sharing the Prize: The Economics of the Civil Rights Revolution in the American South.*

29. Black and Black, *The Rise of Southern Republicans*; Hood, Kidd, and Morris, "The Republican Party in the American South."

30. For example, Key, *Southern Politics*, chap. 14.

31. Key, *Southern Politics.*

32. Quadagno, "From Old-Age Assistance to Supplemental Security Income."

33. For example, Soss and Weaver, "Police Are Our Government."

34. Fraga, *Turnout Gap*, 48, 110.

35. Marschall and Rutherford, "Voting Rights for Whom?"

36. Powell, "Political Representation in Comparative Politics," 277.

37. Lee and Oppenheimer, *Sizing Up the Senate.*

38. Ansolabehere and Snyder, *End of Inequality*, 194.

39. The data for this chart are based on a number of different sources. The data for 1937 and 1955 are from table 4 in David and Eisenberg, *Devaluation* and is based on the original data in Dauer and Kelsay, "Unrepresentative States." The data for 1960 are from table 3.1 Ansolabehere

and Snyder, *End of Inequality*. The data for 1962 and 1967 are from National Municipal League, "Apportionment in the Nineteen Sixties." Finally, we assume that all states had equipopulous districts by the 1972 elections. Values for other years are linearly interpolated.

40. Dauer and Kelsay, "Unrepresentative States," 572, 574.

41. David and Eisenberg, *Devaluation*; White and Thomas, "Urban and Rural Representation and State Legislative Apportionment."

42. Ansolabehere, Gerber, and Snyder, "Equal Votes, Equal Money."

43. Cox and Katz, *Elbridge Gerry's Salamander*. Cox and Katz also argue that because court-ordered redistricting coincided with a high point of their electoral fortunes and dominance of the federal judiciary, Democrats were able to use their control over district drawing to lock in long-term electoral advantages in many states.

44. Ansolabehere and Snyder, *End of Inequality*.

45. States where the median district shifted to the left also increased state funding levels; Ansolabehere and Snyder, *End of Inequality*.

46. Ansolabehere and Snyder, *End of Inequality*; Stephanopoulos and McGhee, "Partisan Gerrymandering and the Efficiency Gap."

47. Rodden, *Why Cities Lose*, chap. 6.

48. McGhee, "Partisan Gerrymandering and Political Science."

49. But see J. Chen and Rodden, "Unintentional Gerrymandering."

50. McGhee, "Measuring Efficiency in Redistricting." Other metrics include partisan symmetry, median-mean difference, and the declination; see, respectively, Gelman and King, "A Unified Method of Evaluating Electoral Systems and Redistricting Plans"; Best et al., "Considering the Prospects for Establishing a Packing Gerrymandering Standard"; Warrington, "Quantifying Gerrymandering Using the Vote Distribution."

51. The efficiency gap can be calculated from statewide election results using the formula $EG = S - 0.5 - 2(V - 0.5)$, where S is the two-party proportion of legislative seats won by the focal party (in our case, Democrats) and V is the two-party proportion of statewide votes won by that party. For the bulk of our analysis, we estimate the EG for each state by decade between decennial redistricting cycles. This implicitly means we are generally capturing the average partisan advantage embedded in each legislative map; Stephanopoulos and McGhee, "Partisan Gerrymandering and the Efficiency Gap." Prior to the 1970s, there is uneven availability of election results in state legislative elections. As a result, we use statewide elections to calculate V. Specifically, we average the two-party Democratic vote share in statewide elections in each decade using data from Eggers et al., "On the Validity of the Regression Discontinuity Design for Estimating Electoral Effects," and Shiro Kuriwaki, "Ticket Splitting in a Nationalized Era," as well as from https://ballotpedia.org. We adjust the raw vote shares to estimate the statewide normal vote by adding or subtracting estimates of the incumbency advantage in each decade based on figure 2 and table A.2 in Ansolabehere and Snyder, "The Incumbency Advantage in US Elections," and on figure 8 in Jacobson, "Driven to Extremes."

52. For plots showing similar trends, see Rodden, *Why Cities Lose*, 191; Stephanopoulos and McGhee, "Partisan Gerrymandering and the Efficiency Gap."

53. On the decline in partisan bias after the Reapportionment Revolution, see Ansolabehere and Snyder, *End of Inequality*, 251.

54. Here, the South is defined to include Kentucky and Oklahoma. On the generally pro-Republican bias of congressional districts outside the South in the malapportionment era, see Erikson, "Malapportionment, Gerrymandering, and Party Fortunes in Congressional Elections."

55. Democrats in the South were also aided by their party's vestigial strength in rural areas, which made it easier for them to draw maps that efficiently distributed their supporters across districts.

56. In terms of political geography, Democrats are less spatially concentrated in the West, particularly the Southwest, than in other areas, especially the Midwest; Rodden, *Why Cities Lose*, 65, 170.

57. These forces have affected both parties, but in recent years Democrats have generally been less aggressive about gerrymandering states that they control, though there are certainly exceptions (e.g., Maryland). Democrats also tend to be more supportive of nonpartisan districting commissions and other reforms designed to weaken political control of redistricting, and in states such as Colorado have taken advantage of their control of state government to pass such reforms. See, for example, Mutnick, "How Democrats Are 'Unilaterally Disarming' in the Redistricting Wars." Partisan advantage in the districting process has also proved remarkably durable in recent years. This durability is partially due to the initial maps and partially due to the fact that feedback effects from gerrymandering impede numerous party functions at both the congressional and state house levels. Parties are less likely to contest districts when their party is disadvantaged by a districting plan. Candidates that do choose to run are more likely to have weak résumés. Donors are less willing to contribute money. And ordinary voters are less apt to support the targeted party. See Stephanopoulos and Warshaw, "The Impact of Partisan Gerrymandering on Political Parties."

58. Spicuzza and Hall, "Walker Defeats Barrett to Win Governor's Race."

59. Wines, "Judges Find Wisconsin Redistricting Unfairly Favored Republicans"; J. Chen, "The Impact of Political Geography on Wisconsin Redistricting."

60. Niemi and Jackman, "Bias and Responsiveness in State Legislative Districting"; Gelman and King, "Enhancing Democracy through Legislative Redistricting"; McGhee, "Measuring Partisan Bias in Single-Member District Electoral Systems"; Stephanopoulos, "The Causes and Consequences of Gerrymandering."

61. Figure 9.7 is derived from two-way FE model of the efficiency gap in years just after decennial redistricting (e.g., 2012) as a function of partisan control of government during the redistricting process. We do not include states with nonpartisan commissions in the analysis.

62. See also Ansolabehere and Snyder, *End of Inequality*, 254.

63. This analysis of the representational consequences of partisan gerrymandering draws heavily on Caughey Tausanovitch, and Warshaw, "Partisan Gerrymandering."

64. Rodden, "The Geographic Distribution of Political Preferences."

65. See also Shor and McCarty, "Ideological Mapping."

66. This assumes that district ideology and partisanship are positively correlated (i.e., more conservative districts are more likely to elect Republicans).

67. In this analysis, legislative conservatism is measured by the median Shor-McCarty ideal point, averaged across chambers. Policy conservatism is measured with the results of our standard mixed factor-analysis model, fitted to all policies as opposed to separately by domain.

68. Kaiser Family Foundation, "Status of State Medicaid Expansion Decisions: Interactive Map."

69. Davey, "Twinned Cities Now Following Different Paths."

Chapter 10

1. Morone, *The Democratic Wish*.

2. Wilentz, *The Rise of American Democracy*.

3. Foner, *Reconstruction*.

4. Lax and Phillips, "Democratic Deficit," 158. Though popularized by a 1932 Supreme Court dissent penned by Justice Louis Brandeis, the idea of states as laboratories of democracy has a much longer history. For example, Chief Justice Charles Hughes, who joined the majority opinion from which Brandeis dissented, had as governor of New York two decades earlier given a speech in which he lauded state government as "a laboratory of experimentation in free institutions"; see Teaford, *Rise of the States*, 90.

5. Bateman, *Disenfranchising Democracy*.

6. Perman, *Pursuit of Unity*, 170.

7. Bridges, *Morning Glories*.

8. Lichtenstein, *State of the Union*. According to opinion polls conducted in the late 1930s and 1940s, labor leader John L. Lewis was far and away the most unpopular man in America; Schickler and Caughey, "Public Opinion, Organized Labor, and the Limits of New Deal Liberalism, 1936–1945."

9. For a helpful overview of institutional variation across states, see LaCombe, "Measuring Institutional Design in US States."

10. Kubin, "Case for Redistricting Commissions"; Bates, "Congressional Authority to Require State Adoption of Independent Redistricting Commissions"; Stephanopoulos, "Arizona and Anti-Reform," 477–507, 14; Seabrook, *Drawing the Lines*.

11. "Redistricting Commissions," Ballotpedia; Stephanopoulos, "Arizona and Anti-Reform"; National Conference of State Legislatures, "Redistricting Law 2010."

12. Another claim made in favor of nonpartisan commissions is that they increase electoral competition, but there is little evidence that they do; see Henderson, Hamel, and Goldzimer, "Gerrymandering Incumbency."

13. Kogan and McGhee, "Redistricting California"; Stephanopoulos, "The Consequences of Consequentialist Criteria," 669; Stephanopoulos, "Arizona and Anti-Reform."

14. The results do change if the state FEs are replaced with a lagged dependent variable; as expected, commissions are indeed estimated to reduce the absolute EG in this specification. It is not clear which of these models is more plausible theoretically, but the FE model fits the data much better. Due to the small number of decades in the analysis, a full dynamic panel model with both FEs and an LDV would be subject to substantial bias; see Nickell, "Biases in Dynamic Models with Fixed Effects."

15. For a recent review, see Matsusaka, "Public Policy and the Initiative and Referendum."

16. For evidence that direct democracy promotes policy innovation, but in ways conditioned by states' ideological leanings, see LaCombe and Boehmke, "Initiative Process and Policy Innovation."

17. Gerber, "Legislative Response to the Threat of Popular Initiatives."

18. Matsusaka, *For the Many or the Few*.

19. Some studies find that direct democracy enhances representation, at least in some policy areas; see, for example, Arceneaux, "Direct Democracy and the Link between Public Opinion and State Abortion Policy"; Gerber, "Legislative Response to the Threat of Popular Initiatives"; Matsusaka, "Popular Control." Others, however, find that it has no effect; see, for example, Monogan, Gray, and Lowery, "Public Opinion, Organized Interests, and Policy Congruence in Initiative and Noninitiative US States"; Lascher, Hagen, and Rochlin, "Gun Behind the Door? Ballot Initiatives, State Policies and Public Opinion"; Lax and Phillips, "Gay Rights"; Lax and Phillips, "Democratic Deficit"; Tausanovitch and Warshaw, "Representation in Municipal Government." One reason might be that initiatives tend to have a strong status quo bias so that even

very popular initiatives often lose; Barber et al., "Status Quo Bias in Ballot Wording"; Robinson, Sides, and Warshaw, *When Mass Opinion Goes to the Ballot Box*.

20. Garrett, "Term Limitations and the Myth of the Citizen-Legislator."

21. Clark and Williams, "Parties, Term Limits, and Representation in the US States"; Fouirnaies and Hall, "How Do Electoral Incentives Affect Legislator Behavior? Evidence from U.S. State Legislatures"; T. Kousser, *Term Limits and the Dismantling of State Legislative Professionalism*.

22. Lax and Phillips, "Democratic Deficit."

23. Data on these reforms were obtained from Springer, *How the States Shaped the Nation*. We updated Springer's data using information from the National Conference of State Legislatures and verified it against a variety of Internet sources.

24. Wolfinger and Rosenstone, *Who Votes?*; Springer, *How the States Shaped the Nation*; Xu, "Generalized Synthetic Control Method: Causal Inference with Interactive Fixed Effects Models"; Cantoni and Pons, *Does Context Outweigh Individual Characteristics in Driving Voting Behavior?*

25. Kaplan and Yuan, "Early Voting Laws, Voter Turnout, and Partisan Vote Composition: Evidence from Ohio"; Cantoni and Pons, *Does Context Outweigh Individual Characteristics in Driving Voting Behavior?*; Thompson et al., "Universal Vote-by-Mail Has No Impact on Partisan Turnout or Vote Share."

26. We obtain data on the prevalence of voter ID laws from various websites and National Conference of State Legislatures, "Voter Identification Requirements | Voter ID Laws." Like most previous studies, we include both strict and nonstrict photo identification laws; see Fraga, *Turnout Gap*, 179.

27. Goel et al., "One Person, One Vote."

28. Graham, "What's the Goal of Voter-ID Laws?"

29. Highton, "Voter Identification Laws and Turnout in the United States"; Fraga and Miller, "Who Does Voter ID Keep from Voting?"

30. Fraga, *Turnout Gap*; Hopkins et al., "Voting but for the Law."

31. Data on campaign contribution limitations were obtained from state statutes, various editions of *The Book of the States* and the FEC's *Analysis of Federal and State Campaign Finance Law*, and several reference works and academic analyses, including Ford, *Regulation of Campaign Finance*; Alexander and Denny, *Regulation of Political Finance*; Stratmann and Aparicio-Castillo, "Competition Policy for Elections"; La Raja and Schaffner, "The Effects of Campaign Finance Spending Bans on Electoral Outcomes."

32. On the representational distortions induced by campaign contributions, see Bartels, *Unequal Democracy*; Gilens, *Affluence and Influence*; Erikson, "Income Inequality and Policy Responsiveness."

33. La Raja and Schaffner, "Effects of Campaign Finance Spending Bans."

34. Barber, "Ideological Donors, Contribution Limits, and the Polarization of American Legislatures"; La Raja and Schaffner, *Campaign Finance and Political Polarization*.

35. Besley and Case, "Political Institutions and Policy Choices"; Werner and Coleman, "Assessing the Potential Effects of *Citizens United*: Policy and Corporate Governance in the States."

36. Besley and Case find that bans on contributions from corporations lead to more liberal outcomes on two of the five policies they examine, lead to more conservative outcomes on one policy, and have no effect at all on two other policies; Besley and Case, "Political Institutions and Policy Choices." Two more recent studies focus on the impact of campaign finance limits on

other policy outputs using more complex dynamic panel models. Werner and Coleman find that bans on contributions from unions and corporations have no effect on minimum wage laws; Werner and Coleman, "Assessing the Potential Effects of *Citizens United*." La Raja and Schaffner find that bans on contributions from corporations and unions have no effect on corporate tax revenues and that contribution limits have little effect on the partisan composition of government; La Raja and Schaffner, "Effects of Campaign Finance Spending Bans."

37. Ahlquist, "Labor Unions, Political Representation, and Economic Inequality."

38. Data on right-to-work laws are from Eren and Ozbeklik, "What Do Right-to-Work Laws Do?" and National Conference of State Legislatures, "Right-to-Work Resources."

39. Hertel-Fernandez, "Policy Feedback as Political Weapon."

40. Ellwood and Fine, "The Impact of Right-to-Work Laws on Union Organizing"; Eren and Ozbeklik, "What Do Right-to-Work Laws Do?"; Lyon, "Heroes, Villains, or Something in Between?"

41. Macdonald, "Labor Unions and White Democratic Partisanship."

42. Kerrissey and Schofer, "Union Membership and Political Participation in the United States."

43. Feigenbaum, Hertel-Fernandez, and Williamson, *From the Bargaining Table to the Ballot Box.*

44. Data on collective bargaining laws come from a variety of sources, including Lovenheim and Willen, "The Long-Run Effects of Teacher Collective Bargaining" and Valletta and Freeman, "The NBER Public Sector Collective Bargaining Law Data Set."

45. Anzia and Moe, "Do Politicians Use Policy to Make Politics?"

46. Keefe, "Laws Enabling Public-Sector Collective Bargaining Have Not Led to Excessive Public-Sector Pay."

47. Hertel-Fernandez, "Policy Feedback as Political Weapon."

48. Saltzman, "Bargaining Laws as a Cause and Consequence of the Growth of Teacher Unionism"; Moe, *Special Interest.*

49. Flavin and Hartney, "When Government Subsidizes Its Own."

50. Paglayan, "Public-Sector Unions and the Size of Government."

51. Imai, Kim, and Wang, "Matching Methods for Causal Inference with Time-Series Cross-Sectional Data."

52. Benjamini and Hochberg, "Controlling the False Discovery Rate." We consider the set of estimates in each figure a "family" for the purposes of FDR correction.

53. The limited partisan effects of voting-related reforms is consistent with the general finding that such reforms—and higher turnout generally—do not strongly favor one party; see, for example, Barber and Holbein, "The Participatory and Partisan Impacts of Mandatory Vote-by-Mail"; Cantoni and Pons, *Does Context Outweigh Individual Characteristics in Driving Voting Behavior?*; Thompson et al., "Universal Vote-by-Mail Has No Impact on Partisan Turnout or Vote Share"; Shaw and Petrocik, *The Turnout Myth.*

54. See also Feigenbaum, Hertel-Fernandez, and Williamson, *From the Bargaining Table to the Ballot Box.*

55. Dark, *The Unions and the Democrats.*

56. For more on the politics of collective bargaining laws, see Anzia and Moe, "Do Politicians Use Policy."

57. Right to work and collective bargaining for state employees are both in our policy data set, but when we estimate their effects on policy conservatism we drop them from the data.

58. See also Matsusaka, "Public Policy."

59. Indirect evidence for this claim is provided by the fact that campaign donors—who are presumably more similar to politicians than the average citizen is—are more socially liberal (and more economically conservative) than voters in general; Francia et al., "Limousine Liberals and Corporate Conservatives"; Broockman and Malhotra, "What Do Partisan Donors Want?"

60. Stone, *Gay Rights at the Ballot Box.*

61. Contra Matsusaka, "Public Policy."

62. On tax cuts, see, for example, Sears and Citrin, *Tax Revolt*; on Missouri, see Suntrup and Erickson, "Democrats, Unions Declare Victory as 'Right to Work' Loses by Wide Margin in Missouri."

63. Erikson, Wright, and McIver, *Statehouse Democracy*, 93–94.

64. Matsusaka, "Problems with a Methodology."

65. For example, Lax and Phillips, "Democratic Deficit"; Tausanovitch and Warshaw, "Representation in Municipal Government"; Caughey and Warshaw, "Policy Preferences and Policy Change"; Schaffner, Rhodes, and La Raja, *Hometown Inequality*. This dearth of evidence may be due to the greater difficulty of detecting interaction effects relative to main effects, but it is worth noting that we were able to detect at least some interaction effects in chapter 7 (table 7.1). On interactions being harder to estimate, see Gelman, Hill, and Vehtari, *Regression and Other Stories*.

66. To avoid confusing institutional effects for secular trends toward increasing responsiveness, the models underlying this figure also include interactions with era (like columns 2 and 5 of table 7.1).

67. For a cross-national study that comes to similar conclusions, see Rasmussen, Reher, and Toshkov, "Opinion-Policy Nexus."

68. For example, J. Kousser, *The Shaping of Southern Politics*; Wright, *Sharing the Prize.*

Chapter 11

1. Lax and Phillips, "Democratic Deficit"; Rogers, "Electoral Accountability"; Gilens, *Affluence and Influence*; Achen and Bartels, *Democracy for Realists*.

2. Achen, "Mass Political Attitudes and the Survey Response," 1220; see also Bartels, "Democracy with Attitudes," 50–51.

3. Compare Erikson, Wright, and McIver, *Statehouse Democracy*, 94.

4. Although Erikson, Wright, and McIver acknowledge the divergence of party elites' *positions* within states, their structural equation estimates indicate that Democratic control of the legislature has no net effect on policy liberalism (the negative direct effect almost exactly cancels the positive indirect effect mediated through legislative liberalism). They therefore conclude that when it comes to policymaking, Democrats and Republicans "respond to state opinion—perhaps even to the point of enacting similar policies when in legislative control"; Erikson, Wright, and McIver, "Political Parties, Public Opinion, and State Policy," 735, 743; see also Erikson, Wright, and McIver, *Statehouse Democracy*, 130.

5. Mayhew, *Congress: The Electoral Connection*; Kingdon, *Congressmen's Voting Decisions*; Arnold, *The Logic of Congressional Action*; Stimson, MacKuen, and Erikson, "Dynamic Representation."

6. Achen and Bartels, *Democracy for Realists*, 249.

7. Dahl, *Polyarchy.*

8. May, "Defining Democracy."

9. Rigby and Wright, "Whose Statehouse Democracy"; see also Gilens, "Inequality and Democratic Responsiveness"; Bartels, *Unequal Democracy*; Hajnal, *Dangerously Divided*; Schaffner, Rhodes, and La Raja, *Hometown Inequality*.

10. O'Donnell, "On the State."

11. Key, *Southern Politics*; Mickey, *Paths Out of Dixie*.

12. Midterm turnout among Blacks remains substantially lower than among Whites; see Fraga, *Turnout Gap*, 41, 48.

13. Valentino and Sears, "Old Times."

14. Downs, *An Economic Theory of Democracy*.

15. McKee, "The Past, Present, and Future of Southern Politics"; McKee and Springer, "A Tale of 'Two Souths.'"

16. Black and Black, *The Rise of Southern Republicans*, 151.

17. Pierson, "When Effect Becomes Cause."

18. Louisiana passed a right-to-work law in 1954 but repealed it two years later. A permanent law was adopted in 1976. See Canak and Miller, "Gumbo Politics: Unions, Business, and Louisiana Right-to-Work Legislation."

19. On complementarities across institutions in capitalist political economies, see Hall and Soskice, *Varieties of Capitalism*.

20. For a similarly positive assessment of national responsiveness, see Erikson, MacKuen, and Stimson, *The Macro Polity*.

21. Matsusaka, "Public Policy."

22. LaCombe and Boehmke, "Initiative Process and Policy Innovation," 12.

23. Hopkins, *Increasingly United States*.

24. On polarization across states, see Grumbach, "From Backwaters to Major Policymakers"; on overresponsiveness, see Lax and Phillips, "Democratic Deficit."

25. See Hirano and Snyder, *Primary Elections in the United States*, chap. 10.

26. Matsusaka, "Public Policy."

27. Daniel Hopkins, *Increasingly United States*.

28. Darr, Hitt, and Dunaway, "Newspaper Closures Polarize Voting Behavior."

29. Hayes and Lawless, *News Hole*.

30. Snyder and Strömberg, "Press Coverage and Political Accountability."

31. Darr, Hitt, and Dunaway, "Newspaper Closures"; Moskowitz, "Local News, Information, and the Nationalization of US Elections."

32. For evidence from comparative politics that a free press is a vital part of the democratic process, see Hiaeshutter-Rice, Soroka, and Wlezien, "Freedom of the Press and Public Responsiveness."

33. Hertel-Fernandez, *State Capture*.

34. Valelly, *Two Reconstructions*; more generally, see Mettler and Lieberman, *Four Threats*.

35. Levitsky and Ziblatt, *How Democracies Die*.

36. Future work on interest groups could build on Julia Payson's work about how local governments' lobbying efforts affects the political process in the states; Payson, *When Cities Lobby*.

37. Lowery and Gray, *The Population Ecology of Interest Representation*.

38. For an exemplary use of newspapers as data, see Ban et al., "How Newspapers Reveal Political Power."

Bibliography

Abramowitz, Alan I. *The Great Alignment: Race, Party Transformation, and the Rise of Donald Trump*. New Haven, CT: Yale University Press, 2018.

Achen, Christopher H. "Mass Political Attitudes and the Survey Response." *American Political Science Review* 69, no. 4 (1975): 1218–31.

———. "Measuring Representation." *American Journal of Political Science* 22, no. 3 (1978): 475–510.

Achen, Christopher H., and Larry M. Bartels. *Democracy for Realists: Why Elections Do Not Produce Responsive Government*. Princeton, NJ: Princeton University Press, 2016.

Adams, James, and Samuel Merrill. "Candidate and Party Strategies in Two-Stage Elections Beginning with a Primary." *American Journal of Political Science* 52, no. 2 (2008): 344–59.

Ahlquist, John S. "Labor Unions, Political Representation, and Economic Inequality." *Annual Review of Political Science* 20 (2017): 409–32.

Aisch, Gregor, Robert Gebeloff, and Kevin Quealy. "Where We Came From and Where We Went, State by State." *The Upshot* (blog), *New York Times*, August 19, 2014. https://nyti.ms/2jRA6xh.

Aldrich, John H., and David W. Rohde. "The Consequences of Party Organization in the House: The Roles of the Majority and Minority Parties in Conditional Party Government." In *Polarized Politics: Congress and the President in a Partisan Era*, edited by J. R. Bond and R. Fleisher, 37–72. Washington, DC: CQ Press, 2000.

Alesina, Alberto. "Credibility and Policy Convergence in a Two-Party System with Rational Voters." *American Economic Review* 78, no. 4 (1988): 796–805.

Alesina, Alberto, John Londregan, and Howard Rosenthal. "A Model of the Political Economy of the United States." *American Political Science Review* 87, no. 1 (1993): 12–33.

Alesina, Alberto, and Howard Rosenthal. *Partisan Politics, Divided Government, and the Economy*. New York: Cambridge University Press, 1995.

Alexander, Herbert E., and Laura L. Denny. *Regulation of Political Finance*. Berkeley: Institute of Governmental Studies, University of California, 1966.

Alt, James E. "The Impact of the Voting Rights Act on Black and White Voter Registration in the South." In *Quiet Revolution in the South: The Impact of the Voting Rights Act, 1965–1990*, edited by Chandler Davidson and Bernard Grofman, 351–77. Princeton, NJ: Princeton University Press, 1994.

Anderson, Carol. *One Person, No Vote: How Voter Suppression Is Destroying Our Democracy.* New York: Bloomsbury, 2018.

Anonymous. "The Limits of Representation: Revisiting the Democratic Deficit in the States." Unpublished manuscript, 2018.

Ansolabehere, Stephen, Alan Gerber, and James Snyder. "Equal Votes, Equal Money: Court-Ordered Redistricting and Public Expenditures in the American States." *American Political Science Review* 96, no. 4 (2002): 767–77.

Ansolabehere, Stephen, and Eitan Hersh. "Validation: What Big Data Reveal about Survey Misreporting and the Real Electorate." *Political Analysis* 20, no. 4 (2012): 437–59.

Ansolabehere, Stephen, Jonathan Rodden, and James M. Snyder Jr. "The Strength of Issues: Using Multiple Measures to Gauge Preference Stability, Ideological Constraint, and Issue Voting." *American Political Science Review* 102, no. 2 (2008): 215–32.

Ansolabehere, Stephen, and James M. Snyder Jr. *The End of Inequality: One Person, One Vote and the Transformation of American Politics.* New York: Norton, 2008.

———. "The Incumbency Advantage in US Elections: An Analysis of State and Federal Offices, 1942–2000." *Election Law Journal* 1, no. 3 (2002): 315–38.

Ansolabehere, Stephen, James M. Snyder Jr., and Charles Stewart III. "Candidate Positioning in U.S. House Elections." *American Journal of Political Science* 45, no. 1 (2001): 136–59.

Anzia, Sarah F., and Terry M. Moe. "Do Politicians Use Policy to Make Politics? The Case of Public-Sector Labor Laws." *American Political Science Review* 110, no. 4 (2016): 763–77.

Arceneaux, Kevin. "Direct Democracy and the Link between Public Opinion and State Abortion Policy." *State Politics and Policy Quarterly* 2, no. 4 (2002): 372–87.

Arnold, R. Douglas. *The Logic of Congressional Action.* New Haven, CT: Yale University Press, 1990.

Ashworth, Scott. "Electoral Accountability: Recent Theoretical and Empirical Work." *Annual Review of Political Science* 15 (2012): 183–201.

Atkinson, Mary Layton, K. Elizabeth Coggins, James A. Stimson, and Frank R. Baumgartner. *The Dynamics of Public Opinion.* Elements in American Politics. Cambridge, UK: Cambridge University Press, 2021.

Bafumi, Joseph, Robert S. Erikson, and Christopher Wlezien. "Balancing, Generic Polls and Midterm Congressional Elections." *Journal of Politics* 72, no. 3 (2010): 705–19.

Bafumi, Joseph, and Michael C. Herron. "Leapfrog Representation and Extremism: A Study of American Voters and Their Members in Congress." *American Political Science Review* 104, no. 3 (2010): 519–42.

Ban, Pamela, Alexander Fouirnaies, Andrew B. Hall, and James M. Snyder Jr. "How Newspapers Reveal Political Power." *Political Science Research and Methods* 7, no. 4 (2019): 661–78.

Barber, Michael, David Gordon, Ryan Hill, and Joseph Price. "Status Quo Bias in Ballot Wording." *Journal of Experimental Political Science* 4, no. 2 (2017): 151–60.

Barber, Michael, and John B. Holbein. "The Participatory and Partisan Impacts of Mandatory Vote-by-Mail." *Science Advances* 6, no. 35 (2020): EABC7685.

Barber, Michael J. "Ideological Donors, Contribution Limits, and the Polarization of American Legislatures." *Journal of Politics* 78, no. 1 (2016): 296–310.

Bartels, Larry M. "Democracy with Attitudes." In *Electoral Democracy*, edited by Michael B. MacKuen and George Rabinowitz, 48–82. Ann Arbor: University of Michigan Press, 2003.

―――. *Unequal Democracy: The Political Economy of the New Gilded Age*. Princeton, NJ: Princeton University Press, 2008.

Bateman, David A. *Disenfranchising Democracy: Constructing the Electorate in the United States, the United Kingdom, and France*. New York: Cambridge University Press, 2018.

Bates, Ryan P. "Congressional Authority to Require State Adoption of Independent Redistricting Commissions." *Duke Law Journal* 55, no. 2 (2005): 333–71.

Baumgartner, Frank R., and Bryan D. Jones. "Agenda Dynamics and Policy Subsystems." *Journal of Politics* 53, no. 4 (1991): 1044–74.

―――. *Agendas and Instability in American Politics*. 2nd ed. Chicago: University of Chicago Press, 2009.

Beck, Kent M. "What Was Liberalism in the 1950s?" *Political Science Quarterly* 102, no. 2 (1987): 233–58.

"Ben Nelson (D)." In *The Almanac of American Politics*. 2008. https://advance.lexis.com/api/document?collection=directories&id=urn:contentItem:4TRB-7KP0-001F-V0DN-00000-00&context=1516831.

Benedictis-Kessner, Justin de, and Christopher Warshaw. "Accountability for the Local Economy at All Levels of Government in United States Elections." *American Political Science Review* 114, no. 3 (2020): 660–76.

Benjamini, Yoav, and Yosef Hochberg. "Controlling the False Discovery Rate: A Practical and Powerful Approach to Multiple Testing." *Journal of the Royal Statistical Society: Series B (Statistical Methodology)* 57, no. 1 (1995): 289–300.

Berinsky, Adam J. "American Public Opinion in the 1930s and 1940s: The Analysis of Quota-Controlled Sample Survey Data." *Public Opinion Quarterly* 70, no. 4 (2006): 499–529.

Berlin, Ira. *Many Thousands Gone: The First Two Centuries of Slavery in North America*. Cambridge, MA: Belknap Press, 1998.

Berry, William D., Michael B. Berkman, and Stuart Schneiderman. "Legislative Professionalism and Incumbent Reelection: The Development of Institutional Boundaries." *American Political Science Review* 94, no. 4 (2000): 859–74.

Berry, William D., Richard C. Fording, and Russell L. Hanson. "An Annual Cost of Living Index for the American States, 1960–1995." *Journal of Politics* 62, no. 2 (2000): 550–67.

Besley, Timothy, and Anne Case. "Political Institutions and Policy Choices: Evidence from the United States." *Journal of Economic Literature* 41, no. 1 (2003): 7–73.

Besley, Timothy, and Stephen Coate. "An Economic Model of Representative Democracy." *Quarterly Journal of Economics* 112, no. 1 (1997): 85–114.

Best, Robin E., Shawn J. Donahue, Jonathan Krasno, Daniel B. Magleby, and Michael D. McDonald. "Considering the Prospects for Establishing a Packing Gerrymandering Standard." *Election Law Journal* 17, no. 1 (2018): 1–20.

Bisbee, James. "BARP: Improving Mister P Using Bayesian Additive Regression Trees." *American Political Science Review* 113, no. 4 (2019): 1060–65.

Black, Earl, and Merle Black. *The Rise of Southern Republicans*. Cambridge, MA: Belknap Press, 2002.

Bloom, Nicholas Dagen. *How States Shaped Postwar America: State Government and Urban Power*. Chicago: University of Chicago Press, 2019.

Boehmke, Frederick J., and Paul Skinner. "State Policy Innovativeness Revisited." *State Politics and Policy Quarterly* 12, no. 3 (2012): 303–29.

Bonica, Adam. "Inferring Roll-Call Scores from Campaign Contributions Using Supervised Machine Learning." *American Journal of Political Science* 62, no. 4 (2018): 830–48.

———. "Mapping the Ideological Marketplace." *American Journal of Political Science* 58, no. 2 (2014): 367–86.

Bonica, Adam, and Gary W. Cox. "Ideological Extremists in the US Congress: Out of Step but Still in Office." *Quarterly Journal of Political Science* 13, no. 2 (2018): 207–36.

Bridges, Amy. *Morning Glories: Municipal Reform in the Southwest.* Princeton, NJ: Princeton University Press, 1997.

Bromley-Trujillo, Rebecca, and Mirya R. Holman. "Climate Change Policymaking in the States: A View at 2020." *Publius: The Journal of Federalism* 50, no. 3 (2020): 446–72.

Broockman, David, and Neil Malhotra. "What Do Partisan Donors Want?" *Public Opinion Quarterly* 84, no. 1 (2020): 104–18.

Broockman, David E. "Approaches to Studying Policy Representation." *Legislative Studies Quarterly* 41, no. 1 (2016): 181–215.

Brown-Dean, Khalilah, Zoltan Hajnal, Christina R. Rivers, and Ismail K. White. *50 Years of the Voting Rights Act: The State of Race in Politics.* Joint Center for Political and Economic Studies, 2015. https://jointcenter.org/wp-content/uploads/2019/11/VRA-report-3.5.15-1130-am updated.pdf.

Brunner, Eric, Stephen L. Ross, and Ebonya Washington. "Does Less Income Mean Less Representation?" *American Economic Journal: Economic Policy* 5, no. 2 (2013): 53–76.

Bryan, Frank M. *Yankee Politics in Rural Vermont.* Hanover, NH: University Press of New England, 1974.

Burnham, Walter Dean. "Party Systems and the Political Process." In *The American Party Systems: Stages of Political Development,* edited by W. N. Chambers and Walter Dean Burnham, 277–307. New York: Oxford University Press, 1967.

Burstein, Paul. *American Public Opinion, Advocacy, and Policy in Congress: What the Public Wants and What It Gets.* New York: Cambridge University Press, 2014.

———. "The Impact of Public Opinion on Public Policy: A Review and an Agenda." *Political Research Quarterly* 56, no. 1 (2003): 29–40.

Buttice, Matthew K., and Benjamin Highton. "How Does Multilevel Regression and Poststratification Perform with Conventional National Surveys?" *Political Analysis* 21, no. 4 (2013): 449–67.

Cadigan, John, and Eckhard Janeba. "A Citizen-Candidate Model with Sequential Elections." *Journal of Theoretical Politics* 14, no. 4 (2002): 387–407.

Cain, Andrew. "Sunday Q&A with James B. Alcorn, State Board of Elections Chairman." *Richmond Times-Dispatch,* January 9, 2016. https://www.richmond.com/news/local/sunday-q-a -with-james-b-alcorn-state-board-of/article_a731413e-06c0-5fa2-a0b5-1cfc5daed7f0.html.

Calonico, Sebastian, Matias D. Cattaneo, Max H. Farrell, and Rocío Titiunik. *rdrobust: Robust Data-Driven Statistical Inference in Regression-Discontinuity Designs.* R package version 1.0.2. 2021. https://CRAN.R-project.org/package=rdrobust.

———. "Regression Discontinuity Designs Using Covariates." *Review of Economics and Statistics* 101, no. 3 (2019): 442–51.

Campbell, Andrea Louise. "Policy Makes Mass Politics." *Annual Review of Political Science* 15 (2012): 333–51.

Campbell, Angus, Philip Converse, Warren Miller, and Donald Stokes. *The American Voter.* New York: Wiley, 1960.

Canak, William, and Berkeley Miller. "Gumbo Politics: Unions, Business, and Louisiana Right-to-Work Legislation." *Industrial and Labor Relations Review* 43, no. 2 (1990): 258–71.

Canes-Wrone, Brandice, David W. Brady, and John F. Cogan. "Out of Step, Out of Office: Electoral Accountability and House Members' Voting." *American Political Science Review* 96, no. 1 (2002): 127–40.

Cantoni, Enrico, and Vincent Pons. *Does Context Outweigh Individual Characteristics in Driving Voting Behavior? Evidence from Relocations within the US.* Working paper 27998. National Bureau of Economic Research, August 2021. https://doi.org/10.3386/w27998.

Carmines, Edward G., and James A. Stimson. *Issue Evolution: Race and the Transformation of American Politics.* Princeton, NJ: Princeton University Press, 1989.

Carpenter, Tim. "New Poll Ranks Gov. Sam Brownback as Nation's Least Popular Governor." *Topeka Capital Journal*, September 21, 2016. https://www.cjonline.com/story/news/politics/state/2016/09/20/new-poll-ranks-gov-sam-brownback-nations-least-popular-governor/16574005007/.

Cascio, Elizabeth U., and Ebonya Washington. "Valuing the Vote: The Redistribution of Voting Rights and State Funds Following the Voting Rights Act of 1965." *Quarterly Journal of Economics* 129, no. 1 (2014): 379–433.

Caughey, Devin. *The Unsolid South: Mass Politics and National Representation in a One-Party Enclave.* Princeton, NJ: Princeton University Press, 2018.

Caughey, Devin, Adam J. Berinsky, Sara Chatfield, Erin Hartman, Eric Schickler, and Jasjeet J. Sekhon. *Target Estimation and Adjustment Weighting for Survey Nonresponse and Sampling Bias.* Elements in Quantitative and Computational Methods for the Social Sciences. Cambridge, UK: Cambridge University Press, 2020. https://doi.org/10.1017/9781108879217.

Caughey, Devin, Michael C. Dougal, and Eric Schickler. "Policy and Performance in the New Deal Realignment: Evidence from Old Data and New Methods." *Journal of Politics* 82, no. 2 (2020): 494–508.

Caughey, Devin, James Dunham, and Christopher Warshaw. "The Ideological Nationalization of Partisan Subconstituencies in the American States." *Public Choice* 70, no. 2 (2018): 1–19.

Caughey, Devin, Tom O'Grady, and Christopher Warshaw. "Policy Ideology in European Mass Publics, 1981–2016." *American Political Science Review* 113, no. 3 (2019): 674–93.

Caughey, Devin, and Jasjeet S. Sekhon. "Elections and the Regression Discontinuity Design: Lessons from Close U.S. House Races, 1942–2008." *Political Analysis* 19, no. 4 (2011): 385–408.

Caughey, Devin, Chris Tausanovitch, and Christopher Warshaw. "Partisan Gerrymandering and the Political Process: Effects on Roll-Call Voting and State Policies." *Election Law Journal* 16, no. 4 (2017): 453–69.

Caughey, Devin, and Christopher Warshaw. "Policy Preferences and Policy Change: Dynamic Responsiveness in the American States, 1936–2014." *American Political Science Review* 112, no. 2 (2018): 249–66.

———. "Public Opinion in Subnational Politics." *Journal of Politics* 81, no. 1 (Symposium on Subnational Policymaking 2019): 352–63.

———. "The Dynamics of State Policy Liberalism, 1936–2014." *American Journal of Political Science* 60, no. 4 (2016): 899–913.

Caughey, Devin, Christopher Warshaw, and Yiqing Xu. "Incremental Democracy: The Policy Effects of Partisan Control of State Government." *Journal of Politics* 79, no. 4 (2017): 1342–58.

Cebul, Brent, Karen Tani, and Mason B. Williams. "Clio and the Compound Republic." *Publius: The Journal of Federalism* 47, no. 2 (2017): 235–59.

Chen, Anthony S. *The Fifth Freedom: Jobs, Politics, and Civil Rights in the United States, 1941–1972.* Princeton, NJ: Princeton University Press, 2009.

Chen, Jowei. "The Impact of Political Geography on Wisconsin Redistricting: An Analysis of Wisconsin's Act 43 Assembly Districting Plan." *Election Law Journal* 16, no. 4 (2017): 443–52.

Chen, Jowei, and Jonathan Rodden. "Unintentional Gerrymandering: Political Geography and Electoral Bias in Legislatures." *Quarterly Journal of Political Science* 8, no. 3 (2013): 239–69.

Clark, Jennifer Hayes, and R. Lucas Williams. "Parties, Term Limits, and Representation in the US States." *American Politics Research* 42, no. 1 (2014): 171–93.

Cohen, Jeffery E., ed. *Public Opinion in State Politics.* Stanford, CA: Stanford University Press, 2006.

Converse, Philip E. "Popular Representation and the Distribution of Information." In *Information and Democratic Processes*, edited by John Ferejohn and James Kuklinski, 369–88. Chicago: University of Illinois Press, 1990.

———. "The Nature of Belief Systems in Mass Publics." In *Ideology and Discontent*, edited by David E. Apter, 206–61. London: Free Press, 1964.

Cowie, Jefferson. *Stayin' Alive: The 1970s and the Last Days of the Working Class.* New York: The New Press, 2010.

Cox, Gary W., and Jonathan N. Katz. *Elbridge Gerry's Salamander: The Electoral Consequences of the Reapportionment Revolution.* New York: Cambridge University Press, 2002.

Cox, Gary W., Thad Kousser, and Mathew D. McCubbins. "Party Power or Preferences? Quasi-Experimental Evidence from American State Legislatures." *Journal of Politics* 72, no. 3 (2010): 799–811.

Dahl, Robert A. *How Democratic Is the American Constitution?* 2nd ed. New Haven, CT: Yale University Press, 2003.

———. *Polyarchy: Participation and Opposition.* New Haven, CT: Yale University Press, 1971.

———. "The Concept of Power." *Behavioral Science* 2, no. 2 (1957): 201–15.

Dark, Taylor E. *The Unions and the Democrats: An Enduring Alliance.* Ithaca, NY: Cornell University Press, 1999.

Darr, Joshua P., Matthew P. Hitt, and Johanna L. Dunaway. "Newspaper Closures Polarize Voting Behavior." *Journal of Communication* 68, no. 6 (2018): 1007–28.

Dauer, Manning J., and Robert G. Kelsay. "Unrepresentative States." *National Municipal Review* 44, no. 11 (1955): 571–75.

Davey, Monica. "Twinned Cities Now Following Different Paths." *New York Times*, January 12, 2014. https://www.nytimes.com/2014/01/13/us/twinned-cities-now-following-different-paths.html.

David, Paul Theodore, and Ralph Eisenberg. *Devaluation of the Urban and Suburban Vote: A Statistical Investigation of Long-Term Trends in State Legislative Representation.* Vol. 1. Bureau of Public Administration, University of Virginia, 1961.

De Boef, Suzanna, and Luke Keele. "Taking Time Seriously." *American Journal of Political Science* 52, no. 1 (2008): 184–200.

Derthick, Martha. *Keeping the Compound Republic: Essays on American Federalism.* Washington, DC: Brookings, 2001.

Downs, Anthony. *An Economic Theory of Democracy.* New York: Harper & Row, 1957.

Dye, Thomas R. *Politics, Economics, and the Public: Political Outcomes in the American States.* Chicago: Rand McNally, 1966.

Eggers, Andrew C., Anthony Fowler, Jens Hainmueller, Andrew B. Hall, and James M. Snyder Jr. "On the Validity of the Regression Discontinuity Design for Estimating Electoral Effects: New Evidence from Over 40,000 Close Races." *American Journal of Political Science* 59, no. 1 (2015): 259–74.

Ellwood, David T., and Glenn Fine. "The Impact of Right-to-Work Laws on Union Organizing." *Journal of Political Economy* 95, no. 2 (1987): 250–73.

Eren, Ozkan, and Serkan Ozbeklik. "What Do Right-to-Work Laws Do? Evidence from a Synthetic Control Method Analysis." *Journal of Policy Analysis and Management* 35, no. 1 (2016): 173–94.

Erikson, Robert S. "Income Inequality and Policy Responsiveness." *Annual Review of Political Science* 18 (2015): 11–29.

———. "Malapportionment, Gerrymandering, and Party Fortunes in Congressional Elections." *American Political Science Review* 66, no. 4 (1972): 1234–45.

———. "The Puzzle of Midterm Loss." *Journal of Politics* 50, no. 4 (1988): 1011–29.

Erikson, Robert S., Olle Folke, and James M. Snyder Jr. "A Gubernatorial Helping Hand? How Governors Affect Presidential Elections." *Journal of Politics* 77, no. 2 (2015): 491–504.

Erikson, Robert S., Michael B. MacKuen, and James A. Stimson. *The Macro Polity*. New York: Cambridge University Press, 2002.

Erikson, Robert S., Gerald C. Wright, and John P. McIver. "Political Parties, Public Opinion, and State Policy in the United States." *American Political Science Review* 83, no. 3 (1989): 729–50.

———. "Public Opinion in the States: A Quarter Century of Change and Stability." In *Public Opinion in the States*, edited by Jeffrey E. Cohen, 229–53. Stanford, CA: Stanford University Press, 2006.

———. *Statehouse Democracy: Public Opinion and Policy in the American States*. New York: Cambridge University Press, 1993.

Fairclough, Adam. "Historians and the Civil Rights Movement." *Journal of American Studies* 24, no. 3 (1990): 387–98.

Farhang, Sean, and Ira Katznelson. "The Southern Imposition: Congress and Labor in the New Deal and Fair Deal." *Studies in American Political Development* 19, no. 1 (Spring 2005): 1–30.

Fausset, Richard. "North Carolina, in Political Flux, Battles for Its Identity." *New York Times*, September 23, 2014. http://nyti.ms/1oeYCUc.

Fearon, James D. "Electoral Accountability and the Control of Politicians: Selecting Good Types versus Sanctioning Poor Performance." In *Democracy, Accountability, and Representation*, edited by Adam Przeworski, Susan Carol Stokes, and Bernard Manin, 55–97. New York: Cambridge University Press, 1999.

Feigenbaum, James, Alexander Hertel-Fernandez, and Vanessa Williamson. *From the Bargaining Table to the Ballot Box: Political Effects of Right to Work Laws*. Working paper 24259. National Bureau of Economic Research, February 2019. https://doi.org/10.3386/w24259.

Feigenbaum, James J., Alexander Fouirnaies, and Andrew B. Hall. "The Majority-Party Disadvantage: Revising Theories of Legislative Organization." *Quarterly Journal of Political Science* 12, no. 3 (2017): 269–300.

Fiorina, Morris. "The Reagan Years: Turning to the Right or Groping for the Middle?" In *The Resurgence of Conservatism in Anglo-American Democracies*, edited by Barry Cooper, Allan Kornberg, and William Mishler, 430–59. Durham, NC: Duke University Press, 1988.

Flavin, Patrick. "Policy Representation and Evaluations of State Government." *State and Local Government Review* 45, no. 3 (2013): 139–52.

Flavin, Patrick, and Michael T. Hartney. "When Government Subsidizes Its Own: Collective Bargaining Laws as Agents of Political Mobilization." *American Journal of Political Science* 59, no. 4 (2015): 896–911.

Folke, Olle, and James M. Snyder Jr. "Gubernatorial Midterm Slumps." *American Journal of Political Science* 56, no. 4 (2012): 931–48.

Foner, Eric. *Reconstruction: America's Unfinished Revolution, 1863–1877.* New York: Harper & Row, 1988.

Ford, Pamela S. *Regulation of Campaign Finance.* Bureau of Public Administration, University of California, 1955.

Fouirnaies, Alexander, and Andrew B. Hall. "How Do Electoral Incentives Affect Legislator Behavior? Evidence from U.S. State Legislatures." Unpublished working paper, September 28, 2018. http://www.andrewbenjaminhall.com/Fouirnaies_Hall_Electoral_Incentives.pdf.

Fowler, Anthony, and Andrew B. Hall. "Disentangling the Personal and Partisan Incumbency Advantages: Evidence from Close Elections and Term Limits." *Quarterly Journal of Political Science* 9, no. 4 (2014): 501–31.

Fraga, Bernard L. *The Turnout Gap: Race, Ethnicity, and Political Inequality in a Diversifying America.* Cambridge, UK: Cambridge University Press, 2018.

Fraga, Bernard L., and Michael G. Miller. "Who Does Voter ID Keep from Voting?" *Journal of Politics,* 2021. https://doi.org/10.1086/716282.

Francia, Peter L., John C. Green, Paul S. Herrnson, Lynda W. Powell, and Clyde Wilcox. "Limousine Liberals and Corporate Conservatives: The Financial Constituencies of the Democratic and Republican Parties." *Social Science Quarterly* 86, no. 4 (2005): 1–18.

Franses, Philip Hans. "Distributed Lags." In *The New Palgrave Dictionary of Economics,* 3rd ed., 2955–59. London: Palgrave Macmillan, 2018.

Gabriel, Trip. "Virginia Official Pulls Republican's Name from Bowl to Pick Winner of Tied Race." *New York Times,* January 4, 2018. https://nyti.ms/2E6H5Mi.

Gais, Thomas, and R. Kent Weaver. *State Policy Choices under Welfare Reform.* Policy brief 21. Washington, DC: The Brookings Institution, April 2002. https://www.brookings.edu/wp-content/uploads/2016/06/pb21.pdf.

Garrett, Elizabeth. "Term Limitations and the Myth of the Citizen-Legislator." *Cornell Law Review* 81 (1996): 623–97.

Gelman, Andrew, Jennifer Hill, and Aki Vehtari. *Regression and Other Stories.* New York: Cambridge University Press, 2021.

Gelman, Andrew, and Gary King. "A Unified Method of Evaluating Electoral Systems and Redistricting Plans." *American Journal of Political Science* 38, no. 2 (1994): 514–54.

———. "Enhancing Democracy through Legislative Redistricting." *American Political Science Review* 88, no. 3 (1994): 541–59.

Gelman, Andrew, and Thomas C. Little. "Poststratification into Many Categories Using Hierarchical Logistic Regression." *Survey Methodology* 23, no. 2 (1997): 127–35.

Gerber, Elisabeth R. "Legislative Response to the Threat of Popular Initiatives." *American Journal of Political Science* 40, no. 1 (1996): 99–128.

Gerring, John. *Party Ideologies in America, 1828–1996.* New York: Cambridge University Press, 1998.

Gerstle, Gary. *Liberty and Coercion: The Paradox of American Government from the Founding to the Present.* Princeton, NJ: Princeton University Press, 2015.

Gilens, Martin. *Affluence and Influence: Economic Inequality and Political Power in America.* Princeton, NJ: Princeton University Press, 2012.

———. "Inequality and Democratic Responsiveness." *Public Opinion Quarterly* 69, no. 5 (2005): 778–96.

Gilens, Martin, and Benjamin I. Page. "Testing Theories of American Politics: Elites, Interest Groups, and Average Citizens." *Perspectives on Politics* 12, no. 3 (2014): 564–81.

Goel, Sharad, Marc Meredith, Michael Morse, David Rothschild, and Houshmand Shirani-Mehr. "One Person, One Vote: Estimating the Prevalence of Double Voting in US Presidential Elections." *American Political Science Review* 114, no. 2 (2020): 456–69.

Goodnough, Abby. "After Years of Trying, Virginia Finally Will Expand Medicaid." *New York Times*, May 30, 2018. https://nyti.ms/2xsDyJV.

———. "Gay Rights Groups Celebrate Victories in Marriage Push." *New York Times*, April 9, 2009. https://nyti.ms/2rkFG1B.

Graham, David A. "What's the Goal of Voter-ID Laws?" *Atlantic Monthly*, May 2, 2016. https://www.theatlantic.com/politics/archive/2016/05/jim-demint-voter-id-laws/480876/.

Gray, Virginia, David Lowery, Matthew Fellowes, and Andrea McAtee. "Public Opinion, Public Policy, and Organized Interests in the American States." *Political Research Quarterly* 57, no. 3 (2004): 411–20.

Green, Donald, Bradley Palmquist, and Eric Schickler. *Partisan Hearts and Minds: Political Parties and the Social Identities of Voters*. New Haven, CT: Yale University Press, 2002.

Grofman, Bernard. "Downs and Two-Party Convergence." *Annual Review of Political Science* 7 (2004): 25–46.

Grossmann, Matt. *Red State Blues: How the Conservative Revolution Stalled in the States*. New York: Cambridge University Press, 2019.

Grumbach, Jacob. "From Backwaters to Major Policymakers: Policy Polarization in the States, 1970–2014." *Perspectives on Politics* 16, no. 2 (2018): 416–35.

———. *Laboratories against Democracy: How National Parties Transformed State Politics*. Princeton, NJ: Princeton University Press, 2022.

Hajnal, Zoltan L. *Dangerously Divided: How Race and Class Shape Winning and Losing in American Politics*. New York: Cambridge University Press, 2020.

Hall, Andrew B. "What Happens When Extremists Win Primaries?" *American Political Science Review* 109, no. 1 (2015): 18–42.

Hall, Andrew B., and James M. Snyder Jr. "Candidate Ideology and Electoral Success." Unpublished working paper, September 29, 2015. http://www.andrewbenjaminhall.com/Hall_Snyder_Ideology.pdf.

Hall, Andrew B., and Daniel M. Thompson. "Who Punishes Extremist Nominees? Candidate Ideology and Turning Out the Base in US Elections." *American Political Science Review* 112, no. 3 (2018): 509–24.

Hall, Peter A., and David Soskice, eds. *Varieties of Capitalism: The Institutional Foundations of Comparative Advantage*. New York: Oxford University Press, 2001.

Hall, Richard L. *Participation in Congress*. New Haven, CT: Yale University Press, 1996.

Handley, Lisa, and Bernard Grofman. "The Impact of the Voting Rights Act on Minority Representation: Black Officeholding in Southern State Legislatures and Congressional Delegations." In *Quiet Revolution in the South: The Impact of the Voting Rights Act, 1965–1990*, edited by Chandler Davidson and Bernard Grofman, 351–77. Princeton, NJ: Princeton University Press, 1994.

Hare, Christopher, and James E. Monogan. "The Democratic Deficit on Salient Issues: Immigration and Healthcare in the States." *Journal of Public Policy* 40, no. 1 (2020): 116–43.

Hayes, Danny, and Jennifer L. Lawless. *News Hole: The Demise of Local Journalism and Political Engagement*. New York: Cambridge University Press, 2021.

Henderson, John A. "Issue Distancing in Congressional Elections." Unpublished working paper, March 14, 2019. http://www.jahenderson.com/research.

Henderson, John A., Brian T. Hamel, and Aaron M. Goldzimer. "Gerrymandering Incumbency: Does Nonpartisan Redistricting Increase Electoral Competition?" *Journal of Politics* 80, no. 3 (2018): 1011–16.

Hertel-Fernandez, Alex. *State Capture: How Conservative Activists, Big Businesses, and Wealthy Donors Reshaped the American States—and the Nation.* New York: Oxford University Press, 2019.

Hertel-Fernandez, Alexander. "Policy Feedback as Political Weapon: Conservative Advocacy and the Demobilization of the Public Sector Labor Movement." *Perspectives on Politics* 16, no. 2 (2018): 364–79.

Hiaeshutter-Rice, Dan, Stuart Soroka, and Christopher Wlezien. "Freedom of the Press and Public Responsiveness." *Perspectives on Politics* 19, no. 2 (2021): 479–91.

Highton, Benjamin. "Voter Identification Laws and Turnout in the United States." *Annual Review of Political Science* 20 (2017): 149–67.

Highton, Benjamin, and Cindy D. Kam. "The Long-Term Dynamics of Partisanship and Issue Orientations." *Journal of Politics* 73, no. 1 (2011): 202–15.

Hill, Seth. *Frustrated Majorities: How Issue Intensity Enables Smaller Groups of Voters to Get What They Want.* Forthcoming, Cambridge, UK: Cambridge University Press, 2022.

Hill, Seth J., and Gregory A. Huber. "On the Meaning of Survey Reports of Roll-Call 'Votes.'" *American Journal of Political Science* 63, no. 3 (2019): 611–25.

Hill, Seth J., and Chris Tausanovitch. "A Disconnect in Representation? Comparison of Trends in Congressional and Public Polarization." *Journal of Politics* 77, no. 4 (2016): 1058–75.

Hirano, Shigeo, and James M. Snyder Jr. *Primary Elections in the United States.* New York: Cambridge University Press, 2019.

Hofferbert, Richard I. "The Relation between Public Policy and Some Structural and Environmental Variables in the American States." *American Political Science Review* 60, no. 1 (1966): 73–82.

Hood, M. V., Quentin Kidd, and Irwin L. Morris. "The Republican Party in the American South: From Radical Fringe to Conservative Mainstream." In *The Oxford Handbook of Southern Politics,* edited by Charles S. Bullock III and Mark J. Rozell, 330–54. New York: Oxford University Press, 2012.

Hopkins, Anne H., and Ronald E. Weber. "Dimensions of Public Policies in the American States." *Polity* 8, no. 3 (1976): 475–89.

Hopkins, Daniel J. *The Increasingly United States: How and Why American Political Behavior Nationalized.* Chicago: University of Chicago Press, 2018.

Hopkins, Daniel J., Marc Meredith, Michael Morse, Sarah Smith, and Jesse Yoder. "Voting but for the Law: Evidence from Virginia on Photo Identification Requirements." *Journal of Empirical Legal Studies* 14, no. 1 (2017): 79–128.

Hopkins, David. *Red Fighting Blue: How Geography and Electoral Rules Polarize American Politics.* New York: Cambridge University Press, 2017.

Huber, John D., and G. Bingham Powell Jr. "Congruence between Citizens and Policymakers in Two Visions of Liberal Democracy." *World Politics* 46, no. 3 (1994): 291–326.

Hyytinen, Ari, Jaakko Meriläinen, Tuukka Saarimaa, Otto Toivanen, and Janne Tukiainen. "When Does Regression Discontinuity Design Work? Evidence from Random Election Outcomes." *Quantitative Economics* 9, no. 2 (2018): 1019–51.

Idaho Secretary of State, Election Division. "Idaho Initiative History," 2020. Accessed January 13, 2020. https://sos.idaho.gov/elect/inits/inithist.htm.

Imai, Kosuke, In Song Kim, and Erik Wang. "Matching Methods for Causal Inference with Time-Series Cross-Sectional Data." *American Journal of Political Science*, forthcoming. https://imai.fas.harvard.edu/research/files/tscs.pdf.

Jacobson, Gary C. "Driven to Extremes: Donald Trump's Extraordinary Impact on the 2020 Elections." *Presidential Studies Quarterly* 51, no. 3 (2021): 492–521.

———. "The Electoral Origins of Polarized Politics: Evidence from the 2010 Cooperative Congressional Election Study." *American Behavioral Scientist* 56, no. 12 (2012): 1612–30.

James, David Ray. "The Transformation of Local State and Class Structures and Resistance to the Civil Rights Movement in the South." PhD diss., University of Wisconsin–Madison, 1981.

Jennings, Edward T. Jr. "Some Policy Consequences of the Long Revolution and Bifactional Rivalry in Louisiana." *American Journal of Political Science* 21, no. 2 (1977): 225–46.

Jennings, M. Kent, and Harmon Zeigler. "The Salience of American State Politics." *American Political Science Review* 64, no. 2 (1970): 523–35.

Jessee, Stephen A. "(How) Can We Estimate the Ideology of Citizens and Political Elites on the Same Scale?" *American Journal of Political Science* 60, no. 4 (2016): 1108–24.

Kaiser Family Foundation. "Status of State Medicaid Expansion Decisions: Interactive Map," August 10, 2021. https://www.kff.org/medicaid/issue-brief/status-of-state-medicaid-expansion-decisions-interactive-map/.

Kaplan, Ethan, and Haishan Yuan. "Early Voting Laws, Voter Turnout, and Partisan Vote Composition: Evidence from Ohio." *American Economic Journal: Applied Economics* 12, no. 1 (2020): 32–60.

Karch, Andrew. "Emerging Issues and Future Directions in State Policy Diffusion Research." *State Politics and Policy Quarterly* 7, no. 1 (2007): 54–80.

Keefe, Jeffrey. "Laws Enabling Public-Sector Collective Bargaining Have Not Led to Excessive Public-Sector Pay." Economic Policy Institute, October 16, 2015. https://www.epi.org/publication/laws-enabling-public-sector-collective-bargaining-have-not-led-to-excessive-public-sector-pay/.

Keele, Luke, William Cubbison, and Ismail White. "Suppressing Black Votes: A Historical Case Study of Voting Restrictions in Louisiana." *American Political Science Review* 115, no. 2 (2021): 694–700.

Keith, Bruce E., David B. Magleby, Candice J. Nelson, Elizabeth Orr, Mark C. Westlye, and Raymond E. Wolfinger. "The Partisan Affinities of Independent 'Leaners.'" *British Journal of Political Science* 16, no. 2 (1986): 155–85.

Kerrissey, Jasmine, and Evan Schofer. "Union Membership and Political Participation in the United States." *Social Forces* 91, no. 3 (2013): 895–928.

Key, V. O. Jr. *Southern Politics in State and Nation*. New York: Knopf, 1949.

Keyssar, Alexander. *The Right to Vote: The Contested History of Democracy in the United States*. New York: Basic Books, 2000.

Killian, Mitchell, and Clyde Wilcox. "Do Abortion Attitudes Lead to Party Switching?" *Political Research Quarterly* 61, no. 4 (2008): 561–73.

King, Desmond, Robert C. Lieberman, Gretchen Ritter, and Laurence Whitehead, eds. *Democratization in America: A Comparative-Historical Analysis*. Baltimore: Johns Hopkins University Press, 2009.

Kingdon, John W. *Congressmen's Voting Decisions*. Ann Arbor: University of Michigan Press, 1989.

Klar, Samara, and Yanna Krupnikov. *Independent Politics: How American Disdain for Parties Leads to Political Inaction*. New York: Cambridge University Press, 2016.

Klingman, David, and William W. Lammers. "The 'General Policy Liberalism' Factor in American State Politics." *American Journal of Political Science* 28, no. 3 (1984): 598–610.

Kogan, Vladimir, and Eric McGhee. "Redistricting California: An Evaluation of the Citizens Commission Final Plans." *California Journal of Politics and Policy* 4, no. 1 (2012): 1–32.

Kousser, J. Morgan. *The Shaping of Southern Politics: Suffrage Restriction and the Establishment of the One-Party South.* New Haven, CT: Yale University Press, 1974.

Kousser, Thad. *Term Limits and the Dismantling of State Legislative Professionalism.* New York: Cambridge University Press, 2005.

Kousser, Thad, Jeffrey B. Lewis, and Seth E. Masket. "Ideological Adaptation? The Survival Instinct of Threatened Legislators." *Journal of Politics* 69, no. 3 (2007): 828–43.

Krehbiel, Keith. *Pivotal Politics: A Theory of U.S. Lawmaking.* Chicago: University of Chicago Press, 1998.

Kreitzer, Rebecca J. "Politics and Morality in State Abortion Policy." *State Politics and Policy Quarterly* 15, no. 1 (2015): 41–66.

Krimmel, Katherine, Jeffrey R. Lax, and Justin H. Phillips. "Gay Rights in Congress: Public Opinion and (Mis)representation." *Public Opinion Quarterly* 80, no. 4 (2016): 888–913.

Kubin, Jeffrey C. "Case for Redistricting Commissions." *Texas Law Review* 75, no. 4 (1996): 837–72.

Kuriwaki, Shiro. "Ticket Splitting in a Nationalized Era." SocArXiv, May 29, 2019. https://doi .org/10.31235/osf.io/bvgz3.

Kuziemko, Ilyana, and Ebonya Washington. "Why Did the Democrats Lose the South? Bringing New Data to an Old Debate." *American Economic Review* 108, no.10 (2018): 2830–67.

La Raja, Raymond J., and Brian F. Schaffner. *Campaign Finance and Political Polarization: When Purists Prevail.* Ann Arbor: University of Michigan Press, 2015.

———. "The Effects of Campaign Finance Spending Bans on Electoral Outcomes: Evidence from the States about the Potential Impact of *Citizens United v. FEC*." *Electoral Studies* 33 (March 2014): 102–14.

Lacombe, Matthew J. "The Political Weaponization of Gun Owners: The National Rifle Association's Cultivation, Dissemination, and Use of a Group Social Identity." *Journal of Politics* 81, no. 4 (2019): 1342–56.

LaCombe, Scott J. "Measuring Institutional Design in US States." *Social Science Quarterly* 102, no. 4 (2021): 1511–33.

LaCombe, Scott J., and Frederick J. Boehmke. "The Initiative Process and Policy Innovation in the American States." *State Politics and Policy Quarterly* 21, no. 3 (2021): 286–305.

Ladd, Everett Carll. "The 1994 Congressional Elections: The Postindustrial Realignment Continues." *Political Science Quarterly* 110, no. 1 (1995): 1–23.

Lahey, Joanna. "State Age Protection Laws and the Age Discrimination in Employment Act." *Journal of Law and Economics* 51, no. 3 (2008): 433–60.

Langehennig, Stefani, Joseph Zamadics, and Jennifer Wolak. "State Policy Outcomes and State Legislative Approval." *Political Research Quarterly* 72, no. 4 (2019): 929–43.

Lascher, Edward L., Michael G. Hagen, and Steven A. Rochlin. "Gun Behind the Door? Ballot Initiatives, State Policies and Public Opinion." *Journal of Politics* 58, no. 3 (1996): 760–75.

Lax, Jeffrey, and Justin Phillips. "Gay Rights in the States: Public Opinion and Policy Responsiveness." *American Political Science Review* 103, no. 3 (2009): 367–86.

———. "How Should We Estimate Public Opinion in the States?" *American Journal of Political Science* 53, no. 1 (2009): 107–21.

———. "The Democratic Deficit in the States." *American Journal of Political Science* 56, no. 1 (2012): 148–66.

Layman, Geoffrey C., and Thomas M. Carsey. "Party Polarization and 'Conflict Extension' in the American Electorate." *American Journal of Political Science* 46, no. 4 (2002): 786–802.

———. "Party Polarization and Party Structuring of Policy Attitudes: A Comparison of Three NES Panel Studies." *Political Behavior* 24, no. 3 (2002): 199–236.

Layman, Geoffrey C., Thomas M. Carsey, John C. Green, Richard Herrera, and Rosalyn Cooperman. "Activists and Conflict Extension in American Party Politics." *American Political Science Review* 104, no. 2 (2010): 324–46.

Lee, David S. "Randomized Experiments from Non-random Selection in US House Elections." *Journal of Econometrics* 142 (2008): 675–97.

Lee, Frances E. *Beyond Ideology: Politics, Principles and Partisanship in the U.S. Senate.* Chicago: University of Chicago Press, 2009.

Lee, Frances E., and Bruce I. Oppenheimer. *Sizing Up the Senate: The Unequal Consequences of Equal Representation.* Chicago: University of Chicago Press, 1999.

Levitsky, Steven, and Lucan A. Way. "Elections without Democracy: The Rise of Competitive Authoritarianism." *Journal of Democracy* 13, no. 2 (2002): 51–65.

Levitsky, Steven, and Daniel Ziblatt. *How Democracies Die.* New York: Crown, 2018.

Lewis, Jeffrey B., and Chris Tausanovitch. "When Does Joint Scaling Allow for Direct Comparisons of Preferences?" Paper presented at the Conference on Ideal Point Models, Massachusetts Institute of Technology, Cambridge, MA, May 1, 2015. http://idealpoint.tahk.us/papers/lewisTausanovitch.pdf.

Lichtenstein, Nelson. *State of the Union: A Century of American Labor.* Princeton, NJ: Princeton University Press, 2002.

Lovenheim, Michael F., and Alexander Willen. "The Long-Run Effects of Teacher Collective Bargaining." *American Economic Journal: Economic Policy* 11, no. 3 (2019): 292–324.

Lowery, David, and Virginia Gray. *The Population Ecology of Interest Representation: Lobbying Communities in the American States.* Ann Arbor: University of Michigan Press, 2000.

Lyon, Melissa Arnold. "Heroes, Villains, or Something in Between? How 'Right to Work' Policies Affect Teachers, Students, and Education Policymaking." *Economics of Education Review* 82 (2021): 102–5.

Macdonald, David. "Labor Unions and White Democratic Partisanship." *Political Behavior* 43 (2021): 859–79.

MacKuen, Michael B., Robert S. Erikson, and James A. Stimson. "Macropartisanship." *American Political Science Review* 83, no. 4 (1989): 1125–42.

Manin, Bernard, Adam Przeworski, and Susan Carol Stokes. "Elections and Representation." In *Democracy, Accountability, and Representation*, edited by Adam Przeworski, Susan Carol Stokes, and Bernard Manin, 29–55. New York: Cambridge University Press, 1999.

Mann, Thomas J., and Norman J. Ornstein. *It's Even Worse Than It Looks: How the American Constitutional System Collided with the New Politics of Extremism.* New York: Basic Books, 2012.

Marschall, Melissa J., and Amanda Rutherford. "Voting Rights for Whom? Examining the Effects of the Voting Rights Act on Latino Political Incorporation." *American Journal of Political Science* 60, no. 3 (2016): 590–606.

Matsusaka, John G. *For the Many or the Few: The Initiative, Public Policy, and American Democracy.* Chicago: University of Chicago Press, 2008.

———. "Popular Control of Public Policy: A Quantitative Approach." *Quarterly Journal of Political Science* 5, no. 2 (2010): 133–67.

———. "Problems with a Methodology Used to Evaluate the Voter Initiative." *Journal of Politics* 63, no. 4 (2001): 1250–56.

———. "Public Policy and the Initiative and Referendum: A Survey with Some New Evidence." *Public Choice* 174, no. 1 (2018): 107–43.

May, John D. "Defining Democracy: A Bid for Coherence and Consensus." *Political Studies* 26, no. 1 (1978): 1–14.

Mayhew, David R. *Congress: The Electoral Connection.* New Haven, CT: Yale University Press, 1974.

———. *Placing Parties in American Politics: Organization, Electoral Settings, and Government Activity in the Twentieth Century.* Princeton, NJ: Princeton University Press, 1986.

McCarty, Nolan, Keith T. Poole, and Howard Rosenthal. "Does Gerrymandering Cause Polarization?" *American Journal of Political Science* 53, no. 3 (2009): 666–80.

———. *Polarized America: The Dance of Ideology and Unequal Riches.* Cambridge, MA: MIT Press, 2006.

McGhee, Eric. "Measuring Efficiency in Redistricting." *Election Law Journal* 16, no. 4 (2017): 417–42.

———. "Measuring Partisan Bias in Single-Member District Electoral Systems." *Legislative Studies Quarterly* 39, no. 1 (2014): 55–85.

———. "Partisan Gerrymandering and Political Science." *Annual Review of Political Science* 23 (2020): 171–85.

McKee, Seth C. "The Past, Present, and Future of Southern Politics." *Southern Cultures* 18, no. 3 (2012): 95–117.

McKee, Seth C., and Melanie J. Springer. "A Tale of 'Two Souths': White Voting Behavior in Contemporary Southern Elections." *Social Science Quarterly* 96, no. 2 (2015): 588–607.

McLean, Dylan S., and Jason Sorens. "The Changing Ideological Politics of U.S. State Firearms Regulation." *Politics and Policy* 42, no. 1 (2019): 327–35.

Mebane, Walter R. "Coordination, Moderation, and Institutional Balancing in American Presidential and House Elections." *American Political Science Review* 94, no. 1 (2000): 37–57.

Mettler, Suzanne, and Robert C. Lieberman. *Four Threats: The Recurring Crises of American Democracy.* New York: St. Martin's Press, 2020.

Michener, Jamila. *Fragmented Democracy: Medicaid, Federalism, and Unequal Politics.* New York: Cambridge University Press, 2018.

Mickey, Robert W. *Paths Out of Dixie: The Democratization of Authoritarian Enclaves in America's Deep South.* Princeton, NJ: Princeton University Press, 2015.

Mislevy, Robert J. "Item Response Models for Grouped Data." *Journal of Educational Statistics* 8, no. 4 (1983): 271–88.

Moe, Terry M. *Special Interest: Teachers Unions and America's Public Schools.* Washington, DC: Brookings Institution Press, 2011.

Monogan, James, Virginia Gray, and David Lowery. "Public Opinion, Organized Interests, and Policy Congruence in Initiative and Noninitiative US States." *State Politics and Policy Quarterly* 9, no. 3 (2009): 304–24.

Monroe, Alan D. "Public Opinion and Public Policy, 1980–1993." *Public Opinion Quarterly* 62, no. 1 (1998): 6–28.

Mooney, Christopher Z. "Measuring State House Speakers' Formal Powers, 1981–2010." *State Politics and Policy Quarterly* 13, no. 2 (2013): 262–73.

Morone, James A. *The Democratic Wish: Popular Participation and the Limits of American Government*. New York: Basic Books, 1990.

Moskowitz, Daniel J. "Local News, Information, and the Nationalization of US Elections." *American Political Science Review* 115, no. 1 (2021): 114–29.

Mutnick, Ally. "How Democrats Are 'Unilaterally Disarming' in the Redistricting Wars." *Politico*, June 21, 2021. https://www.politico.com/news/2021/06/21/democrats-redistricting-wars-495303.

National Conference of State Legislatures. "Redistricting Law 2010." November 2009. https://www.ncsl.org/research/redistricting/redistricting-law-2010.aspx.

———. "Right-to-Work Resources." 2021. https://www.ncsl.org/research/labor-and-employment/right-to-work-laws-and-bills.aspx.

———. "Voter Identification Requirements | Voter ID Laws." August 9, 2021. https://www.ncsl.org/research/elections-and-campaigns/voter-id.aspx.

National Municipal League. "Apportionment in the Nineteen Sixties: State Legislatures, Congressional Districts." National Municipal League, 1967.

Neumark, David. "Age Discrimination Legislation in the United States." *Contemporary Economic Policy* 21, no. 3 (2003): 297–317.

New York Times. "The 1994 Elections: State by State." November 10, 1994, B9–B11.

Nickell, Stephen. "Biases in Dynamic Models with Fixed Effects." *Econometrica* 49 (1981): 1417–26.

Niemi, Richard G., and Simon Jackman. "Bias and Responsiveness in State Legislative Districting." *Legislative Studies Quarterly* 16, no. 2 (1991): 183–202.

Noel, Hans. *Political Ideologies and Political Parties in America*. New York: Cambridge University Press, 2014.

Norrander, Barbara. "Measuring State Public Opinion with the Senate National Election Study." *State Politics and Policy Quarterly* 1, no. 1 (2001): 111–25.

Novak, William J. *The People's Welfare: Law and Regulation in Nineteenth-Century America*. Chapel Hill: University of North Carolina Press, 1996.

O'Donnell, Guillermo. "On the State, Democratization and Some Conceptual Problems: A Latin American View with Glances at Some Postcommunist Countries." *World Development* 21, no. 8 (1993): 1355–69.

Olson, Michael P., and James M. Snyder Jr. "Dyadic Representation in the American North and South: The Case of Prohibition." *Journal of Politics* 83, no. 3 (2021): 1030–45.

Pacheco, Julianna. "Using National Surveys to Measure Dynamic US State Public Opinion: A Guideline for Scholars and an Application." *State Politics and Policy Quarterly* 11, no. 4 (2011): 415–39.

Pacheco, Julianna. "The Thermostatic Model of Responsiveness in the American States." *State Politics and Policy Quarterly* 13, no. 3 (2013): 306–32.

Page, Benjamin I., and Robert Y. Shapiro. "Effects of Public Opinion on Policy." *American Political Science Review* 77, no. 1 (1983): 175–90.

———. *The Rational Public: Fifty Years of Trends in Americans' Policy Preferences*. Chicago: University of Chicago, 1992.

Paglayan, Agustina S. "Public-Sector Unions and the Size of Government." *American Journal of Political Science* 63, no. 1 (2019): 21–36.

Park, David K., Andrew Gelman, and Joseph Bafumi. "Bayesian Multilevel Estimation with Poststratification: State-Level Estimates from National Polls." *Political Analysis* 12, no. 4 (2004): 375–85.

Patashnik, Eric M., and Julian E. Zelizer. "The Struggle to Remake Politics: Liberal Reform and the Limits of Policy Feedback in the Contemporary American State." *Perspectives on Politics* 11, no. 4 (2013): 1071–87.

Payson, Julia. *When Cities Lobby: How Local Governments Compete for Power in State Politics.* New York: Oxford University Press, 2022.

Pearson, Elizabeth. "Saying Yes to Taxes: The Politics of Tax Reform Campaigns in Three Northwestern States, 1965–1973." *American Journal of Sociology* 119, no. 5 (2014): 1279–323.

Perman, Michael. *Pursuit of Unity: A Political History of the American South.* Chapel Hill: University of North Carolina Press, 2009.

Pettersson-Lidbom, Per. "Do Parties Matter for Economic Outcomes? A Regression-Discontinuity Approach." *Journal of the European Economic Association* 6, no. 5 (2008): 1037–56.

Pierson, Paul. "When Effect Becomes Cause: Policy Feedback and Political Change." *World Politics* 45, no. 4 (1993): 595–628.

Poll, Marquette Law School. "New Marquette Law School Poll Finds Some Issues Less Divisive Amid Continuing Partisan Divide," January 24, 2019. https://www.marquette.edu/news -center/2019/new-marquette-law-school-poll-finds-some-issues-less-divisive-amid-continu ing-partisan-divide.php.

Poole, Keith T., and Howard Rosenthal. *Ideology and Congress.* New Brunswick, NJ: Transaction, 2007.

———. "The Polarization of American Politics." *Journal of Politics* 46, no. 4 (1984): 1061–79.

Powell, G. Bingham Jr. "Political Representation in Comparative Politics." *Annual Review of Political Science* 7 (2004): 273–96.

Quadagno, Jill. "From Old-Age Assistance to Supplemental Security Income: The Political Economy of Relief in the South, 1935–1972." In *The Politics of Social Policy in the United States,* edited by Margaret Weir, Ann Shola Orloff, and Theda Skocpol, 235–64. Princeton, NJ: Princeton University Press, 1988.

Quinn, Kevin M. "Bayesian Factor Analysis for Mixed Ordinal and Continuous Responses." *Political Analysis* 12, no. 4 (2004): 338–53.

Ramey, Adam. "Vox Populi, Vox Dei? Crowdsourced Ideal Point Estimation." *Journal of Politics* 78, no. 1 (2016): 281–95.

Rasinski, Kenneth A. "The Effect of Question Wording on Public Support for Government Spending." *Public Opinion Quarterly* 53, no. 3 (1989): 388–94.

Rasmussen, Anne, Stefanie Reher, and Dimiter Toshkov. "Opinion-Policy Nexus." *European Journal of Political Research* 58, no. 2 (2019): 412–34.

"Redistricting Commissions." Ballotpedia, 2021. https://ballotpedia.org/Independent_redistricting _commissions.

Rigby, Elizabeth, and Gerald C. Wright. "Whose Statehouse Democracy? Policy Responsiveness to Poor versus Rich Constituents in Poor versus Rich States." In *Who Gets Represented?*, edited by Peter K. Enns and Christopher Wlezien, 189–222. New York: Russell Sage Foundation, 2011.

Roanoke Times. "How an Election in 1991 Led to Virginia's 2018 Medicaid Vote." Editorial. June 1, 2018. https://www.roanoke.com/opinion/editorials/editorial-how-an-election-in-led-to-virginia -s-medicaid/article_f0c8d7a6-d02d-5790-820a-e51839978fe5.html.

Robinson, Jonathan, John Sides, and Christopher Warshaw. *When Mass Opinion Goes to the Ballot Box: A National Assessment of State Level Issue Opinion and Ballot Initiative Results.* AAPOR Conference Presentation, 2021.

Rocco, Philip, Ann C. Keller, and Andrew S. Kelly. "State Politics and the Uneven Fate of Medicaid Expansion." *Health Affairs* 39, no. 3 (2020): 494–501.

Rodden, Jonathan. "The Geographic Distribution of Political Preferences." *Annual Review of Political Science* 13, no. 1 (2010): 321–40.

Rodden, Jonathan A. *Why Cities Lose: The Deep Roots of the Urban–Rural Political Divide.* New York: Basic Books, 2019.

Roemer, John E. *Political Competition: Theory and Applications.* Cambridge, MA: Harvard University Press, 2001.

Rogers, Steven. "Electoral Accountability for State Legislative Roll Calls and Ideological Representation." *American Political Science Review* 111, no. 3 (2017): 555–71.

———. "National Forces in State Legislative Elections." *The Annals of the American Academy of Political and Social Science* 667 (September 2016): 207–25.

Rosenfeld, Sam. *The Polarizers: Postwar Architects of Our Partisan Era.* Chicago: University of Chicago Press, 2018.

Saltzman, Gregory M. "Bargaining Laws as a Cause and Consequence of the Growth of Teacher Unionism." *ILR Review* 38, no. 3 (1985): 335–51.

Saxon, Wolfgang. "Deane Chandler Davis Dies at 90; Vermont Governor for Two Terms." *New York Times*, December 10, 1990, B12. https://www.nytimes.com/1990/12/10/obituaries/deane-chandler-davis-dies-at-90-vermont-governor-for-two-terms.html.

Schaffner, Brian F., Jesse H. Rhodes, and Raymond J. La Raja. *Hometown Inequality: Race, Class, and Representation in American Local Politics.* New York: Cambridge University Press, 2020.

Schattschneider, E. E. *The Semisovereign People: A Realist's View of Democracy in America.* New York: Hold, Rinehart, Winston, 1960.

Schickler, Eric. "New Deal Liberalism and Racial Liberalism in the Mass Public, 1937–1968." *Perspectives on Politics* 11, no. 1 (2013): 75–98.

———. *Racial Realignment: The Transformation of American Liberalism, 1932–1965.* Princeton, NJ: Princeton University Press, 2016.

Schickler, Eric, and Devin Caughey. "Public Opinion, Organized Labor, and the Limits of New Deal Liberalism, 1936–1945." *Studies in American Political Development* 25, no. 2 (2011): 1–28.

Schlozman, Kay Lehman, Henry E. Brady, and Sidney Verba. *Unequal and Unrepresented: Political Inequality and the People's Voice in the New Gilded Age.* Princeton, NJ: Princeton University Press, 2018.

Schuman, Howard. "Ordinary Questions, Survey Questions, and Policy Questions." *Public Opinion Quarterly* 50, no. 3 (1986): 432–42.

Scott, Dylan. "What Virginia's Drawing-Bowl Tiebreaker Means for the State's Medicaid Expansion." Vox, January 4, 2018. https://www.vox.com/policy-and-politics/2018/1/4/16621732/virginia-house-democrats-medicaid-expansion.

Seabrook, Nicholas R. *Drawing the Lines: Constraints on Partisan Gerrymandering in US Politics.* Ithaca, NY: Cornell University Press, 2017.

Sears, David O., and Jack Citrin. *Tax Revolt: Something for Nothing in California.* Cambridge, MA: Harvard University Press, 1982.

Sears, David O., and Carolyn L. Funk. "Evidence of the Long-Term Persistence of Adults' Political Predispositions." *Journal of Politics* 61, no. 1 (1999): 1–28.

Sekar, Samantha. "Misrepresented: Understanding the Gap between US Public Opinion and Policy on Climate Change." PhD diss., Stanford University, 2020.

Shafer, Byron E., and Richard Johnston. *The End of Southern Exceptionalism: Class, Race, and Partisan Change in the Postwar South.* Cambridge, MA: Harvard University Press, 2006.

Sharkansky, Ira, and Richard I. Hofferbert. "Dimensions of State Politics, Economics, and Public Policy." *American Political Science Review* 63, no. 3 (1969): 867–79.

Shaw, Daron, and John Petrocik. *The Turnout Myth: Voting Rates and Partisan Outcomes in American National Elections.* New York: Oxford University Press, 2020.

Shirley, Kenneth E., and Andrew Gelman. "Hierarchical Models for Estimating State and Demographic Trends in US Death Penalty Public Opinion." *Journal of the Royal Statistical Society: Series A (Statistics in Society)* 178, no. 1 (2015): 1–28.

Shor, Boris, and Nolan McCarty. "The Ideological Mapping of American Legislatures." *American Political Science Review* 105, no. 3 (2011): 530–51.

Shorman, Jonathan. "The Brownback Legacy: Tax Cut Push Led to Sharp Backlash." *Wichita Eagle,* July 26, 2017.

Simonovits, Gabor, Andrew M. Guess, and Jonathan Nagler. "Responsiveness without Representation: Evidence from Minimum Wage Laws in U.S. States." *American Journal of Political Science* 22, no. 3 (2018): 401–10.

Smith, Rogers M. *Civic Ideals: Conflicting Visions of Citizenship in U.S. History.* New Haven, CT: Yale University Press, 1997.

Snyder, James M. Jr., and David Strömberg. "Press Coverage and Political Accountability." *Journal of Political Economy* 118, no. 2 (2010): 355–408.

Snyder, James M. Jr., and Michael M. Ting. "Roll Calls, Party Labels, and Elections." *Political Analysis* 11, no. 4 (2003): 419–44.

Sorens, Jason, Fait Muedini, and William P. Ruger. "US State and Local Public Policies in 2006: A New Database." *State Politics and Policy Quarterly* 8, no. 3 (2008): 309–26.

Soroka, Stuart N., and Christopher Wlezien. *Degrees of Democracy: Politics, Public Opinion, and Policy.* New York: Cambridge University Press, 2012.

Soss, Joe, and Vesla Weaver. "Police Are Our Government: Politics, Political Science, and the Policing of Race–Class Subjugated Communities." *Annual Review of Political Science* 20 (2016): 565–91.

Spicuzza, Mary, and Dee J. Hall. "Walker Defeats Barrett to Win Governor's Race." *Wisconsin State Journal,* November 3, 2010. https://madison.com/wsj/news/local/govt-and-politics/elections/walker-defeats-barrett-to-win-governors-race/article_d112cfd0-e6f9-11df-83c9-001cc4c002e0.html.

Springer, Melanie Jean. *How the States Shaped the Nation: American Electoral Institutions and Voter Turnout, 1920–2000.* Chicago: University of Chicago Press, 2014.

Stanley, Harold W. *Voter Mobilization and the Politics of Race: The South and Universal Suffrage, 1952–1984.* New York: Praeger, 1987.

Stephanopoulos, Nicholas, and Christopher Warshaw. "The Impact of Partisan Gerrymandering on Political Parties." *Legislative Studies Quarterly* 45, no. 4 (2020): 609–43.

Stephanopoulos, Nicholas O. "Arizona and Anti-reform." *University of Chicago Legal Forum* 2015 (2016): 14.

———. "The Causes and Consequences of Gerrymandering." *William and Mary Law Review* 59 (2018).

———. "The Consequences of Consequentialist Criteria." *UC Irvine Law Review* 3 (2013): 669.

Stephanopoulos, Nicholas O., and Eric M. McGhee. "Partisan Gerrymandering and the Efficiency Gap." *University of Chicago Law Review* 82, no. 2 (2015): 831–900.

Stimson, James A. *Public Opinion in America: Moods, Cycles, and Swings*. 2nd ed. Boulder, CO: Westview, 1999.

Stimson, James A., Michael B. MacKuen, and Robert S. Erikson. "Dynamic Representation." *American Political Science Review* 89, no. 3 (1995): 543–65.

Stoker, Laura, and Jake Bowers. "Designing Multi-level Studies: Sampling Voters and Electoral Contexts." *Electoral Studies* 21 (2002): 235–67.

Stoker, Laura, and M. Kent Jennings. "Of Time and the Development of Partisan Polarization." *American Journal of Political Science* 52, no. 3 (2008): 619–35.

Stokes, Leah Cardamore. *Short Circuiting Policy: Interest Groups and the Battle Over Clean Energy and Climate Policy in the American States*. New York: Oxford University Press, 2020.

Stone, Amy L. *Gay Rights at the Ballot Box*. Minneapolis: University of Minnesota Press, 2012.

Stratmann, Thomas, and Francisco J. Aparicio-Castillo. "Competition Policy for Elections: Do Campaign Contribution Limits Matter?" *Public Choice* 127, nos. 1–2 (2006): 177–206.

Suntrup, Jack, and Kurt Erickson. "Democrats, Unions Declare Victory as 'Right to Work' Loses by Wide Margin in Missouri." *St. Louis Post-Dispatch*, August 8, 2018. https://www.stltoday .com/news/local/govt-and-politics/right-to-work-opponents-hold-early-advantage-as -precincts-begin/article_d75fc640-45e0-5ecc-93c9-91cecca36113.html.

Tausanovitch, Chris. "Why Are Subnational Governments Responsive?" *Journal of Politics* 81, no. 1 (2019): 334–42.

Tausanovitch, Chris, and Christopher Warshaw. "Does the Ideological Proximity between Candidates and Voters Affect Voting in US House Elections?" *Political Behavior* 40, no. 1 (2018): 223–45.

———. "Estimating Candidates' Political Orientation in a Polarized Congress." *Political Analysis* 25, no. 2 (2017): 167–87.

———. "Representation in Municipal Government." *American Political Science Review* 108, no. 3 (2014): 605–41.

Teaford, Jon C. *The Rise of the States: Evolution of American State Government*. Baltimore: Johns Hopkins University Press, 2002.

Thompson, Daniel M., Jennifer A. Wu, Jesse Yoder, and Andrew B. Hall. "Universal Vote-by-Mail Has No Impact on Partisan Turnout or Vote Share." *Proceedings of the National Academy of Sciences* 117, no. 25 (2020): 14052–56.

Thomsen, Danielle M. "Ideological Moderates Won't Run: How Party Fit Matters for Partisan Polarization in Congress." *Journal of Politics* 76, no. 3 (2014): 786–97.

Time. "The Lonely One." February 20, 1956, 22.

Treier, Shawn, and Simon Jackman. "Democracy as a Latent Variable." *American Journal of Political Science* 52, no. 1 (2008): 201–17.

Tversky, Amos, and Daniel·Kahneman. "The Framing of Decisions and the Psychology of Choice." *Science* 211, no. 4481 (1981): 453–58.

United States Commission on Civil Rights. *Hearings Before the United States Commission on Civil Rights*. Washington, DC: US Government Printing Office, 1965. https://catalog.hathi trust.org/Record/000588551.

Usher, Brian. "The Lausche Era, 1945–1957." In *Ohio Politics*, edited by Alexander P. Lamis with the assistance of Mary Anne Sharkey, 18–41. Kent, OH: Kent State University Press, 1994.

Valelly, Richard M. *The Two Reconstructions: The Struggle for Black Enfranchisement*. Chicago: University of Chicago Press, 2004.

Valentino, Nicholas A., and David O. Sears. "Old Times There Are Not Forgotten: Race and Partisan Realignment in the Contemporary South." *American Journal of Political Science* 49, no. 3 (2005): 672–88.

Valletta, Robert G., and Richard B. Freeman. "The NBER Public Sector Collective Bargaining Law Data Set." In *When Public Employees Unionize*, edited by Richard B. Freeman and Casey Ichniowski, 399–419. Appendix B. Chicago: NBER / University of Chicago Press, 1988.

Vozzella, Laura. "A Rare, Random Drawing Helped Republicans Win a Tied Virginia Election but It May Not End There." *Washington Post*, January 4, 2018. https://www.washing tonpost.com/local/virginia-politics/republican-yancey-picked-in-random-lottery-declared -winner-of-pivotal-va-house-race/2018/01/04/9c9caa5a-f0a1-11e7-b390-a36dc3fa2842_story .html.

Walker, Jack L. "The Diffusion of Innovations among the American States." *American Political Science Review* 63, no. 3 (1969): 880–99.

Warrington, Gregory S. "Quantifying Gerrymandering Using the Vote Distribution." *Election Law Journal* 17, no. 1 (2018): 39–57.

Warshaw, Christopher, and Jonathan Rodden. "How Should We Measure District-Level Public Opinion on Individual Issues?" *Journal of Politics* 74, no. 1 (2012): 203–19.

Weatherby, James B., and Randy Stapilus. *Governing Idaho: Politics, People and Power.* Caldwell, ID: Caxton Press, 2005.

Weaver, Vesla M., and Gwen Prowse. "Racial Authoritarianism in U.S. Democracy." *Science* 369, no. 6508 (2020): 1176–78.

Werner, Timothy, and John J. Coleman. "Assessing the Potential Effects of *Citizens United*: Policy and Corporate Governance in the States." Paper prepared for the Meeting of the Public Choice Society, New Orleans, LA. 2013. http://users.polisci.wisc.edu/coleman/wernercole manpcs2013.pdf.

White, John P., and Norman C. Thomas. "Urban and Rural Representation and State Legislative Apportionment." *Western Political Quarterly* 17, no. 4 (1964): 724–41.

Wildavsky, Aaron B. *The Politics of the Budgetary Process.* Boston: Little, Brown, 1964.

Wilentz, Sean. *The Rise of American Democracy: Jefferson to Lincoln.* New York: W. W. Norton, 2005.

Wilkins, Arjun S. "Is Polarization Hurting the Re-election Prospects of US House Incumbents? The Effect of Roll-Call Voting Records on Election Results, 1900–2010." Unpublished working paper, 2013. https://politicalscience.stanford.edu/events/polarization-hurting-re-election -chances-house-incumbents-effect-roll-call-voting-records.

Wilson, James Q. *The Amateur Democrat: Club Politics in Three Cities.* Chicago: University of Chicago Press, 1962.

Wines, Michael. "Judges Find Wisconsin Redistricting Unfairly Favored Republicans." *New York Times*, November 21, 2016. https://www.nytimes.com/2016/11/21/us/wisconsin-redistricting -found-to-unfairly-favor-republicans.html.

Witt, Stephanie L., and Gary Moncrief. "Religion and Roll Call Voting in Idaho: The 1990 Abortion Controversy." *American Politics Quarterly* 21, no. 1 (1990): 140–49.

Wlezien, Christopher. "The Public as Thermostat: Dynamics of Preferences for Spending." *American Journal of Political Science* 39, no. 4 (1995): 981–1000.

Wolfinger, Raymond E., and Steven J. Rosenstone. *Who Votes?* New Haven, CT: Yale University Press, 1980.

Wortman, Marlene Stein, ed. *From Colonial Times to the New Deal.* Vol. 1. Women in American Law. New York: Holmes & Meier, 1985.

Wright, Gavin. *Sharing the Prize: The Economics of the Civil Rights Revolution in the American South.* Cambridge, MA: Harvard University Press, 2013.

Wright, Gerald C., and Nathaniel Birkhead. "The Macro Sort of the State Electorates." *Political Research Quarterly* 67, no. 2 (2014): 426–39.

Wright, Gerald C., Robert S. Erikson, and John P. McIver. "Measuring State Partisanship and Ideology with Survey Data." *Journal of Politics* 47, no. 2 (1985): 469–89.

———. "Public Opinion and Policy Liberalism in the American States." *American Journal of Political Science* 31, no. 4 (1987): 980–1001.

Xu, Yiqing. "Generalized Synthetic Control Method: Causal Inference with Interactive Fixed Effects Models." *Political Analysis* 25, no. 1 (2017): 57–76.

Yglesias, Matthew. "How Did Democrats Lose Maryland? Meet the Rain Tax." Vox, November 6, 2014. https://www.vox.com/2014/11/6/7159239/rain-tax.

Zaller, John, and Stanley Feldman. "A Simple Theory of the Survey Response: Answering Questions versus Revealing Preferences." *American Journal of Political Science* 36, no. 3 (1992): 579–616.

Index

abortion laws, 1–6, 13, 23, 53, 116, 128, 169, 179n16, 185n14. See also *Roe v. Wade*

Achen, Christopher, 113, 161

adaptation (partisan), 99, 102, 107–8

Affluence and Influence (Gilens), 161

Affordable Care Act (ACA), 3, 119, 125, 145, 169

agency theory, 81

agreement (policy), 123–24, 128, 135, 139, 145, 158–59

Aid to Families with Dependent Children (AFDC), 52–54

Alabama, 165

Alaska, 4, 174n24

Alcorn, James, 63–64

alignment (partisan), 7, 36–37, 44–46, 50, 62, 75

American National Election Studies (ANES), 35–37, 175n22, 177n8

Ansolabehere, Stephen, 138. See also legislative malapportionment; reapportionment revolution

authoritarianism, 165

Baker v. Carr, 137–39

balancing (electoral), 92–93

Bartels, Larry, 161, 175n13

Bayesian model, 22. See also measurement models

bias: conservative, 122–23, 146; districting, 142, 149–50; ideological, 114, 119, 123; liberal, 122; partisan, 141–42, 167, 188n54; policy, 8, 122, 185n19; status quo, 122–23, 129; in study samples, 21–22

Birkhead, Nathaniel, 46

black Americans, 130–36, 146–47, 160, 165

Bonica, Adam, 88. See also DW-DIME scores

Brownback, Sam, 90–91

"brown spots" (O'Donnell), 130, 164

Brown v. Board of Education, 34

budgetary incrementalism, 174n26

California, 180n5

campaign contributions (corporate), 151, 158–59, 191n36

campaign contributions (individual), 151, 157–59

Church of Jesus Christ of Latter-Day Saints (Mormons), 52

citizen governance, 148–51, 154–58

citizen-legislator, 150

citizen's preferences. *See* public opinion

civil rights, 34, 42, 48, 50, 107, 140

climate change mitigation, 113–14, 185n5, 185n7

Clinton, Bill, 78

collective bargaining, 151–59, 192n57

Confederate states, 132, 165

congruence (policy), 124–28, 134–35, 139, 145, 158–59

Connecticut, 91

conservatism: bias in, 122–23; cultural, 7, 37, 43–46, 59, 74–79, 84–87, 108, 157; and the Democratic Party, 48, 74; economic, 7, 37, 41, 46–49, 74–79, 84–85, 106–8; of elected officials, 8; and elections, 89; of governors, 68; and issues, 23, 28; legislative, 144, 189n67; mass, 8, 27–30, 40–50, 60–64, 79–80, 85–87, 92–94, 99–112, 153–58, 178n37; policy, 27, 32, 54–76, 91, 99–111, 123, 138–44, 156–59, 166, 189n67; racial, 7, 37, 40–42, 46–47, 84–85, 178n28; and the Republican Party, 48–50, 74; of the South, 107; states', 44–45, 101; trajectory of, 42; variation in, 31; of voters, 107

constant-difficulty model, 56. *See also* measurement models